IT'S OFFICIAL!

Second Edition

IT'S OFFICIAL!

The Real Stories Behind Arkansas's State Symbols

David Ware

Second Edition

BUTLER
CENTER
BOOKS

The Butler Center for Arkansas Studies
Central Arkansas Library System
100 Rock Street
Little Rock, Arkansas 72201

BUTLER
CENTER
BOOKS

www.butlercenter.org

Second edition: October 2017

ISBN 978-1-935106-84-5
ISBN 978-1-935106-85-2 (e-book)

Manager: Rod Lorenzen
Book & cover design: Jen Hughes
Copyeditor/proofreader: Ali Welky

(Library of Congress cataloging-in-publication data has been applied for)

Butler Center Books, the publishing division of the Butler Center for Arkansas Studies,
was made possible by the generosity of Dora Johnson Ragsdale and John G. Ragsdale Jr.

Printed in the United States of America

This book is printed on archival-quality paper that meets requirements of the
American National Standard for Information Sciences, Permanence of Paper,
Printed Library Materials, ANSI Z39.48-1984.

For Sarah — *"She must be from Arkansas"*

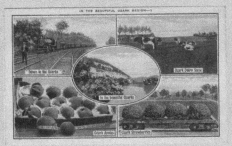

CONTENTS

Acknowledgements

This book has been, in a way, over sixteen years in the making. It started in my first week as historian of the Arkansas State Capitol, when a constituent wrote to me for information on Arkansas's state songs; since then, questions about the various state symbols have continued to appear in my email, on my voicemail, and even in the form of the occasional letter. Thus, my first acknowledgement is of the many individuals who have asked me for this information: Your questions have given me the opportunity to look for answers. This is all your fault. And I thank you.

I have been fortunate in my employers. Secretaries of State Sharon Priest, Charlie Daniels, and Mark Martin have given me both opportunity and responsibility for delving into Arkansas's history, culture, and geography in order to answer such questions and to develop exhibits and programs for the capitol. They have given me a roving commission, and I know how lucky I have been.

I have been just as lucky in my colleagues in the Secretary of State's Office. They have given me advice, asked me for help, edited my work, and egged me on, while making sure that I held on to both humor and perspective. There are too many in this group to name, but a couple require particular designation. Jen Hughes has been my collaborator in exhibits, archives management, and book production; she has frequently been the voice of reason when I have been too far gone into one topic or another. She did a great job designing this book, as you can see. Another is Ann Pryor Clements, my predecessor, who was the first capitol historian. As a mentor, supervisor, colleague, and friend, she has been solid, supportive, and great fun.

To the Arkansas historians and other scholars, academic and public, who welcomed this "damyankee" and made him feel at home, I offer deep thanks. These include, in no particular order, Tom DeBlack, Ben Johnson, Jerry Canerday, Charles Bolton, Carl Moneyhon, Ken Barnes, Pat Ramsey, Dr. ReBecca Hunt-Foster, Starr Mitchell, Johanna Miller Lewis, Jay Barth, Missy McSwain, Tim Nutt, Wes Goodner, Bill Worthen, Swannee Bennett, Jo Maack, Michael Lewis, Jane Wilkerson, Julienne Crawford, the staff of the Arkansas State Archives, and, as they say, "many, many more." Special thanks go to three gifted archivists/historians: Linda Pine, Tom Dillard, and Russell Baker, for their generosity and good counsel. I also owe debts of gratitude to the staff of the Central Arkansas Library System's Butler Center for Arkansas Studies and its Encyclopedia of Arkansas History & Culture (EOA); many of these chapters began as articles for the EOA but seem to have grown…

Acknowledgements are also due to a pair of Arkansas scholars who are sorely missed: Dr. John Ferguson and Dr. C. Fred Williams. I am grateful to them for stories, suggestions, and the welcome they extended me, and for the work they did over their long careers to help Arkansans, native and naturalized alike, learn about and appreciate their state's complex story.

The staff of Butler Center Books has been understanding, supportive, and suspiciously patient with me. Rod Lorenzen originally proposed this project and has kept me focused on it. Ali Welky has been a sensitive and good-humored editor who has managed to cut some of the mickey out of my prose.

A special thanks goes to the Secretary of State's Office summer fellow Alex Wright, who applied her classroom-sharpened eye and a mean markup pen to several of these chapters.

And one more, to close: my wife Marlene and our daughter Sarah have been subjected, almost as long as I have held my job, to my telling—endlessly—stories associated with the capitol, Arkansas history, and the various state symbols. More recently, they have lived with stacks of books and notes piled high on too many domestic surfaces, plus the sounds of typewriter and computer keyboards going late into the night. They've put up with me and with the detritus of the project, and now I get to say that this book is for them.

Introduction
Substitutes, Salutes, Sigils, and Signposts: Why State Symbols Matter

My "desktop Webster"—technically, the *American Heritage Collegiate Dictionary*, third edition (1997)—affords a broad definition of the word *symbol*. A symbol is a thing that "represents something else by association, resemblance or convention; especially a material object representing something invisible." The word comes down to us in a time-honored way, as a term borrowed (in the tradition of reverse cultural imperialism) by the Romans from the Greeks: *symbolum*—a token or mark. Lost in translation was the Greek sense of the token being used for identification, by being compared with others.

For over two centuries, Arkansas's leaders have been guilty of the sporadic practice of symbolism—representing things by means of symbols, or attributing larger meanings to objects and events—and the cumulative effect of this enthusiasm has been the compilation of a significant pile of things which are meant to represent, for the benefit both of residents and outsiders, the cultural heritage and natural resources of the state. As of 2017, after the newest addition, there are twenty-five official symbols, plus a nickname, a motto, and even a state creed. With this many in hand, it is fair to ask: Why so many? And what for?

Some symbols function as representatives or substitutes for the state itself. In this category of stand-ins may be grouped the earliest of our symbols, the state seal, as well as the state flag, the state anthem, and, perhaps, the state motto and creed. When presented or delivered in the presence of others, they are effectively substitutes for the physical and cultural construct we call "Arkansas." For residents, particularly natives, they are foci of state pride, of patriotism. They remind us of the polity that is Arkansas, of which we sing, to which we belong.

Other symbols have a less lofty aim: to draw attention to things that are points of pride for the state. These may be things shared with other states but which have nonetheless been determined to be standout elements of life and culture in Arkansas. Thus, Arkansas has extended official salutes and designation to such agricultural products as rice, tomatoes, pecans, apples (in the form of apple blossoms), and milk, as well as commodities severed from the soil such as pine trees, bauxite, quartz, and even diamonds. Our state mammal may fall into this category, too. Although the white-tailed deer is common throughout much of the nation, Arkansas's connection to it is special, in that it represents a great success for wildlife management and population restoration. These are symbols in the old Greek sense of things that may be compared with equivalents of other states; by their fruits (and vegetables, and minerals) ye shall know them or, for that matter, us.

Still others speak to sentiment, ideals, and past times. The state folk dance, the state cooking vessel, the state musical instrument, the state songs, and even the state dinosaur trade in idealizations of Arkansas's past, although it may be stretching credibility to mention idealization and a strapping carnivorous beast in the same sentence. These are sigils—designs or symbols that seem to possess some supernatural or mystical element. For Arkansawyers of the twenty-first century, these official symbols help to conjure "culture memories" and are links to our roots, real or imagined, and to the land. Even the state's flying symbols, the Diana fritillary butterfly, the honeybee, and the mockingbird, may belong here as well; magic might be defined as a Diana sighting on Mount Magazine, the buzz of a busy honeybee, or a mockingbird doing its best squeaky-hinge mimicry outside a neighbor's window.

For me, though, Arkansas's state symbols have served best as signposts, for they have helped me navigate my way toward understanding a little, at least, about my adopted home state. Symbols are seldom chosen inadvertently; their proposers almost always have a particular aim in mind, be it promotion of a particular crop or industry or celebration of a particular ideal. Following the history of the symbol allows us to observe the processes of change, adaptation, and economic ebbs and flows. Thus, we have the hopeful-sounding state nicknames, which are revised every few years to reflect evolving notions of how to promote the state to outsiders. Designation of the apple blossom was in its day a promotion and celebration of the orchards of Arkansas, once robust although today offering only a shadow of their past glories. The choice of a state beverage drew attention to the state's thriving dairy industry, which, since the designation, has condensed and compacted in recent decades to reflect the realities of mass-market milk. Happily, not all symbols' stories are ones of decline. Rice, the official state grain, was a latecomer to staple-crop production in Arkansas, but today it is an economic mainstay and a source of pride and growth. The stories of these state symbols and others are narratives of change over time: expansion, decline, mutation, the stuff of which historians make...well, books, for one thing—while our developers, promoters, and agriculturalists have made hay.

The best of these, or my favorites, are the symbols that carry more than one level of meaning, or hold a surprise in their story. Examples? Here are a few: the Cynthiana grape, it turns out, has a twin named Norton, resident outside our borders—these genetically identical twins produce subtly different wines, a potent and happy reminder of the power exerted by place (particularly a place in which until recently there were more dry counties than wet ones); a farm field yields a rich harvest of diamonds; a distinctive, simple flag design is tinkered with thrice by committee and yet manages to retain its distinctiveness; an instrument perfected in Baroque-era Italian workshops proves to be equally at home in the backwoods of Arkansas. These dualities add spice to the contemplation of state symbols, allowing them to be something more than mere curiosities.

These are signposts, one and all. Threads of Arkansas's settlement, Arkansas's development, even Arkansas's pride run through each story. They speak of past aspirations, of large ventures, of discoveries and recoveries, and of practical politicians engaging in activities that are not as frivolous as they might seem. They are generally discussed in primary school, often in conjunction with a coloring book distributed by the Secretary of State's Office, then set aside; by the time students return to studying Arkansas in middle school and high school, their attention will be directed toward conventional history, civics, geography, and economics in a manner both deep and rigorous. In place of these signposts, students will be directed toward College, Career, and Civic Life—and rightly so; for them, there is serious work in prospect. Happily, the symbols will be waiting for them when, as adults, they have time to savor the stories they come with, the pride and affection they embody and engender, and the magic they spread.

CHAPTER 1: STATE SEAL

Signed, Sealed, Delivered—It's Yours

The term "seal" derives from the Latin *sigillum*, meaning a sign, mark, or token. A seal is, physically, a piece of wax, clay, lead, or other compound which will attach to a thing, and which will accept a design of words or symbols impressed upon it. It can also be a design impressed into the surface of a document. Legally, a seal may also consist of the particular design engraved or impressed or even scribbled, when the occasion demands. Seals have often been used in place of signatures; in English law, seals were used to authenticate documents, either being affixed directly to the document or being attached by cord or ribbon. Courts have long attached a particular significance to sealed documents, as distinguished from those merely signed.

A state seal is both a design incorporating particular symbolic or artistic elements created for use by the state government and a device that embosses, prints, or otherwise puts replicas of the design onto official documents. Affixing the official seal to a document is meant to signify its authenticity as a document of state, in lieu of or in addition to the signature of the issuing official or officials. Seals were once commonly pressed into "sealing wax" (a heat-softened compound of shellac, other resins, chalk or plaster, and pigment) but today are more usually embossed into the document's surface or affixed as a metal-foil sticker.

What's in a seal? A lot, to put it mildly: hopes, dreams, and bright ideas. Official state seals are often amalgams of classical or religious allusions, generic patriotic icons or sentiments, and representations of things deemed significant or near and dear to the hearts of those whom the seal is supposed to represent. Sometimes they incorporate geographical or landscape elements, or themes from the state's natural history. Alabama's, for instance, offers a riverine map of the state, while Alaska's includes mountains, fjords, and forests, along with an optimistic farmer on a hay rake, a sourdough's cabin with smoke rising from its chimney, and, tucked into the woods, modern buildings not unlike the state's capitol, a onetime federal office block. Iowa's seal shows what might be taken for the towering mountains of Nebraska, visible across a river, while the foreground is emphatically flat land. Other elements commonly encountered on state seals include male figures of miners, farmers, other laborers, Native Americans, and even soldiers and mariners. Female figures, usually clad in flowing garments, allude to classical themes or characters. State seals are not noted for their visual humor or wit; they are, after all, serious business.

◊ ◊ ◊

The present official state seal of Arkansas is descended from the territorial seal believed to have been designed and drawn in 1820 by Samuel Calhoun Roane, engrossing clerk of the Territorial General Assembly. Roane was a significant and well-liked character in early Arkansas. Born in North Carolina in 1793, he moved with his family to Tennessee. He read law and was admitted to the Tennessee bar; he served in the War of 1812 under Andrew Jackson and in 1819 removed to the newly created Arkansaw Territory, where he established a law practice and was admitted to the bar of the territorial superior court. Roane was then appointed engrossing clerk of the Territorial Assembly, which met at Arkansas Post in February 1820. Roane reportedly drew up a preliminary design before the assembly met; "tradition" (a powerful and usual source of information about early Arkansas) holds that on the second day of the session, it was adopted.

What did Roane's seal look like? An 1822 document printed by William Woodruff bears what purports to be the seal of "Arkansaw Territory." The design consists of concentric circles; arching over the top in the space between the circles is emblazoned "Arkansaw Territory," a spelling that persisted until 1823, with eight stars bearing a close resemblance to asterisks filling the space of the lower curve. Inside the inner circle is a riot of martial icons: a central shield bearing the image of a sunrise or a starburst is flanked by, on its left, a mortar, and, on the right, a field gun. Below these is scattered an assortment of projectiles large and small, as well as a stalk of wheat. Behind it, left to right, one may espy a flag bearing a martial herald, a musket with bayonet fixed, a liberty pole, liberty cap, a spear, and, finally, a single-starred version of the national flag. Over all of this, a Z-shaped banner floats—its forked ends give it the unfortunate mien of a double-ended serpent.

If this represented Sam Roane's original design, then it underwent

Samuel Calhoun Roane

drastic changes during the early territorial period. The territorial seal in use by the 1830s still contained martial elements but gone were the artillery pieces and cannon balls; transportation, agriculture, and prosperity were the driving themes. As with the 1822 version, the "late-territorial" seal consisted of concentric circles. In addition to "Arkansas Territory," the space between the circles contained on its left a hilted sword, tangled up with the chains of a balance scale. A national shield on the right was supported by a musket and a pole surmounted by a liberty cap.

Territorial seal, earliest known version.

Within the second circle, symbolism became a little more densely packed and diverse. At the top, a goddess of Liberty held a laurel wreath in her right hand while supporting another pole-and-liberty-cap arrangement. The goddess was flanked by two curved, almost parentheses-like, rows of stars, totaling twenty-five (the number of states in the Union at the time). Instead of the predictable cloud, the goddess stood literally on the wings of eagles, the national bird, a pair of which were arranged symmetrically. The leftmost eagle's single visible talon held an olive branch (symbol of peace), while the one on the right clung to an arrow, a more warlike emblem. The twin eagles' inward-pointing beaks supported a shield bearing...still more symbols: a steamboat, representing the commerce of Arkansas's rivers, by this time still the best highways of commerce and social intercourse; a plow, symbolic of the territory's subsistence and staple-crop agricultural potential; a beehive, calling to mind the industriousness and singleness of purpose found among the honeybees[1]; and a sheaf or shock of wheat, standing as a tribute to the fecundity of the land and showing Arkansas's potential for self-support.[2] At the bottom of the shield was a single five-pointed star, whose symbolic import is unclear. Supporting this symbolically top-heavy shield was a pair of cornucopias, or horns-of-plenty; beneath them, a banner bore the state's motto, "the people rule," rendered in Latin as *regnant populi.*

Territorial seal, revised version, ca. 1830.

When Arkansas became a state in 1836, the new constitution provided that there should be a seal kept by the governor and that the then-current seal of the territory should be used by the governor until otherwise directed by the General Assembly. On September 14, a resolution offered by James Boone of Washington County was adopted, calling for a joint committee to decide what devices and emblems should in fact be part of the Great Seal of Arkansas. The committee did its work and on October 24, Senator William Ball of Washington County introduced a bill providing for a seal. Their measure met favor in both legislative chambers and was signed into law by James Conway on October 29, 1836.

---

1   And, presumably, the human population of the territory. For more on the symbolic import of bees, see the chapter on the honeybee, Arkansas's official state insect.

2   Arkansas is more often associated with rice, cotton, and soybean crops, but its roughly 600,000 acres planted in soft red winter wheat, yielding an average of 58 bu/acre, place it in the top ten of wheat-producing states. Who knew?

By its terms, the new seal would be based on the territorial seal, altered by substituting "Seal of the State of Arkansas" for its original territorial designation. In addition, the session produced a measure stipulating that the secretary of state should procure a seal not exceeding one and three-quarters of an inch in diameter, "engraved so as to present, by its impressions, such emblems and devices as shall be approved by the governor, surrounded by the words, 'Seal of the Secretary of State, Arkansas....'" The cost of procuring this seal, the measure noted, was to be covered by "moneys appropriated for defraying the contingent expenses of the office."

An 1856 enactment specified the "impressions, emblems and devices" to be included in all renderings of the state seal. The law named sixteen separate elements, plus the words and phrases *Regnant Populi*, "Mercy," "Justice," and "Seal of the State of Arkansas." In 1864, the legislature adopted a modification of the old design that survives, almost unchanged, to the present. The Act of May 3 of that year specified that the seal contain a single eagle at its bottom, holding a scroll in its beak inscribed *Regnant Populi*, with a bundle of arrows in one claw and an olive branch in the other; a shield covering the breast of the eagle, engraved with a steamboat at the top, a beehive and plow in the middle, and a sheaf of wheat at the bottom; and the Goddess of Liberty at the top, holding a wreath in her right hand, a pole in the left hand, surmounted by a liberty cap and surrounded by a circle of stars (rendered as thirteen, a nod to the thirteen original states, although the act does not specify any particular number) surrounded by a circle of rays. The act added the figure of an angel on the left, holding a belt or banner inscribed "Mercy," and a sword on the right side, inscribed "Justice," the whole surrounded with the words "Seal of the State of Arkansas."

The only substantial alteration of the seal since 1864 occurred in 1907, when *Regnant Populi*, the Latin motto on the 1864 seal, was changed to *Regnat Populus*. This change was apparently the result of recognition that populi indicates a plurality of groups—that is, "peoples" or "some people" rather than "the people." The 1907 revision added a slightly imperative quality to the motto; one imagines it rendered in English as "The People *Rule*" (and make no mistake about it).[3]

Today's state seal retains the symbolic elements of its territorial predecessor. Much about Arkansas's economy has changed over the years, but the symbols, particularly those on the shield, still hold their significance. Railroads and, latterly, highways lessened Arkansas's reliance on river transport and travel, but the Arkansas River remains a vital shipping route for bulk commodities, while the state's nearly 12,000 miles of rivers, plus lesser streams and over 2,000 lakes and reservoirs, yield benefits for agriculture and

State seal, present version.

---

3   The idea of an indefinite quantity of people may be less an issue than the sense that "regnant" conveys a sense of a condition, rather than an action.

Stained-glass rendering of state seal, displayed in the Arkansas Capitol, Little Rock. Colors optional.

16

recreation alike. The plow and beehive, taken together, sum up the ideal of agricultural industriousness; the state's potential, when combined with hard work, produces the lowermost symbol on the shield: a wheat sheaf, a traditional indicator of abundant crops.

The Arkansas Code does not enumerate all the possible uses of the seal, but it stipulates that it "shall be kept by the Governor, used by him." The secretary of state, auditor of state, and treasurer each employ a seal of office embodying the same design elements presented by the state seal. The words surrounding the emblems indicate the respective constitutional offices. Visitors to the Arkansas State Capitol often pose for their pictures in front of an outsize stained-glass rendering of the seal which is displayed in the first floor rotunda area. The seal is colorful, but the hues chosen by the glass artist enjoy no official status; the thousands of schoolchildren who are each year issued the Secretary of State's Office's activity book are therefore free to color the included outline drawing of the seal in any scheme they may desire.

◇ ◇ ◇

The seal of state is with us yet, although the fame of its traditional credited designer, Sam Roane, has faded a little. After the territorial government moved to Little Rock in the fall of 1820, Roane moved his law practice to Arkadelphia and represented Clark County in both the second and third territorial assemblies (1821 and 1823). He later relocated to Pine Bluff, served as county and probate judge of Jefferson County in 1832-33 and returned to Little Rock as state senator from Jefferson County in the First General Assembly of Arkansas, 1836-38, serving as president of the State Senate and acting governor during James Conway's absence from the state. Roane died in 1852 and is buried in Little Rock's Mount Holly cemetery; he lived long enough to see his much-younger brother, John Selden Roane, rise to the rank of governor of Arkansas.[4]

For further reading:

Jenkinson, Sir Hilary. *Guide to Seals in the Public Record Office*. London: Her Majesty's Stationery Office, 1954.

Rankin, Claude A. "Arkansas's Seal Is Wrong." *Arkansas Gazette*, April 18, 1937, Magazine section, p. 1.

———. "Emblematic Meanings of the Great Seal of Arkansas." *Arkansas Gazette*, April 26, 1938, Magazine section, p. 1.

Shearer, Benjamin F., and Barbara Smith Shearer. *State Names, Seals, Flags and Symbols—A Historical Guide*. New York: Greenwood Press, 1989.

4   For correspondence concerning Samuel Calhoun Roane and his accomplishments, I am indebted to Mr. Glenn Railsback III, a Roane descendant, whose scholarship on the family has been featured in articles appearing in the *Jefferson County Historical Quarterly*.

CHAPTER 2:
STATE FLORAL EMBLEM

Or, the Apple of Our Eye

At the dawn of the twentieth century, the Arkansas General Assembly designated the apple blossom as the official floral emblem of Arkansas. When Governor Jeff Davis signed the resolution into law on January 30, 1901, Arkansas became the second state to adopt the bloom (Michigan was the first). The apple blossom consists of clusters of pink or white petals, their shade depending on the variety of apple. The colors can range from a light pink to a dark red. These blooms emit a sweet scent that attracts bees to the trees, where they carry out the work of pollination.

The vogue for designating state flowers first blossomed in 1893 when one state (Minnesota) and one future one (the Indian Territory, later Oklahoma) adopted the ladyslipper orchid and the mistletoe, respectively, as their official flower (Minnesota) or floral emblem (Oklahoma). Both were chosen in response to an invitation for all states and territories to send floral entries to the great Chicago World's Fair, or Columbian Exposition.[1] Other states followed suit, even after the exposition had closed. In 1894, Vermont designated the red clover. In 1895, four more states chose their floral symbols: Delaware (peach blossom), Maine (white pine cone and tassel), Montana (bitterroot), and Nebraska (goldenrod). Two more followed in 1897, and again in 1899. In

---

1   One other state may have taken this step in 1893: Arkansas. More on this anon.

1900, only Louisiana selected a state flower, the perhaps inevitable magnolia. Two more states would take this step in 1901: Texas (bluebonnet) and Arkansas.

Within Arkansas, the initiative to select a state flower came from within the network of women's clubs and organizations that, in pre–women's suffrage years, afforded women both social opportunities and context for influence and action within their communities. In 1900, a group calling itself the Arkansas Floral Emblem Society, which appears to have existed under the umbrella of the Arkansas Federation of Women's Clubs, canvassed other women's groups to gauge sentiment for a choice of state flower or floral emblem. The originator of the group is not known, and its full membership and organizing principles remain mysteries. Two leaders' names are preserved: statewide president Mrs. H. C. Rightor of Helena and Searcy chapter president Mrs. Ed Barton (known as Love Barton).

A number of Arkansas flowers—either native or long established—were considered. They included the holly, honeysuckle, boll, and even the oakleaf and acorn. The two strongest contenders proved to be the apple blossom and the passionflower. The Arkansas Federation of Women's Clubs (now the General Federation of Women's Clubs) supported the passionflower, while the apple blossom was championed by the Arkansas Floral Emblem Society and, in particular, by Love Barton. What ensued was dubbed "the battle of the blooms," which in the end, thanks to some savvy campaigning by Barton, resulted in the apple blossom winning laurels as the state's flower—and with good reason, too. By the end of the twentieth century, much of the prosperity of northern Arkansas rested on a foundation of fruit.

◇ ◇ ◇

The apple is not, of course, an Arkansas native; it is in fact not a native plant of the Americas. *Malus domestica* is a relative of the rose, and its ancestors were wild trees that grew in the mountains of central Asia.[2] The path or process of domesticated apples' emigration is unclear, but it is generally accepted that the apple was one of the first trees to be cultivated and intentionally variegated. In ancient China and Turkey, apples were picked in autumn, then stored in cold dugout cellars, providing important winter fare for peasants and their livestock alike. This practice of "storing over" followed the apple as it migrated from Asia to western Europe.

Along the way, orchardists learned that for best results, one should not simply plant apple seeds, then wait to see what would sprout up. Trees planted from seeds grew tall, but they often produced unpalatable fruit. To ensure propagation of sweet apples, it was better to graft budded "scion" cuttings of sweet apple trees onto seed-grown stock. The result would be a lower-growing tree that bore sweet fruit. Romans, particularly, refined the art of grafting scions.

Apples came to North America with sixteenth-century explorers and, later, colonists. In the early seventeenth century, Lord Baltimore, proprietor of the colony of Maryland, instructed his Catholic settlers to carry across the sea "kernalls of peares and apples, especially of Pippins, Pearemains, and Deesons for maykinge thereafter of Cider and Perry." Instructing his clients to bring seeds reflected the practicalities of colonizing transport; there would be more room for seeds than for barrels of cuttings. Cuttings were brought as well,

---

2   How they spread to the west is unclear, but one tale indicates that gastronomic tourist and gifted imperialist Alexander ("the Great") of Macedonia brought home unknown varieties of apples from today's Kazakhstan in 328 B.C.E.

but they proved in many cases too delicate to thrive in the new soil and harsher weather. Seed-planted trees, ironically, proved hardier and easier to grow, since they required no particular skill, unlike grafting. By the late eighteenth century, apple orchards were established throughout the former English colonies, and as Euro-Americans crossed the Alleghenies and followed Native American trading routes, apples and apple seeds came with them. A farmstead with planted and tended orchards was considered one proved up; land speculators sometimes planted orchards in anticipation of peddling land to new arrivals at a premium.

One participant in this was Massachusetts-born John Chapman, better remembered today by his nickname, "Johnny Appleseed." Chapman is not known to have visited Arkansas, but his enthusiastic propagation of apples makes him one of the "godfathers" of the apple culture economy that included Arkansas. In popular culture, Chapman is depicted as a rural eccentric who traversed the countryside of the old Northwest, sowing apple seeds wherever he wandered.

Chapman was indeed an eccentric who went on foot from town to town clad in castoff clothing, usually bare footed, with a saucepan for a hat and often displaying an almost Jain-like reverence for animal and human life. At the same time, he was a successful nurseryman and land developer. He planted nurseries rather than orchards, built fences around them to protect them from livestock, then left the nurseries in the care of a neighbor who sold trees to other settlers on shares: so much for Chapman, so much for the resident nurseryman-partner.

John Chapman

Chapman would return every year or two to tend the trees. Chapman's first nursery was planted near Warren, Pennsylvania, but he did not stop there. Instead, he moved west, ultimately establishing several nurseries in the Mohican area of north-central Ohio. At his death in 1845, he left an estate of over 1,200 acres of nurseries to his sister; he also owned four plots in Indiana, including a nursery with 15,000 trees.

In spite of his relative prosperity, Chapman lived a spartan, wandering life until its end, following a primitive Christianity shaped by the teachings of Emanuel Swedenborg. Swedenborgian principles also steered Chapman toward propagation by growing from seed, rather than grafting. In this tradition, grafting was explicitly forbidden, since it was believed to cause plants to suffer. Chapman planted all of his orchards from seed, thus his apples were, for the most part, unfit to eat.

They were, however, suitable for making cider, which provided a safe, stable, and healthy beverage. Hard cider was a taste brought by settlers to the New World from the Old; in a time when water could be full of dangerous bacteria, fermented cider could be drunk without worry.[3] In the New World, cider was a characteristic feature of tables and cuisine in the years before and after the American Revolution; it

---

3   And, if consumed in sufficient quantities, could considerably ease any pre-existing ones.

played its part in creating what historian William Rorabaugh dubbed "the alcoholic republic." As the new Americans moved west after the revolution, they took with them both this taste and the means to satisfy it.

Scholarship has addressed how the phenomenon of excess production of grain, coupled with transportation difficulties, led to the widespread distillation of whiskey, but along with the grain grew the fruit of the orchards. Grain might be turned into beer as well, but why waste it this way, when you could make whiskey from it? For a temperate beverage, cider was preferable, and, besides, if something stronger were desired, cider might be fortified, either by leaving it to freeze, then discarding the watery part and saving the alcoholic concentrate, known commonly as "applejack," or by distillation into apple brandy. Once-pressed apples could be soaked with clean water, then pressed again to produce the basis for "ciderkin," a mildly alcoholic cider often served to women and children. Transplanted New Englanders on the frontier drank a reported half-gallon or more of hard cider per day; it was as common as meat or bread and probably healthier.[4]

---

4   Modern cider enthusiasts and promoters point to the presence of antioxidants and the lack of sodium in cider. On the other hand, cider is as carbohydrate-rich as beer, thanks to its high sugar content, and is only a minor source of calcium and vitamins.

◇◇◇

Anglo-American settlers arriving in Arkansas from the East Coast brought both apple seeds and graftable cuttings with them. The *Arkansas Gazette* reported in 1822 that apples were being grown on the farm of future governor James Sevier Conway west of Little Rock. Ultimately, orchards were planted throughout Arkansas, but the Ozark Plateau proved particularly suited for their culture and became the state's dominant region for apple production.

Nurseries were established at Cane Hill in Washington County in 1835 and at Bentonville in Benton County in 1836 to meet the need for apple trees. Others followed. Excess production from expansion of kitchen orchards was sold to freighters who hauled apples to distant markets in open wagons. In 1852, a wagon train to Van Buren in Crawford County delivered Ozarks apples, to be sent by boat downriver to Little Rock. This may have been, however, something of a "stunt"; in practice, overland hauling by wagon was inefficient for bulk crops, and apples certainly promised to become such. As larger orchards were planted in postwar years, production grew past overland freighters' carrying capacity. The "Apple Belt" of the Ozarks could not efficiently distribute its production.

The Iron Mountain route appeals to orchardists, ca. 1878.

Salvation came in the form of iron rails.

The entry of railroad lines into the state—such as one that reached Fayetteville in 1881 and Lincoln in 1901—offered access to distant markets as well as improving shipping efficiency within the state borders. The new access to markets outside of Arkansas ultimately resulted in a great increase in commercial orchard plantings in northwest Arkansas. Acreage grew from a few hundred acres to many thousands. By 1900, orchards occupied some 40,000 acres in Benton County and nearly that many in Washington County, thus making them the two largest apple-producing counties in the United States.

Apple production swelled, and, with it, the number of varieties grown. At the turn of the century, more than 400 varieties of apple were said to grow in Arkansas orchards, out of the reported thousands found across the nation. The Collins Red, Summer Queen, August Beauty, and Summer Champion were well-represented in the orchards of northwest Arkansas.

Another popular variety, a mainstay of Washington County orchards, was the Ben Davis, a rugged apple known for its qualities as a "keeper" and also as a reliable producer that would drop its fruit late in the season. The Ben Davis won few awards for its flavor—one description characterized it as "cottonlike"—but it would grow and produce reliably, so provided dependable production for cider making and drying. A local variant, the "Black Ben Davis," may have first sprouted in a refuse pile next to an apple dryer located near Lincoln in Washington County. The farm on which the dryer was located had once been owned by a certain Parson Black, hence the variety was dubbed the "Black Ben Davis." Contrary to the name, though, the fruit was colored a bright red. It proved to be very popular when exhibited at the state fair in Little Rock.

Just why the Arkansas Federation of Women's Clubs chose 1900 as the year to advance the cause of a state flower is unknown; perhaps the floral zeitgeist brought inspiration to the group. In April, at the statewide convention held at Texarkana, some 105 representatives of the state's women's clubs gathered for what the *Arkansas Democrat* described as "three days' sessions...brimful of business and bubbling over with good things from the brainy and brilliant women."[5] On Friday, April 19, the convention heard a brief discussion of the floral emblem idea from State President Mrs. Frederick Hanger, followed by a series of five presentations from champions of various flowers.

The apple blossom, of course, was advocated by Love Barton of Searcy. The greatest impact, however, was made by Miss Clara Eno of Van Buren, who read a paper penned by the absent Mrs. Jessie Fuller, also of Van Buren, which revealed that what was being contemplated was a change, rather than an institution. According to Fuller, the state already had chosen a floral emblem, the passionflower. The choice, she revealed, had been made in 1893 in response to the call for state flowers by the organizers of the great Columbian Exposition and World's Fair in Chicago. The "Columbian Clubs" of Arkansas and the state directorate of the World's Fair had requested Senator Adams of Jefferson County to advance the cause of the passionflower in the state

APPLE ORCHARD IN BLOOM, SPRINGDALE, ARK.

legislature, so that it might take its place in the Arkansas pavilion at the Chicago exposition. Adams obliged, introducing a measure, Senate Bill 185, on February 13, 1893, designating the passionflower. It won approval, asserted Fuller, in March of that year. The passionflower had been worked into the mural decorations of the Arkansas pavilion by their artist, Mrs. Mary Trivet of Cincinnati. The mural was described by a visitor thus: "Her work is exquisite, merely a June blue and white clouded sky and, windblown across it, in vines and tendrils, leaf and petal, the Passion Flower, the state's emblem."

5   "The Annual Meeting of the A.F.W.C." *Arkansas Democrat*, April 28, 1900, p. 6.

Fuller concluded, "It cannot be denied that we have gone before the whole world as the Passion Flower State and it will be sad and humiliating for this beautiful emblem to be cast aside, and its sacred legend to find no place in our Christian hearts."[6] There was, she admitted, one teensy cloud over the passionflower's status: the bill was not recorded in the *Acts of Arkansas*, the sessional compendium of enacted legislation. Senate staffer J. T. Ginocchio explained to an AFWC representative that the bill had been "a concurrent bill" (which may in fact indicate a concurrent resolution), but he could not explain why the measure did not appear in the *Acts*. Perhaps unhelpfully, he noted that in that year, five bills that never passed were recorded, while three known measures that had been approved were missing in print.

Fuller's fervent advocacy for the designation or, more properly, the *retention* of the passionflower won the day. The AFWC voted to nominate the passionflower as the state's floral emblem. Newspaper coverage gave no indication of any dissent—the next topic for discussion was the burning issue of considering a uniform date for club elections throughout the state—and the issue was doubtless considered settled. And so it may have been, except for a few hearty enthusiasts of other blooms. One of these was Love Barton.

Given the apple's importance to Arkansas's farmers, the selection of its blossom as the state's floral emblem may have seemed an obvious choice, particularly for solons from the Ozark counties. To make this manifest to others, between April 1900 and January 1901, Mrs. Barton added her deep enthusiasm. On January 18, 1901, State Senator Hal L. Norwood introduced Senate Concurrent Resolution 3, advancing the apple blossom as the state floral emblem with a ripping, enthusiastic speech. On January 25, the measure was debated in the state House chamber.

By this time, Mrs. Barton had done good work on behalf of her chosen flower. She had written letters to local papers statewide, as well as to the *Arkansas Gazette*, in support of the apple blossom. The importance of the apple as a cash crop bolstered her case: as many as 400 varieties were grown in Arkansas, and its apples had won blue ribbons at the Chicago Exposition of 1893 and the Paris Exposition of 1900. Mrs. Barton's espousal of the apple blossom cause inspired the *Gazette*'s editorialist to quip, in the January 25 issue, "This is Senate day in the House and it is hoped that body will take up Senator Norwood's concurrent resolution...and dispose of it, one way or another."[7] On the same page was printed a letter from former Arkansas governor Thomas Churchill, who upheld the passionflower's pride of place and professed himself surprised that the "young and gallant" Senator Norwood would sponsor a measure taking the choice of the state flower "out of the hands of the ladies." Churchill asserted that for all of its many charms, the apple was not a native: "But the tree was not found in Arkansas by the first settlers. It is an imported fruit....Its real home is further north."[8]

The communications from Barton and Churchill set the stage for extended morning debate in the House chamber, as SCR 3 was considered; further inspiration came from a pile of shiny red Arkansas apples deposited on the speaker's desk, courtesy of Barton. On the walls hung "tapestries" depicting the passionflower, believed to

---

6   "Our Floral Emblem." *Arkansas Democrat*, April 26, 1900, p. 3. The "sacred legend" alluded to is in fact a practice of early Catholic missionaries in the New World, who used the unique physical structures of this plant, particularly the numbers of its various flower parts, as reminders of the last days of Jesus and, especially, his crucifixion.

7   *Arkansas Gazette*, January 25, 1901, p. 4.

8   Ibid.

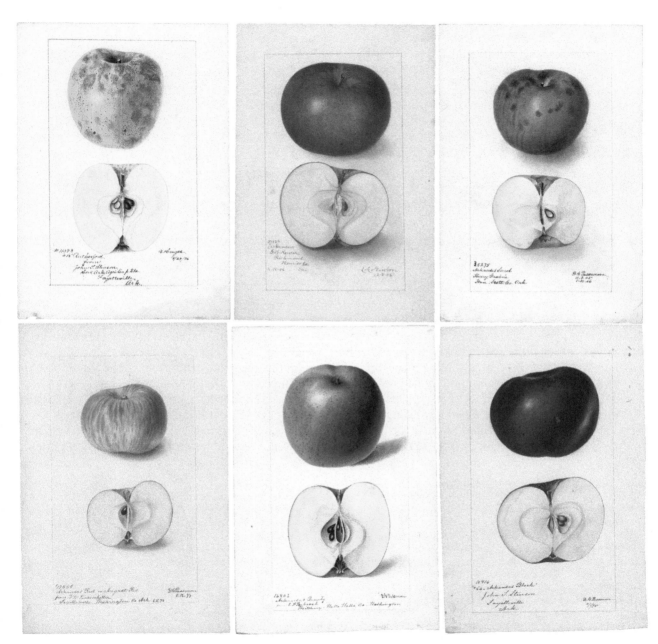

Exemplars of Arkansas apple cultivars, late 19th and early 20th centuries.

have been prepared by the AFWC for display at the upcoming St. Louis Exposition.[9] Outside the House chamber, George Williams of Pulaski County spoke against the Norwood resolution, citing the legendary linkage between the passionflower and Christianity, before echoing Churchill's characterization of the apple as a non-native plant and embracing "the flower indigenous to our soil."

Several other speakers continued in this vein, suggesting that the choice of state flower be left to the AFWC and in several cases complaining that adopting the apple blossom would be merely a commercial move and would misrepresent the state in the eyes of the rest of the nation. Randolph Comstock of Crawford County summed up this position neatly: "We don't want the people abroad to think we have nothing else in Arkansas besides apples. We [want] a flower for our emblem, not a fruit."[10]

In the end, the apples had it. Whether it was because of Barton's efforts or as a result of the state's apple-based economy cannot be determined, but before noon the House voted 70 to 19 in favor of the apple blossom's designation as the state floral emblem. As one club woman later quipped, "and again man was beguiled by the apple."

With bloviation accomplished and the vote taken, SCR 3 was passed along to Governor Jeff Davis for his signature, which was affixed on January 30, 1901.[11]

Arkansas's orchardists and farmers continued to ride high on the apple bandwagon through the second decade of the twentieth century. In 1920, Washington and Benton counties alone produced more than five million bushels of apples. Hard times, however, were in store. Over-reliance on varieties like the Ben Davis made Arkansas apples less popular for snacking or cooking than sweeter or tastier types. The apple-drying industry, which had used much of the region's low-grade fruit, began to decline after the enactment of the Pure Food and Drug Act of 1906. Before the act, some 250 evaporators had been in production; by 1920, the industry was all but extinct. Disease, insects, and late frosts beset Arkansas's orchards in the 1920s, and the onset of the Great Depression made matters worse. By 1935, Arkansas produced fewer than two million bushels of apples, whose market value had plunged to a fraction of its former level. These and other factors led farmers to diversify, thus ending their dependence on fruit production. In years to come, poultry would become a more characteristic

---

9   Or, perhaps not; the St. Louis World's Fair was scheduled for 1904, which would make these murals an example of extreme pre-need planning and execution. On the other hand, the magnificent murals from the 1893 Arkansas Pavilion at the Chicago Columbian exposition may have been preserved; language in Jessie Fuller's report of April 1900 raises this possibility ("Our Floral Emblem." *Arkansas Democrat*, April 26, 1900, p. 3).

10   *Arkansas Gazette*, January 26, 1901, p. 3 c1-5. With tongue possibly in cheek, the *Gazette*'s headline read "AGONY OVER." According to an account by Jane Kinley, who was Barton's great-granddaughter, Barton, running a 103° fever, wore a red dress to the State House on the day of the debate and passed out apples on the steps. With each apple came a note asserting that "These are the results of our beautiful apple blossoms, but what is the results [sic] of a passion flower? A dried shriveled pod!" Barton was also no great respecter of the passionflower's native status, dismissing it as "a pretty but rank and disagreeable weed, which isn't a native of Arkansas at all but will grow anywhere the farmer's hoe will let it." *The Arkansas News*, Fall 1984. http://67.220.50.228/collections/classroom/arkansas_news.aspx (accessed July 10, 2015).

11   With the legislature's vote in place, the AFWC seems to have fallen into step behind the gentlemen's choice. Writing in the *Arkansas Historical Quarterly* in 1943, Clara Eno, the onetime upholder of the passionflower (and founding member of the Arkansas History Commission), asserted that "When Mrs. Frederick Hanger was made president in 1899, the Federation...succeeded in getting the apple blossom designated as the official state flower." *What?*

agricultural product of the region.[12]

The apple blossom remains the state's floral emblem despite the apple's decline in importance as an Arkansas market crop. Or, perhaps that should be worded as "Arkansas's decline as a market producer of apples." Apples are one of the most valuable fruit crops in the United States. The 2014 U.S. apple crop, as reported in the USDA's annual statistics report of noncitrus fruits and nuts, totaled over 5.6 million tons and was valued at nearly three billion dollars. In that same report, twenty-nine states were listed as having commercial apple production, but Arkansas was not one of them. In 2004, the most recent year in which Arkansas was listed in the survey, Arkansas ranked thirty-second in apple production. Arkansas's 550 acres of commercial orchards produced about 1.9 million pounds of apples, 1.1 million of which were utilized, with a cash value of $390,000.

Brown Betty

Peel, core, and slice or chop six large apples. Set aside, covered. Grease or butter a small Dutch oven or deep baking pan and set aside. In a separate bowl, mix one cup melted butter, two cups rolled oats, two cups white or graham flour, two cups brown sugar, a scant handful of currants or raisins, two teaspoons of ground cinnamon, and a half-teaspoon of baking powder. Set aside. In another large bowl, mix well two tablespoons of cornstarch and the juice of two large lemons. Add apples and toss to coat the fruit with the lemon mixture.

Divide the oatmeal mixture. Line the bottom of the oven or pan with one-third, then spread the fruit over it. Cover the fruit with the rest of the oatmeal. Bake uncovered in a warm oven about one-half hour or more until the top is brown. Eat with heavy cream, sweetened, or custard.

Source: Original author unknown, recipe card in author's collection

If the industry has declined, there remains considerable sentimental support—and a steady local market demand—for the Arkansas apple. Every October, Lincoln holds its Apple Festival, featuring a weekend full of crafts, demonstrations, music, and other entertainment, as well as, of course, consumption of apples in pies, cakes, butter, and sauce—baked, stewed, fried, and even fresh. The festival concludes on a Sunday afternoon with an apple core–throwing contest.

There remain fewer than 150 growers in the state, located mainly in northern Arkansas. They grow for local farmers' markets and also in roadside stands. Their orchards are small, and most grow familiar market varieties such as Red and Golden Delicious, Galas, and Jonathans. Some, however, produce quantities of "heirloom" apples, ones that would have been familiar to nurserymen and farmers of a century ago. Of these, the best-known and highly prized may be the Arkansas Black. In the late nineteenth century, the Black may have accounted for as much as ten percent of Arkansas's apple production, but today it is a rarity in the marketplace—not extinct, or even particularly threatened, just respectably hard to find.

The Arkansas Black apple is not particularly black, at least not when on the tree or first picked. It is believed to be a Winesap variant and like other Winesaps, its skin is a deep red when ripe. Its meat or flesh is hard when

---

12   Leading Arkansas horticulturist Thomas Rothrock blamed the decline of the apple industry mainly on the codling moth, whose larva is known as the common apple worm.

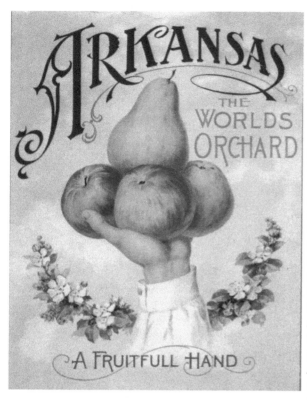

ARKANSAS
THE WORLDS ORCHARD
A FRUITFULL HAND

fresh, and tart, though not as tart as a good Granny Smith. Arkansas Blacks are medium sized and are slightly "flat"—that is, wide, rather than long. They are fine when fresh, but are traditionally prized as good "keepers"—apples that hold up well in storage. Stored properly, they soften and slightly mellow in flavor, and the skin darkens into the shade that gives the variety claim to its name.

The Arkansas Black appears sometimes in organic markets and farmers' markets, more often in roadside stands but, at least for its devotees, not often enough. The Black is also grown outside of the state; Missouri orchards produce quantities of it, although one might quibble that these might more honestly be sold as "Expatriate Blacks." This, however, would be unfair; the Missouri-grown fruit fits the profile of the old Arkansas Black in shape, shade, and savor. They are good stewed, dried, eaten fresh from the peck basket, and, when slightly sweetened, form the heart of ambrosial pies, Brown Betty, and Dutch oven cobblers. There are even anecdotal indications that the commercial fortunes of the Arkansas Black are on the rise, making it possible that it will be more widely available in markets far from where it is grown. Success to this, but perhaps not too much. Were the Arkansas Black to challenge the Red Delicious in national markets, it might lose a little of the savor of being a local semi-secret, a hardy survivor beloved by its intimates and initiates.

For further reading:

Arkansas State Flower vertical file, Arkansas History Commission.

Brown, C. Allan. "Horticulture in Early Arkansas." *Arkansas Historical Quarterly* 43, no. 2 (Summer 1984): 99–123.

Eno, Clara B. "Some Accomplishments of Arkansas Federation of Women's Clubs." *Arkansas Historical Quarterly* 2, no. 3 (September 1943).

"Fruit-Full Arkansas: Apples." Special Collections. University of Arkansas Libraries, Fayetteville, Arkansas. http://scipio.uark.edu/cdm4/index_apples.php?CISOROOT=/apples (accessed July 10, 2015).

Geiling, Natasha. "The Real Johnny Appleseed Brought Apples—and Booze—to the American Frontier." Smithsonian.com. http://www.smithsonianmag.com/arts-culture/real-johnny-appleseed-brought-applesand-booze-american-frontier-180953263/#AOHYh3PViH5vHm7t.99 (accessed July 10, 2015).

"Nutritional Information for Hard Apple Cider." http://www.livestrong.com/article/533509-the-nutritional-information-for-hard-apple-cider/ (accessed July 10, 2015).

Pollan, Michael. *The Botany of Desire: A Plant's-Eye View of the World*. New York: Random House, 2001.

Ragsdale, John G. "Arkansas Black Apple." *Encyclopedia of Arkansas History & Culture*. http://www.encyclopediaofarkansas.net/encyclopedia/entry-detail.aspx?entryID=2100 (accessed July 10, 2015).

Rom, Roy Curt. "Apple Industry." *Encyclopedia of Arkansas History & Culture*. http://www.encyclopediaofarkansas.net/encyclopedia/entry-detail.aspx?entryID=2098 (accessed July 10, 2015).

Rothrock, Thomas. "A King that Was." *Arkansas Historical Quarterly* 39, no. 4 (Winter 1974).

United States Department of Agriculture, National Agricultural Statistics Service. *Crop Production, 2014 Summary*. Washington: USDA, January 2015. http://www.usda.gov/nass/PUBS/TODAYRPT/cropan15.pdf (accessed July 10, 2015).

Ware, David. "Official State Floral Emblem, a.k.a Apple Blossom." *Encyclopedia of Arkansas History & Culture*. http://www.encyclopediaofarkansas.net/encyclopedia/entry-detail.aspx?entryID=3145 (accessed July 10, 2015).

For A Buttered Apple Pie:

Pare, quarter and core tart apples, lay in paste No. 3 (butter-crust pastry fortified with egg whites), cover with the same; bake half an hour; when drawn, gently raise the top crust. Add sugar, butter, orange peel and a sufficient quantity of rose water.

Source: *The Cook Not Mad, or Rational Cookery; Being a Collection of Original and Selected Receipts...* (Watertown, NY: Knowlton and Rice, 1831).

CHAPTER 3: STATE FLAG

Diamond Shape, Delta Born

About nineteen miles northeast of Pine Bluff by Arkansas Route 15 and U.S. Highway 79, near the border of Jefferson County, is the small agricultural center of Wabbaseka. Established in the 1870s near the Wataseka Bayou, the town long served as a service town for local cotton plantations. It lies along the route of the Union Pacific, formerly the St. Louis Southwestern Railway, better known as the Cotton Belt. Its shops are few, its population is sparse, and its local high school has been consolidated with that of nearby Altheimer. A small park and picnic ground at the center of Wabbaseka lie close by the railroad tracks. In that park on October 12, 2013, a ceremony marked the dedication of a memorial honoring the memory and legacy of a local woman who "made good," the creator of the Arkansas state flag.

◇ ◇ ◇

A flag—be it national, state, municipal, sectarian, or corporate—is a symbol. It must come from something, represent something, stand for something. As author Arthur C. Clarke observed, "Flags do not wave in a vacuum." For most of its first century of existence, Arkansas designated no such official cloth. In the second decade of the twentieth century, however, this deficiency was remedied. An important occasion coupled with a developing sense of pride and state identity led to the creation of a flag both handsome and distinct, resembling that of no other state.

In late December 1819, a keelboat was moored at the old former colonial town of Arkansas Post, bearing appointed territorial governor James Miller and his party. Established in 1686, Arkansas Post was in 1819 a muddy hamlet populated by French and Spanish Creoles, a group of Quapaw natives, and some recent arrivals from the United States, intent on finding and exploiting such opportunities as might arise in a developing country. It was also the designated capital or administrative center of the new Arkansaw Territory, created by Congress from the southern half of Missouri Territory on July 4, 1819.

To lead the government of the new territory, President James Monroe chose James Miller of New Hampshire, who had distinguished himself during the War of 1812. As a major of the Twenty-First U.S. Infantry at the Battle of Lundy's Lane (present-day Niagara Falls, Ontario) on July 25, 1814, Miller won fame for modestly replying, "I will try, sir!" when asked by his commanding officer to capture a British artillery battery.[1]

Appointed governor of the Arkansas Territory on March 3, 1819, Miller did not leave New England to take up his governorship until September. Instead, he traveled first to Washington DC, then to Pittsburgh, Pennsylvania, where he collected equipment for the territorial militia that he would organize and command. Only then did he head south, sailing down the Ohio and Mississippi Rivers with armaments in tow. Along the way, settlements reportedly staged impromptu festival salutes to the Hero of Lundy's Lane.[2] Somehow, Miller and his entourage managed to survive these patriotic manifestations and sailed down the Mississippi, then hauled their way up the Arkansas River, arriving at Arkansas Post on December 26, 1819.

James Miller, first governor of Arkansas Territory.

Miller's keelboat was decorated with gilt lettering along its cabin sides proclaiming its destination. At its masthead flew a national flag with twenty-one stars. Eyewitnesses noted that the flag was embellished with "Arkansaw" in large letters and Miller's motto "I'll Try, Sir!" emblazoned on the stripes.[3] No record survives of public acknowledgement of or reaction to this design, nor is there any evidence of this flag serving as an official flag for the new territory. Instead, it was a bit of private

---

1   Miller's assault was successful, but the battle ended in an effective draw; commanders of both British and U.S. forces were injured, and the U.S. invasion of Canada was effectively stopped. Much was made of Miller, whose success on the field of battle contrasted with the luck of most American commanders, at least on land, during the war. His response to his commander was sometimes reported as, "I will try, sir" and other times as, "I'll try, sir!" Dallas Herndon, in his *Centennial History of Arkansas* (1922), opts for the latter version, albeit without the exclamation point.

2   Given the bibulous nature of the early American republic, it is not surprising that these tributes to Miller involved spirits both high and ardent. At one (at least), the drinking game ploy involved a question such as, "Can you drink to the health of the Hero of Lundy's Lane?" to which the only worthy response was, "I will try, sir!" One suspects that Miller, as the serial guest of honor, was probably somewhat the worse for this succession of patriotic tributes by the time he finally reached Arkansas Post on Boxing Day.

3   The practice of modifying or elaborating the national flag in this way was not uncommon; at the time, no law or regulation forbade it. Not until 1923 was a code for use and display of the U.S. flag drafted. That code was prepared by the National Flag Conference in an attempt to bring uniformity to the flag-related procedures of the army, the navy and some sixty-six other organizations and was largely adopted as part of the U.S. Code in 1942. Among its recommendations was this: "The flag should never have placed upon it, nor on any part of it, nor attached to it any mark, insignia, letter, word, figure, design, picture, or drawing of any nature." (USC Title 36 Chapter 10 Par. 176)

Conjectural reconstruction of Miller's 1819 flag.

enterprise, a note of cheery patriotic bravado which was well-suited to the challenges faced by Miller as he took over the duties of his office. During Miller's dilatory journey, territorial secretary Robert Crittenden had taken steps to organize the territory's provisional government, convened its court, and had in fact held elections for its first legislature, which would meet in the new year at Arkansas Post.[4]

From 1819 through the territorial period and early statehood, Arkansas (like many other states) survived comfortably without an official state flag, although an official great seal was adopted. The onset of the Civil War does not seem to have spurred any calls for adoption of one, either, and during the war, Arkansans "marched to the sound of the guns" under a variety of flags.

One of the best-remembered Confederate banners was the "Little Blue Flag" carried by Arkansas troops commanded by Major General Patrick Cleburne in Hardee's Corps of the Army of Tennessee. This was a version of the "Hardee" battle flag which was in fact designed by General Simon Buckner, who led a division under General William Hardee.[5] According to an anonymous soldier under Buckner's command, Buckner's wife made flags that had "no artistic taste...but which could not be mistaken." The Hardee pattern battle flag was issued to units beginning in November 1861. It featured a blue field (later modified by the addition of a white border) enclosing a white circle or full moon. This was seen in examples both nearly square and elongatedly rectangular. The regiments of Cleburne's division fought under these "little blue flags" during 1862 and 1863.[6]

In 1864, General Joseph Johnston decreed a new battle flag for the regiments of the Army of Tennessee. Patrick Cleburne protested, and his personality and sterling reputation won the right for his division to retain its flags, slightly revised with a "squared" oval (sometimes referred to as a rectilinear moon), in which regimental mottos, honors, and emblems were often painted.

Arkansas's state flag deficiency persisted into the post-war era. Perhaps the state's unsettled political landscape prevented adoption of one, or perhaps there was simply little perceived need. One partial exception arose in 1876, when the reconstructed state contributed a pavilion to the grounds of the Philadelphia Centennial

---

4   Miller's tenure as governor was not considered particularly successful, but under his guidance the seat of government was moved from rented rooms in an Arkansas Post tavern to a two-room rented structure at the heart of embryonic Little Rock, not far from a tavern.

5   General William Hardee was commandant of cadets at the United States Military Academy before the Civil War. In 1855, he published *Rifle and Light Infantry Tactics for the Exercise and Manoeuvres of Troops When Acting as Light Infantry or Riflemen*, popularly known as *Hardee's Tactics*, which became the best-known drill manual of the Civil War. He is also credited with the design of the so-called "Hardee" hat, a heavy, high-crowned felt dress-uniform cover which sported a brim folded up at one side to further reduce its already limited weather-protection utility.

6   Irish-born Patrick Cleburne was a Helena lawyer and apothecary whose military training prior to the Civil War was limited to less than four years' service in the British army, keeping order in his home country. He immigrated to the United States in 1850 and settled in Helena. In 1861, he was selected as captain of the Yell Guards, a Helena militia. He proved himself to be an able leader and his rise was rapid. By the end of 1862, he held the rank of major general. Cleburne died in battle in late 1864.

Exposition. Apparently a state flag or banner graced the structure; a sketchy mention suggests that it resembled the "little blue flag" of wartime but with the state seal design traced in the central white oval. In this respect, the flag presaged the designs of several state flags adopted during the final decades of the century.

Arkansas Building at the World's Columbian Exposition, Chicago, 1893.

The World's Columbian Exposition, held in Chicago from May through October of 1893, is sometimes identified as having provided impetus for a number of states to create flags for themselves. Most states, including Arkansas, contributed pavilions to the fairgrounds; a photograph of the Arkansas building shows a flag flying in front, but no detail can be made out. The exposition's actual influence on state flag adoptions is debatable, however, as only a handful of states adopted flags anew during the early 1890s or modified earlier existing ones. Some states seem to have adopted official flags to represent them at the Louisiana Purchase Exposition (St. Louis, 1903) or other such expositions. Perhaps it was the net influence of these world's fairs that encouraged some states to think of adopting representative colors, while other states' adoptions seem to have been spurred by the maturation of their respective governments and polities. For whatever reason, it is true that by the second decade of the twentieth century, most states had managed to adopt an official flag. Many of these were variations of what vexillologists[7] have described as the "seal on a bedsheet": a state seal on a single-colored background. Seen in this context, Arkansas's adoption of its own state flag can be seen as timely, rather than delayed, and both ingenious and thoughtful in design.

The first attempt to create a state flag for Arkansas took shape in the spring of 1910, when the Arkansas Federation of Women's Clubs (AFWC) was contacted by the national office of the federation, requesting a state flag to display in an upcoming convention. To the surprise (and, presumably, embarrassment) of the state federation, a quick bit of research revealed that no such flag existed. Undaunted, Mrs. John I. Moore of Helena, art teacher and wife of a prominent Helena attorney, developed a design for a state flag. Her design was shown to State Senator Charles Jacobson of Pulaski County, who urged the federation to submit the flag to the

---

7   These being the legion of scholars who vex themselves and one another with lively discussions of flags, pennants, banners, and related matters.

legislature in the General Assembly's next session for consideration as an official flag for Arkansas.[8]

What was this design? No contemporary description is known to have survived, but a letter to the editor of the *Arkansas Gazette* from April 24, 1910, suggests that it resembled the "little blue flag" of Civil War renown; if this is the case, then it was a conventional design, probably a state seal superimposed on a blue ground, possibly with white borders. In short, it was a design well within the mainstream of state flag designs.

In May 1911, the AFWC's annual meeting in El Dorado voted to present the flag to the legislature in hopes of designation. At the meeting's close, AFWC president Mrs. P. H. Ellsworth and Mrs. Moore traveled to Little Rock. They arrived on May 13, which proved to be a less-than-ideal day for their errand. May 13 marked the last day of the regular session of the Thirty-Eighth General Assembly, which had convened in the new—and, as yet, unfinished—Capitol building. The session had gone long and members were eager to adjourn, either to leave town or to enjoy the spectacle promised by the impending reunion of the United Confederate Veterans, which would bring as many as 40,000 visitors—former Confederates and their families—to the Rose City. In addition, much was being made of the ornamental gaslight fixture installed in front of the new capitol due to be ignited by Governor George Donaghey to celebrate the arrival of natural gas to Little Rock. The session was adjourned at noon on the 13th; thirty minutes later, Governor Donaghey issued his call ordering a special session, to meet at the Capitol on May 22, after the dust, din, and parades of the Confederate reunion were done. With such distractions, the modest proposal of the AFWC was doomed to be overlooked. The matter would, however, like the South itself, rise again.

◊ ◊ ◊

On January 14, 1911, the U.S. Navy's latest Wyoming-class battleship, USS *Arkansas*, was launched and christened at Camden, New Jersey. The *Arkansas* was a massive dreadnought, a fitting instrument of the new global reach of the navy. Stem to stern, she measured 562 feet, 6 inches (171.45 m) long with a beam of 93 feet, 2 inches (28.40 m). The ship was powered by four-shaft steam turbines and twelve coal-fired boilers. The *Arkansas* was armed with a main battery of twelve 12-inch guns in six twin gun turrets. Over the next eighteen months, the *Arkansas* was fitted out at the Philadelphia Navy Yard and was commissioned and accepted for service on September 17, 1912. That December, after sea trials, she would convey President William Howard Taft and other dignitaries to the Panama Canal Zone.

Earlier in 1912, the Pine Bluff chapter of the Daughters of the American Revolution (DAR) resolved to present a stand of colors—that is, a national flag, a naval ensign, and a state flag—to the *Arkansas* as a token of good wishes from its namesake state. The chapter contacted Secretary of State Earle Hodges, who replied indirectly, via a newspaper article, that no official state flag existed.[9] The Pine Bluff DAR, apparently unaware

8   This origin story bears an intriguing resemblance to that of another state's flag: Washington State. In 1914, the national society of the Daughters of the American Revolution (DAR) asked the state organization to send a state flag to Washington DC to be hung in the DAR Memorial Continental Hall. The Washington State DAR "discovered" that no such flag existed, so a committee of the DAR chaired by Mrs. S. J. Chadwick, wife of justice of the Supreme Court Stephen J. Chadwick, created a design having "a green background for the Evergreen State, upon which was the seal of the State of Washington." The banner was used in Memorial Continental Hall and then returned to Washington in April 1916 to hang behind the speaker's table at the annual state assembly of the DAR. In 1929, the DAR presented a state flag to Governor Roland H. Hartley, who received it on behalf of the state.

9   No explanation can be found as to why the secretary of state chose to respond in this way. It must have made sense at the time.

of the earlier initiative of the AFWC, resolved to present a flag for official designation at the next legislature. A competition was announced, advertising for flag designs. Secretary of State Hodges agreed to serve as custodian of the submissions, which were to be considered with their creators' identities concealed.

USS Arkansas *at sea.*

On December 12, 1912, a brief article appeared in the *Arkansas Gazette* indicating that a total of twenty-one flag designs had been submitted to the Secretary of State's Office. In a few days, Hodges would name the members of a commission to judge the assorted entries.

On December 28, the flag design selection judges were announced. The committee consisted of:

Major Clifton Breckenridge, Fort Smith

Dr. J. H. Reynolds, President, University of Arkansas

Mrs. Joseph T. Robinson

Mrs. George W. Donaghey

J. N. Heiskell, of the *Arkansas Gazette*

Mrs. Jo Frauenthal, AFWC

George Rose, Attorney, Little Rock

Julia McAlmont, State Regent, DAR, Pine Bluff

Mrs. Richard Welles, UDC, Fayetteville

George B. Cook, Superintendent of Public Instruction

Dallas Herndon, Arkansas History Commission

Judge Jacob Treiber, Little Rock

Elmer Clarke, Publisher, *Arkansas Democrat*

Dr. V. Y. Cook, Batesville

James Jordan, former Superintendent of Public Instruction

The *Gazette* informed its readers that the committee would meet at the Hotel Marion on January 2, 1913, to choose the flag's design.

This announcement provoked an angry communication from State Senator Charles Jacobsen (10th District, Pulaski and Perry Counties), who reminded readers of the AFWC's 1911 project, complained of Secretary of State Hodges's sponsorship of the DAR initiative, and predicted that the legislature would, in the spirit of "true chivalry," adopt Mrs. Moore's design.

An early January 1913 letter to the *Gazette* from Mrs. W. L. Dewoody of the Pine Bluff DAR attempted to smooth over hurt feelings. Dewoody asserted that the DAR's competition had been undertaken without knowledge of the AFWC's flag initiative. Noting that many designs had been submitted for consideration, Dewoody suggested that the AFWC's choice be added to the mix:

> If our design is more desirable, we hope it will be adopted; if yours (the Federation design) is more resperentative [*sic*] and typical than ours, we trust the legislature will adopt that. We are not working in a partisan spirit for our design, but for a design that will reflect lasting honor and credit upon the great state of Arkansas, something that she can be proud of long after little factions are forgotten.

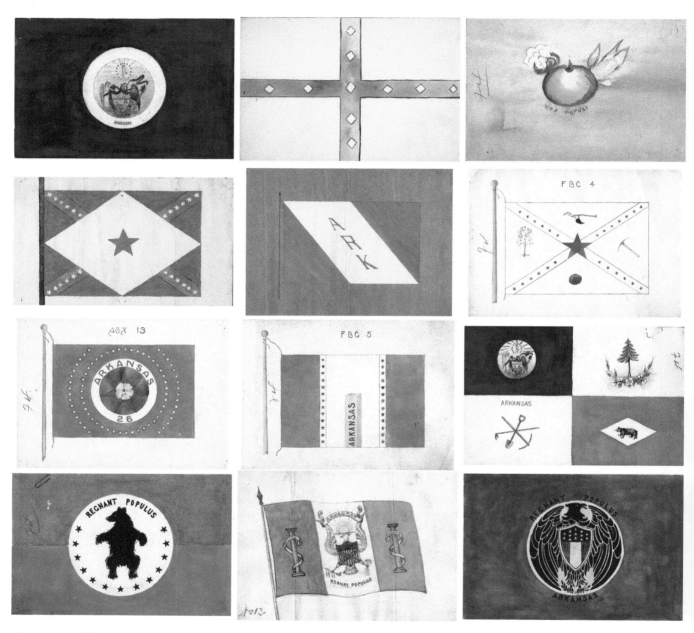

Blossoms and diamonds and bears, oh my! A selection of flag designs submitted to the Arkansas Secretary of State's Office in 1912.

The committee met as scheduled on January 2, 1913, then again a month later, to evaluate and rank an assortment of some sixty-five designs, the work of thirty groups and individuals. Some sent in only one design, others as many as eight. Some were submitted as watercolors or were pasted together from colored paper. Many used one or more elements from the state seal or other items symbolic of the state's heritage and economy.

Several submissions featured the apple blossom, the recently designated state floral emblem. One placed a cotton boll on a blue field, along with James Miller's motto, "I'll Try, Sir." Another submitter suggested two designs, one with a cornucopia or horn-of-plenty, the other exhibiting a dove with an olive branch in its beak, each design bearing the motto *vox populi* (the voice of the people). At least two designs featured bears, harkening back to one of the earliest nicknames for Arkansas. Several designs by various hands overlaid the state seal or a variation of it onto a plain field. One graceful submission placed a crescent moon over a river, with a steamboat plying its way. Yet another, emphatic in its optimism, showed a naked male figure, viewed from his left rear quarter, ascending a wide stairway, torch in hand, headed toward the sun. The theme, the designer asserted, was "progress."

Original design submission by Willie Kavanaugh Hocker.

Willie Hocker re-enacting her creation of the state's flag design.

Ultimately the committee chose a striking design: a field of red, surmounted by a white rhombus or equilateral four-sided diamond shape signifying Arkansas's status as the nation's only diamond-producing state. The diamond was bordered by twenty-five stars on a blue band; centered in the diamond were three blue stars.

The anonymous submitter explained the symbolism thus: the colors meant that Arkansas was one of the United States of America. The three blue stars signified that Arkansas had belonged to <u>three</u> countries (France, Spain, and the United States) before attaining statehood; 1803 was the year of the Louisiana Purchase when the land that is now Arkansas was acquired by the United States; and Arkansas was the <u>third</u> state created from the purchase by the United States. The twenty-five stars in the blue band stood for Arkansas's status as the twenty-fifth state admitted to the Union.

The artist responsible for this design was a Jefferson County schoolteacher, Willie Kavanaugh Hocker of Wabbaseka. Raised on a plantation along the Wataseka Bayou, Hocker spent thirty-four years teaching in the public schools of Pine Bluff and Jefferson County. Hocker was also a member of the Pine Bluff chapter of the Daughters of the American Revolution—the very chapter that originated and sponsored the flag-design competition.

A biographical sketch published in 1923 indicated that "while a guest in Pine Bluff, Miss Hocker designed and drew the winning flag." A memoir by Hocker herself indicated that the design suggested itself in a dream. The committee accorded it unanimous approval, subject to a minor modification: the state's name was added to the diamond, with one star placed above the name and two dropped below. This made possible even more symbolic weight: the twin stars below the state name would suggest the "twin" relationship of Arkansas and Michigan, which were admitted to the Union within approximately seven months of each other, maintaining the balance between free and slave states in Congress.

Governor Joseph T. Robinson signed Senate Concurrent Resolution 11, adopting Hocker's design as the state's official flag, on February 26, 1913. The flag was first shown to the public later that year at the Arkansas State Fair, when it was christened with a bottle of "radium-infused" Hot Springs water by Willie Hocker, who then grasped the halyard and hoisted the state flag aloft before a reported crowd of some 20,000.

The design remained unchanged until 1923, when the General Assembly added a fourth star to the central diamond to represent Arkansas's membership in the Confederate States of America. House Concurrent Resolution 4 asserted that it was "a proper and fitting respect to the memory of the heroic men and women of that period, who, by their matchless sacrifice and unprecedented feats of heroism on the field of battle deserve due and proper recognition as does the cause they served so well." The measure specified that one star should be placed above the letter "R" in Arkansas, with a second one (styled "the present one") should be positioned above the last letter "A." Presumably, the remaining two stars would be located directly below the two on top, but the measure did not so specify. The resulting visual simulation of a horizontally spread letter "H" did not, however, last long. The Extraordinary Session of 1924, at Hocker's suggestion, revised the design. House Concurrent Resolution 11, introduced by Neill Bohlinger of Pulaski County, placed three stars below and one above, with the three lower stars arranged as an inverted triangle.

◇ ◇ ◇

The design of the flag of the United States is strictly laid out in the U.S. Code in terms of proportions, shapes, and colors. By contrast, that of the Arkansas flag is only generally described in the Arkansas Code:

Title 1 General Provisions

Chapter 4 State Symbols, Motto, Etc.

A.C.A. § 1-4-101 (2011)

1-4-101. State flag.

(a) (1) (A) The official state flag shall be a rectangle of red on which is placed a large white diamond, bordered by a wide band of blue on which are twenty-five (25) white stars.

(B) Across the diamond shall be the word "ARKANSAS" and four (4) blue stars, with one (1) star above and three (3) stars below the word "ARKANSAS."

(C) The star above the word "ARKANSAS" shall be below the upper corner of the diamond.

(D) The three (3) stars below the word "ARKANSAS" shall be placed so that one (1) star shall be above the lower corner of the diamond and two (2) stars shall be placed symmetrically, parallel above and to the right and left of the star in the lower corner of the diamond.

In 2011, the legislature added language defining the colors of the flag as "Old Glory Red," white, and "Old Glory Blue," the same colors prescribed for official flags of the United States. Although this established standards for color, the rest of the official description provides room for distinctive variations on the theme of the proud diamond banner. The size of the diamond within the red field varies by maker, as do the angles of the diamond and the proportionate width of its blue border. Stars may be represented in any form and the word "Arkansas" may be rendered in any typeface, so long as the proper number of stars are arranged in the correct pattern, with the state's name resting below the (risen) star of the Confederacy.

In 1916, outgoing Secretary of State Hodges presented the flag-design entries to the Arkansas History Commission. Hocker similarly deeded her original submission, a 2' x 3' silk version. They are preserved there and remain colorful reminders of an episode which presented Arkansans with the opportunity of defining how they represented themselves to the rest of the nation.

Equipped with its stand of colors, including the Arkansas state flag, the *Arkansas* served as one of the navy's beloved capital ships for more than three decades. In early 1914, an international incident with Mexico culminated in the American occupation of Veracruz. Two of the *Arkansas*'s crewmen were killed in the fighting, and another two, John Grady and Jonas H. Ingram, won the Medal of Honor for actions during the occupation. During World War I, she was part of Battleship Division Nine, which was attached to the British Grand Fleet, but she saw no action during the war. During the interwar years, the *Arkansas* performed a variety of duties, including training cruises for midshipmen and goodwill visits overseas.

Following the outbreak of World War II, the *Arkansas* conducted neutrality patrols in the Atlantic prior to America's entry into the war. Thereafter, she escorted convoys to Europe. In the summer of 1944, she supported the D-Day invasion of Normandy and the liberation of southern France. In 1945, she bombarded Japanese positions on Iwo Jima and Okinawa. After the end of the war, she ferried troops back to the United States. Ultimately, the *Arkansas*, the nation's oldest serving battleship, was deemed obsolete; her last cruise was to Bikini Atoll, where she last served as a target in a pair of nuclear bomb tests in July 1946.

◊ ◊ ◊

For the rest of her life, Willie Hocker received honor for her design of the Arkansas state flag. In 1929, she represented Arkansas at the National Federation of Business and Professional Women's Clubs' Pageant of Famous Women of the United States. In 1938, the Wabbaseka School Board named the new high school building for her.

Hocker was a longtime member of Wabbaseka Methodist Church, at which she taught Sunday school. She lived directly behind the church and wrote a brief history of it in 1934. She died on February 6, 1944.

In the decades following Hocker's death, the small town of Wabbaseka waxed and waned, mainly the latter, in size and prosperity, paralleling the fate of much of the surrounding delta. Apart from its modest fame as the home of Willie Hocker, Wabbaseka was known, barely, as the birthplace and childhood home of the writer, political activist, and Black Panther Party leader Eldridge Cleaver (1935–1998). In 1950, its population stood at 375, which shot up to 432 in 1960. By 2000, this number had fallen to 323 and by 2010 to 255.

In 2013, a Wabbaseka native set out to create something that would draw attention to his community and give it a focal point of civic pride. On January 1, author Jason Irby, a native son who had attended Willie K. Hocker Elementary and Junior High Schools, as well as Wabbaseka High School, called a press conference at which he pledged to establish a memorial in the City Park to commemorate the 100th year of Arkansas's flag. By the following week, the Wabbaseka Memorial Committee was formed and, on February 26, ground was broken. On the same day, a resolution was

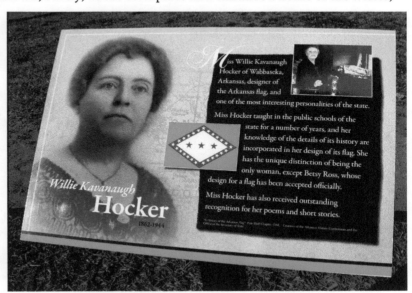

Wabbaseka memorial interpretive panel.

adopted in the Arkansas House saluting Hocker as the creator of the state flag, commemorating the flag's 100th anniversary, and supporting the campaign to create a memorial in Wabbaseka.

On October 12, 2013, the Arkansas Flag/Wabbaseka Memorial site was dedicated. A motorcade began at Oaklawn Park in Hot Springs, where the flag was first flown in 1913 at the Arkansas State Fair. The motorcade stopped in Little Rock, home of the current Arkansas State Fair, and was greeted with a reception and presented with flags to be flown at the memorial site. The motorcade then proceeded to Pine Bluff—where Hocker was staying when she first envisioned the flag design—before proceeding to Wabbaseka, Willie Hocker's home town.

The memorial was completed in February 2014 and dedicated on February 26. Panels developed by the University of Arkansas at Pine Bluff (UAPB) Art Department, using information and elements supplied by the Arkansas History Commission and the Arkansas Secretary of State's Office, were unveiled. UAPB's Agriculture and ROTC Departments participated in and exhibited at the ceremony. Other guests included the Little Rock Air Force Base and Arkansas National Guard units. The Navy Band (Blues City Quintet) from Millington, Tennessee, provided music.

At the memorial, three flagpoles fly the national flag as well as the evolutions of Arkansas's flag. Interpretive plaques tell the stories of Willie Kavanaugh Hocker, the *Arkansas*, and the flag itself. It is not known how many motorists driving along Highway 79 stop to read the panels and reflect on the intertwined stories of a spinster schoolteacher, a capital ship, and a state icon, but perhaps the real significance lies in the fact that the community remembers and celebrates these things. The Arkansas flag came from a daughter of the Delta and a citizen of Wabbaseka, and it stands for something larger: the state itself.

This mural, located at the intersection of Chestnut Street and U.S. 65B in downtown Pine Bluff, honors Willie Hocker and her creation of the Arkansas state flag. It was painted in the 1990s by artists David and Susan Kelly Frye of Houston, Texas.

For further reading:

Acts of Arkansas, 1913.

Acts of Arkansas, 1923.

Acts of Arkansas, Special Session, 1924.

Acts of Arkansas, 2011.

Arkansas Secretary of State. *Protocol for the State Flag*. Little Rock: Secretary of State's Office.

Hanley, Ray, and Steven Hanley. *Arky: The Saga of the USS* Arkansas. Little Rock, AR: Butler Center Books, 2014.

Hocker, Willie K. "A History of the Official Flag of Arkansas." *Arkansas Historical Association Publications* 4. Conway, AR: Arkansas Historical Association, 1917.

Hooker, Jane. "Willie Kavanaugh Hocker." *Encyclopedia of Arkansas History & Culture*. http://www.encyclopediaofarkansas. net/encyclopedia/entry-detail.aspx?search=1&entryID=2948 (accessed July 3, 2015).

Leslie, James W. *Pine Bluff and Jefferson County, a Pictorial History*. Norfolk, VA: The Donning Company, 1981.

Shankle, George Earlie. *State Names, Flags, Seals, Songs, Birds, Flowers, and Other Symbols: A Study Based on Historical Documents Giving the Origin and Significance of the State Names, Nicknames, Mottoes, Seals, Flags, Flowers, Birds, Songs, and Descriptive Comments on the Capitol Buildings and on Some of the Leading State Histories, with Facsimiles of the State Flags and Seals*. Rev. ed. Westport, CT: Greenwood Press, 1970.

Shearer, Benjamin F., and Barbara Smith Shearer. *State Names, Seals, Flags and Symbols: A Historical Guide*. 3rd ed. Westport, CT: Greenwood Press, 2002.

Stokes, Phyllis. "Pride of Wabbaseka: Small Town Celebrates History behind State Flag," *Pine Bluff Commercial*, March 28, 2014. http://m.pbcommercial.com/news/local/pride-wabbaseka-small-town-celebrates-history-behind-state-flag (accessed July 3, 2015).

Ware, David. "Arkansas State Flag." *Encyclopedia of Arkansas History & Culture*. http://www.encyclopediaofarkansas.net/encyclopedia/entry-detail.aspx?search=1&entryID=3151 (accessed July 3, 2015).

CHAPTER 4: STATE BIRD

Or, Who Dares to Mock the Mockingbird?

The craze for designation of state birds began in 1926, when the Kentucky cardinal (*Cardinalis cardinalis*), commonly known as the red bird, was officially selected as the state bird of Kentucky. The resolution of the Senate of Kentucky, the House of Representatives concurring, approved the designation on February 26, 1926. The enthusiasm for selecting avian representatives swelled in the following year. On January 31, 1927, the Texas legislature approved a measure adopting, at the suggestion of the state's Federation of Women's Clubs, the mockingbird as the state bird. This action was quickly followed by one in the Wyoming legislature, which produced a measure adopted on February 27 designating the western meadowlark as that state's chosen bird. Missouri, Maine, Florida, Oregon, and Alabama chose their state birds by year's end.[1]

The next spate of bird designations came in 1929. Three states named their official birds that year—Arkansas was the first out of the gate. The measure to designate the mockingbird as the state bird was sponsored by State Representative Daniel Webster of Saline County, acting at the request of the Arkansas Federation of Women's Clubs. Mrs. W. A. Utley, who directed the campaign, was

---

1   New Hampshire's Federation of Women's Clubs chose the purple finch as their state's bird in 1927, but the legislature may not have noticed; the ladies' choice was not officially ratified until thirty years later.

responsible for promoting the legislation naming the mockingbird as the official state bird. The measure failed in its first outing; on January 30, Webster's proposed House Concurrent Resolution 12 failed to gain approval. In the *Encyclopedia of Arkansas History & Culture*, John Spurgeon noted that the measure "was first perceived as a joke but passed following speeches proclaiming the mockingbird's value to farmers."

Webster's second introduction of the resolution, now bearing the number 22, was successful.[2] On March 5, 1929, Governor Harvey Parnell and the Forty-Seventh General Assembly adopted House Concurrent Resolution Number 22 proclaiming the following: "The mockingbird is declared and everywhere recognized as the state bird of the State of Arkansas." Four other states—Florida, Mississippi, Tennessee, and Texas—have also designated the mockingbird as their official state bird. Only the cardinal and western meadowlark have more state-bird designations.[3]

The mockingbird, *Mimus polyglottos*, is one of the most common and most easily recognized birds in the South, but is not restricted to the region; they are found throughout North America, including southern Canada and Mexico, and as far offshore as Hawaii. However, they are most often encountered in the southern regions of the United States and are most often sighted in Texas and southern Florida (both of which, appropriately, have designated the mockingbird as their own state bird). Mockingbirds prefer open areas and forest edges. They are found in various places, including residential areas, farmlands, roadsides, city parks, open grassy areas with thickets, and brushy deserts. They require a tree or higher perch from which they can defend their territories.

Cigarette package premium card, ca. 1888.

Northern mockingbirds are, technically speaking, migratory. It is true that the majority are "residents" and therefore do not migrate, but some mockingbirds do migrate for the colder months—particularly those that live in northerly regions or elevated altitudes. These migrant mockingbirds sensibly head for the warmer weather of milder geographic locations such as Mexico, the Caribbean islands, and the Bahamas. Most of Arkansas's mockingbirds, however, stay put.

The adult mockingbird is between nine and eleven inches in length and weighs almost two ounces, with a wingspan of thirteen to fifteen inches. It has a slender bill, a light gray coat, whitish undersides and patches on wings, a long tail that is a darker gray with white outer feathers, and black legs.

Males are slightly larger than females but otherwise resemble them, except for having slightly lighter tail feathers. Mockingbirds are usually monogamous, at least within a single breeding season; one ornithological

2   Other birds were not so favored by the 1929 Assembly. HB 67, a measure to protect quail and partridges, failed to pass.

3   Arkansas was followed in designating state birds by Nebraska (western meadowlark, March 22) and Illinois (cardinal, June 4).

Mockingbirds and an
unwelcome visitor,
lithograph by John James
Audubon, from Birds of
America (1840 octavo
edition).

source observes dryly that "polygyny and bigamy seem to occur only rarely in this species." A female may produce as many as three broods, or batches, of chicks in a season; the first produces from four to six eggs, with smaller yields in successive broods. Lifetime mating occurs occasionally.

Arkansas State Bird

Mockingbirds may live as long as eight years in the wild, and some captive examples have lived up to twenty years. They are notably territorial and will defend their nests vigorously. John James Audubon observed that not only the nesting pair but also other adults would rally to defend a threatened nest.[4] The birds also have few flying predators. As Audubon stated in his book *Ornithological biography, or An account of the habits of the birds of the United States of America*:

> Few hawks attack the Mocking Birds, as...they are always ready not only to defend themselves vigorously and with undaunted courage, but to meet the aggressor half way, and force him to abandon his intention. The only hawk that occasionally surprises it is the *Falco stanleii*, which flies low with great swiftness, and carries the bird off without any apparent stoppage. Should it happen that the ruffian misses his prey, the Mocking Bird in turn becomes the assailant, and pursues the Hawk with great courage, calling in the mean time all the birds of its species to its assistance; and although it cannot overtake the marauder, the alarm created by their cries, which are propagated in succession among all the birds in the vicinity, like the watchwords of sentinels on duty, prevents him from succeeding in his attempts.

Mockingbirds are omnivorous, foraging on the ground or while perched on vegetation. Their primary food sources in the wild are insects, berries or fruit, and seeds. They also eat earthworms, and they occasionally consume small crustaceans and lizards. In proximity to humans, they—like other animals—take advantage of any uncovered garbage and have an earned reputation both for foraging in food waste and for snacking on garden fruits and vegetables. They obtain water by drinking from puddles, at stream and lake edges, and from dew and rain droplets that collect on vegetation.

These attributes would add up to a worthy and even useful but unremarkable bird, were it not for the mockingbird's vocal abilities. They can sing for hours on end. Unmated males sing at night (often just outside

---

4   Apparently mockingbirds can also recognize possible nuisance humans. In 2009, a University of Florida biologist published a paper reporting that mockingbirds recognize and remember people whom the birds perceive as threatening their nests. If they spot unwelcome guests, such as humans who repeatedly come too close to a nest, they screech, dive bomb, and even sometimes graze the visitors' heads—while ignoring other passersby or nearby strangers. Observation revealed that mockingbirds could identify individual humans after sixty seconds of exposure. (Douglas J. Levey, Judit Ungvari Martina, Hiersouxa et al., "*Urban Mockingbirds Quickly Learn to Identify Individual Humans*," Proceedings of the National Academy of Sciences of the United States of America, vol. 106, no. 22.

Arkansas

USA 20c

Mockingbird & Apple Blossom

sleeping people's windows, it seems...). Mockingbirds may have inventories of as many as thirty-eight songs.[5] They mimic other bird species as well as dogs, sirens, and even squeaky gates—thus their scientific name, *Mimus polyglottos*, or "mimic of many tongues."[6] This ability may be twined with mating success. Ornithologists have observed that females are attracted to males with the most sounds, which would tend to keep the proclivity for vocal prowess firmly embedded in the mockingbird's genetic makeup.

Audubon observed in his travels through the South that mockingbirds, much prized for their songs, as well as for their consumption of insects, were protected by farmers, stating: "Children seldom destroy the nests of these birds, and the planters generally protect them. So much does this feeling prevail throughout Louisiana, that they will not willingly permit a Mocking Bird to be shot at any time."[7] They were, however, subject to kidnapping: from the 1700s until the early years of the twentieth century, mockingbirds were hunted for sale as pets. A well-known nursery-rhyme lulls the child with the assurance that "poppa's gonna buy you a mocking bird." Audubon noted that "(it) is easily reared by hand from the nest, from which it ought to be removed when eight or ten days old. It becomes so very familiar and affectionate, that it will often follow its owner about the house." There was a price to be paid for this domestication, however. Audubon noted that a domestic, caged bird "never...produce[d] any thing at all approaching in melody to its own natural song."

Today, the northern mockingbird is protected from such predation. The national Migratory Bird Treaty Act of 1918 prohibits the "taking" of any native birds; "taking" can mean killing a wild bird or possessing parts of a wild bird, including feathers, nests, or eggs. It also renders illegal attempts to incubate wild bird eggs; to keep nests or eggs nestlings, even for "show and tell" educational purposes; or to have road-killed birds in one's possession without a permit. The act makes it illegal to remove or move nests that contain eggs or nestlings, even if they are in an inconvenient location, such as above a door or walkway. This protection, plus the mockingbird's willingness to defend itself, has doubtless contributed to the species's robust numbers, estimated at roughly forty-five million worldwide.

---

5   The Texas Parks and Wildlife Department claims, on its website, that their mockingbirds can mimic fifty other birds' songs, as well as other sounds, so perfectly that electronic analysis cannot distinguish between the original and the mockingbird's reproduction; this stands as one of the more plausible Texas superlatives.

6   This designation has supplanted the earlier Linnaean classification *Turdus polyglottos*, which is translated as "multilingual thrush."

7   A sentiment echoed by avian ethicist Atticus Finch, who—in Harper Lee's famous book *To Kill a Mockingbird*—admonished his children, "Shoot all the blue jays you want, if you can hit 'em, but remember it's a sin to kill a mockingbird."

For further reading:

Acts of Arkansas, Regular Session, 1929.

Audubon, John James, and William Macgillivray. *Ornithological biography, or An account of the habits of the birds of the United States of America: accompanied by descriptions of the objects represented in the work entitled The birds of America, and interspersed with delineations of American scenery and manners / v.1.* Digital edition, hosted by the Darlington Digital Library of the University of Pittsburgh, online at http://digital.library.pitt.edu (accessed July 10, 2015).

Derrickson, K. C., and R. Breitwisch. "Northern Mockingbird" in A. C. Poole, P. Stettenheim, and F. Gill, eds., *The Birds of North America* 7 (Philadelphia: American Ornithologists' Union and the Academy of Natural Sciences, 1992): 1–26. Online at https://repository.si.edu/bitstream/handle/10088/4030/Derrickson1992.pdf?sequence=1&isAllowed=y (accessed July 10, 2015).

James, Douglas A., and Joseph C. Neal. *Arkansas Birds: Their Distribution and Abundance.* Fayetteville: University of Arkansas Press, 1986.

"Northern Mockingbird." Cornell Lab of Ornithology. *All About Birds.* http://www.allaboutbirds.org/guide/Northern_Mockingbird/id (accessed July 10, 2015).

Rylander, Kent. "Northern Mockingbird." *The Handbook of Texas Online.* https://tshaonline.org/handbook/online/articles/tbn01 (accessed July 10, 2015).

Shearer, Benjamin F., and Barbara Smith Shearer. *State Names, Seals, Flags and Symbols: A Historical Guide.* 3rd ed. Westport, CT: Greenwood Press, 2002.

Spurgeon, John. "Official State Bird." *Encyclopedia of Arkansas History & Culture.* http://www.encyclopediaofarkansas.net/encyclopedia/entry-detail.aspx?search=1&entryID=3137 (accessed July 10, 2015).

CHAPTER 5: STATE TREE

A pine is a pine is a pine...

In the State Capitol, there is a painting that has long hung behind the receptionist's desk in the Arkansas governor's office. *Arkansas Travelers*, by Arkansas artist Maurice Kellogg, shows a small party of men emerging into a clearing on a height of land, against a background of forested mountains stretching as far as the eye can see or the viewer can imagine. The men wear helmets and armor, not the current sort made of synthetics but rather the old kind: plate steel, kept bright by dint of ashes, sand, and hand. The men are bearded and carry the banners of a distant majesty: Charles V, King of Castile, Aragon, and Sicily, King of Naples, Count of Barcelona, Archduke of Austria, and Holy Roman Emperor—or, for short, the King of Spain.

These are the *conquistadores* of the column led by *adelantado* Hernando de Soto. The year is 1541, and they have come a long way to find themselves on this hill. They have tramped through coastal swamps, the soft Delta muck of the Mississippi River Valley, and more—and wherever they have gone, they have encountered woods, always woods. For these men of the Extremadura—the hot, dry, and rough region of western Spain which has produced its toughest soldiers—encountering thick green forests at every turn must have seemed like a particularly cruel divine jest. For more than a year, they had tramped overland and always their way had been blocked by trees: trees on prairies, trees growing out of swamps, and now trees covering rough mountain terrain. And of what majestic

Arkansas Travelers: De Soto, 1541. *Maurice Kellogg (1919–1984); 1974.*

variety! There were pines, cedars, cypresses like none had seen in Spain for decades if not centuries; oaks, walnut, and other hardwoods, some of which they could not name.

It was much for them to bear. They had been immersed in it, ploughed through it, wandered lost in it and overwhelmed by it. From their journey's lowest point to its most elevated, the trees loomed before them, beside them, and behind them. Even now, as they reach a rock bench on this height of land, the leader and his men realize that there is no escape from their arboreal adversary, this daunting and magnificent verdure. They are as mariners who pray for even an unknown coast for which to steer. A clear path, even a thinning of the wooded cover, would be a godsend, but the green cover confronts them on every side.

The painting shows de Soto and his men in a crisp autumn light and one may hope that some few of the men depicted could, in the flesh, appreciate something of the majesty of what they saw, just as the artist has been able to accomplish in two dimensions. We can imagine that they admired the sublimeness of the view from that hillside but we know that, for the realists of 1541, there could mainly be only fatigued acceptance. They were surely as sailors beyond hope and horizon; mariners far from home, fated to sail a while longer on that ocean of trees.

The earliest human inhabitants of what is now Arkansas chose for their home turf an arboreal fastness: it is estimated that pre–European contact Arkansas was as much as 95 percent forested. Moreover, this forestation was not a stable and unchanging cover. At the end of the last Ice Age, some 13,000 years ago, Arkansas enjoyed a cooler climate than it does today—hence, what are today thought of as northern softwoods such as spruce, jack pine, and firs were found in the Mississippi Alluvial Plains; the uplands featured cool-climate deciduous species. These were the trees seen and used by the first Arkansans.

As glaciers receded and the climate warmed, new forestation came to dominate the uplands, plains, and Delta bottoms of Arkansas. Deciduous forests of oak and hickory with some pines were in the uplands, short-leaf southern pines for eastern and southeastern parts of what would be this state. By four millennia in our past, the dense variety of Arkansas's present-day forests was largely in place. And so was a varying native population: some nomadic and others sedentary, or at least fixed within a range. We know that these Arkansans made good use of the forests. They ate tree seeds and fruits, and they spread some of those seeds around. They also cleared the land for farming, mostly in the south and east.

On these cleared plots, they grew maize (corn), beans, and squash. De Soto saw these fields, marched along them, and no doubt dined from them. Later European entrants into Arkansas would as well, although by the time the French emissaries arrived, a century and a half after de Soto and his men had slogged through the region, the Mississippian cultures that met the Spanish column had themselves vanished. There is a longer, complex story here, but we do not sing of men at this point. We sing of trees.

Were Arkansas's forests rendered in music, their extent and variety would require a handful of the best composers to be found.[1] The forests' diversity is revealed in the accounts of early-nineteenth-century travelers who recorded detailed descriptions of the land through which they passed and its vegetation.

One of the first was William Dunbar, co-captain of an expedition that ascended the Ouachita River in 1804. Heading upriver toward present-day Hot Springs, he noted that the left, or south, side of the river was forested with pines, interspersed with oak, hickory, and dogwood. Around the hot springs, he found oak, pine, cedar, holly, hawthorn, and "others common to this climate." On the upper faces of the hills, he reported cedar, wax myrtle, and *Cassina yaupon*, or Youpon holly, growing out of the clefts of the rocks.

A few years after Dunbar, Henry Schoolcraft noted a great variety of trees, including sycamore, cottonwood, elm, buckeye, walnut, ash, oak of several types, maple, and persimmon. Bluffs and ridges were covered with pines and post oaks; in the Ouachitas, Schoolcraft wrote, large stands of pines were common. Army engineer Stephen Long visited the Ouachitas in 1819 and, like Schoolcraft, reported highlands covered with yellow pine and bramble. Two years later, Thomas Nuttall described a pattern of hills with pine trees growing on south-

---

1   Or Mozart, were he available, in which case one would do very nicely, thank you.

facing slopes and hardwoods on the north-facing sides.[2] An 1832 survey of the Ozarks identified some twenty-nine species in a sample tract of land along the middle fork of the White River, including nine varieties of oak; no pines were reported, but farther south, toward the Arkansas River, they were numerous.[3]

Early European settlement in what would become the state of Arkansas had little impact on the great stretches of forest that covered the land. The state's first steam sawmill began operating at Helena in 1826, and others opened as Arkansas's population gathered and grew, but the wood remained a commodity mainly for local use until some way of getting it to markets outside of Arkansas should appear. In the years before the Civil War, some Arkansas logs were rafted downriver to Louisiana sawmills, but this precocious "export" activity made little impact on the state's virgin forests.[4]

The decades following the Civil War saw Arkansas's population stagnate for a time, rebounding after 1880; by this time, moreover, railroad construction across the state created both a market for crossties and building timber and also a way to transport the forests' riches to markets beyond the state's borders. With the completion of the St. Louis Southwestern Railway ("Cotton Belt")—which stretched from St. Louis, Missouri, through Arkansas to Texas—the way was clear to begin the great export of the great piney forests of southern and eastern Arkansas.[5]

Every American state has designated at least one sort of tree as an official emblem; several have chosen two. Eighteen states have designated softwoods; they include spruce, cedar, pinyon, and several varieties of pines.[6] The earliest known designation dates from 1919, when Texas honored the pecan tree; no states took similar action until the 1930s, when a modest vogue for embracing state trees seems to have swept the nation.

In 1939, five states designated official trees. Arkansas was one of them.[7] House Concurrent Resolution 2 of 1939 designated the pine tree as Arkansas's official state tree. The measure, introduced by State Representative Boyd Tackett of Pike County, cited the state's timber resources as one of its greatest sources of wealth and, notably, "one of the few renewable resources of the state." The resolution was introduced on January 11 and met

2   Stephen Strausberg and Walter Hough, *The Ouachita and Ozark-St. Francis National Forests: A History of the Lands and USDA Forest Tenure* (general technical report SOI-21), Asheville, NC: United States Department of Agriculture, U.S. Forest Service Southern Research Station, 1997, pp. 3-4; Don C. Bragg, "A Brief History of Forests and Tree Planting In Arkansas," *Tree Planters' Notes* 55, no. 1 (2012). http://www.rngr.net/publications/tpn/55-1 (accessed August 14, 2015).

3   Strausberg, 5. The authors cite the research of Phillip L. Chaney incorporated in his 1990 MA thesis, "Geographic Analysis of the Presettlement Vegetation of the Middle Fork of the White River, Arkansas: A GIS Approach." University of Arkansas, Fayetteville.

4   John Gray, "Arkansas Forest History (1993)," Arkansas Forestry Association. http://www.arkforests.org/?page=foresthistory (accessed August 14, 2015).

5   The late Dr. John Gray dubbed this the "pre-forestry exploitation era."

6   At least one state has shown itself to be an inconstant arboreal designator. In 2014, the Utah legislature chose the quaking aspen as the state's official tree, displacing the blue spruce, which had held that position of honor since 1933. There is no indication that the Dutch oven, the state's official cooking vessel since 1997, stands in similar danger but vigilance may be indicated.

7   "Official State Trees," Netstate.com. http://www.netstate.com/states/tables/st_trees_year.htm (accessed August 14, 2015).

no opposition, winning final approval on January 20.[8]

The question might arise: "Why pine?" Markets existed or would exist for virtually any sort of tree, hardwood or soft, but pine, especially the best grades, had long been particularly important in the nation's economy. By the 1880s, southern pine forests represented a particularly attractive resource. Less than three decades into the twentieth century, however, that resource stood plundered, the industries it supported moribund. Yet, within another decade, pine and what came from it were once more a mainstay of this state. The question ought to be, then, not "Why?" but "How?"

In colonial days and in the years of the early Republic, pines supplied both construction timber and stuff vital for national defense, referred to as naval stores: ships' timbers, pine tar, and turpentine. In the eighteenth and early nineteenth centuries, the pine forests of the east—from New England down to the Georgia coast—had supplied tall ships' masts and timbers, plus tar needed for waterproofing and preservation, as well as turpentine, the distilled essence of pine resin useful as external liniment, medicine, solvent, and more.[9]

The white pines of New England and the north woods were the most valued for ship timbers and construction lumber, but as the northern forests were depleted of their tall trees, lumbermen looked south and saw vast stands of pine. Along the coastal plains were longleaf pines and farther inland were shortleaf pines such as slash pine and loblolly. Even as the demand for tall ship timbers declined, America's ongoing building boom needed its raw material. Arkansas could supply it, once a delivery route was established.

That route was paved with ribbons of iron. During the decade of the 1880s, Arkansas's railroads expanded from about 800 miles of track to over 2,000 miles, both main lines and short lines, many of which were laid into timber zones. Northern developers began to acquire timberlands in southern Arkansas, rolling hills covered with shortleaf pine. Timber speculators bought up forested parcels and resold them to the out-of-state developers, whose capital paid for such things as blazing trails and building needed roads, laying company-owned short line railways into the forests, building large sawmills, and hiring local men to work the woods and mills—all the better to efficiently harvest the virgin pine stands. By the beginning of the twentieth century, mills capable of cutting more than 50,000 board feet per day were found throughout southern Arkansas, located thirty to forty miles apart. Large-scale logging depended on rail. Lightly built spur tracks branched into each forty-acre logging parcel, with teams of oxen or horses used to skid logs through the brush to the trackside. There, steam-powered loaders picked the logs up and loaded them for transportation to the mills. When a parcel was cleared or "logged out," the track would be taken up to be re-used in another parcel to harvest the pine fastness.

The early decades of the twentieth century were the halcyon years of the Arkansas lumber industry. In 1909,

---

8   The final clause of the resolution stipulated that "the pine tree be declared and everywhere recognized as the state tree of the State of Arkansas." The first commandment would be no problem; the enforcement of the second, however, was not addressed, leaving the way open for visions of future generations of state police politely enforcing recognition of the pine, rather than the oak, walnut, swamp cypress, or even flowering dogwood, as the official tree (*Acts of Arkansas*, 1939).

9   Including flavoring agent: turps were often added to the cheapest gins in order to suggest the flavor and aroma of juniper berries and other aromatics. The trifling amounts of turpentine needed to produce this effect doubtless added little to the general toxicity of such beverages.

Log train for G. F. Bethel Saw Mill; Mansfield, Arkansas, 1903.

more than 2 billion board feet of lumber, another 2.6 billion board feet[10] of firewood, and vast amounts of other wood products were produced. To those in the lumber business, the woods may have seemed infinite. They were treated as though they could not be depleted; for most companies, the operating rule was "cut out and get out," with little attention paid to reclamation or reforestation of the clear-cut parcels. Farmers were happy to sell their timber to logging operations, since this would result in fields requiring less cutting and burning to prepare for putting in row crops. For farmers, timberland was identical to undeveloped land, valueless until it was ready to be put into pasture or crops.

This attitude complemented, in a perverse way, a common perception of the value of second-growth timber. In the traditional view, only slow-grown virgin timber made desirable lumber. Fast-maturing second-growth pine was long deemed undesirable[11] because it was believed to be weak wood, prone to warping and shrinkage. Thus, lumber companies ignored smaller-diameter trees (below 14" dbh[12]) or cut them for use as crossties on temporary logging railroads. The companies offered their cutover lands to farmers and, as the supplies of prime

---

10   A board foot is a measure of volume: it represents a plank of one square foot surface size, one inch thick.

11   At least as long as suitable quantities of first-growth trees were easily accessible.

12   Dbh=diameter at breast height, roughly five feet above ground level.

Arkansas Lumber Company office.

first-growth pine timber dwindled, many either shut down operations or relocated them to the western states. Small, portable "peckerwood" sawmills, able to economically process the remaining smaller trees, moved into the state but employed a fraction of the lumber industry's former labor force.

By the late 1920s, the "Big Cut" was over. The expanses that had once been the ocean of trees were much reduced. Total forest cover (including both soft and hard woods) once estimated to be 32 million acres was reduced to about 22 million acres by 1930, and most of this had been cut over. Some 85 percent of the once-harvested area had been left to naturally reseed, but much of the land was damaged by wildfires, many set by farmers.[13] Huge stretches of the state's prime pine country had been cut, burnt, converted to farm fields, or simply abandoned.

Had matters been left this way, there would have been little but memories of trees and boomer times for Boyd Tackett to celebrate in 1939. A collapsed industry, cleared farm fields, and scrubby pine thickets would have provided scant excuse for designation, but a combination of new technology, a better understanding of reforestation and forest management, and the economic stimulus provided by World War II brought about a revival of Arkansas's forests' fortunes.

At the same time that lumber companies were logging out Arkansas's old-growth shortleaf pine forests, foresters and scientists studying the cutover former longleaf pine forests of the southeastern coastal plains developed a new appreciation of the qualities of the shortleaf pines such as slash pine and loblolly pine—often grouped together as southern or yellow pine—that succeeded virgin longleaf after the cleared land had been farmed or abandoned. The loblolly, especially, seeded frequently and prolifically. Its relatively small seeds could be blown considerable distances from the seed tree. The seeds were tough and, if they germinated and escaped fire for a few seasons, would grow dense and fast.

This reproductive facility had made the loblolly pine and Cuban or slash pine the darlings of southeastern forestry, particularly when it was shown that these fast-growing pines produced more sap—hence more tar, rosin, and turpentine—than the longleaf pines they had replaced. In Arkansas, the remaining lumber and forest-products companies made good use of the yellow pines' resilience while they took steps to ensure that their lands would continue to supply timber into the future. One such was the Crossett Lumber Company. In 1926, the company hired a professional forester who proposed leaving sufficient seed trees in each timber parcel to ensure reseeding and called for his company to work to interest local farmers in fire suppression. His successor went further, evaluating the state of the company's lands and preparing a plan for their future harvesting through selective cutting of virgin and second-growth pines and hardwoods.

While lumber companies sought ways to continue to harvest construction-quality timber from the Arkansas woods, another industry established itself as a consumer of much wood that would be considered unsuitable for lumber. In 1928, International Paper Company opened the state's first pulp and paper mill, in Camden. In years to come, others would follow, making use of a technological evolution of the early twentieth century which made the leftovers of the Big Cut attractive.

---

13   Burning the woods was a traditional way of killing off insect populations and clearing undergrowth while also fertilizing the soil in the short run.

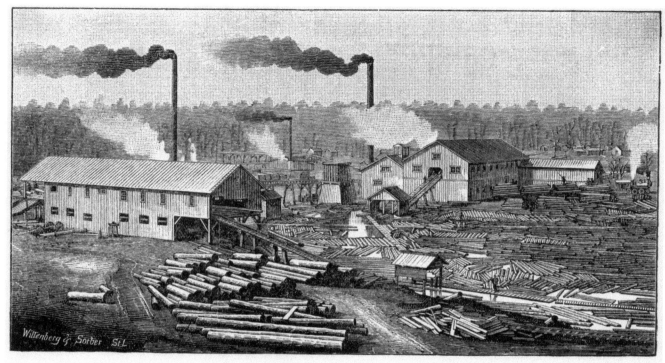

In the Timber Region, Arkansas

What had happened?

The basics of making paper from wood pulp were well-established by the 1860s. Over the years, a wide variety of substances had been used to produce pulp, including various strains of hemp, cotton rags and lint, silkweed, tobacco, sugar cane, mulberry, spider webs, cattails, old fish nets, and even horse manure. Wood pulp, however, proved to be the most versatile (and, when compared with manure, socially acceptable) basis for quantity papermaking. The process was simple in theory, if exhaustive in practice: wood was ground (the product was called, simply, "groundwood"), then bathed in caustic chemicals to break down the bonds of its fibers, then washed, beaten, bleached, then deposited on screens and dried to make sheets of white paper of varying grades.

At first, the spruces and white pines of the Adirondacks and the White Mountains provided most of the wood pulp made in America, but demand outstripped the supply available from these already depleted forests. After 1900, an increasing amount of the wood and other fiber used in American paper mills was imported. This was not for lack of experimentation with southern softwood. A problem, however, lay in (literally) the "pitch." Old-growth and even mature second-growth pines of any species proved to be far too resin-rich; the gooey stuff long prized by turpentiners and vital in making strong, rot-resistant construction lumber gummed up pulpmaking machines. Treating the groundwood with sulphuric acids dissolved the resins, making it possible to produce a strong brown paper: kraft paper. In 1913, a mill was erected at Moss Point, Mississippi, for processing southern pine pulpwood into kraft. This operation, the Southern Paper Company, experienced some initial production difficulties but was ultimately successful. Further experimentation led to processes which made it possible to produce white paper from southern pines, but the extra steps involved limited this process's popularity. For many years to come, southern pines would be made mainly into paperboard and kraft.[14]

International Paper's Camden plant opened in 1928. It was, predictably, built to produce kraft, but it made its debut on the eve of an innovation in papermaking. In the late 1920s, Charles Henty, a retired chemistry professor and longtime advocate of modernizing the uses of southern forests, began research into how to make southern forestry "play well" with making types of paper other than kraft.

Henty ascertained that green pines—twenty years or younger—contained very little resin; the resin-heavy adult trees were to blame for gumming up the paper grinding works, but the kids were alright. This discovery led quickly to a practical demonstration. In 1933, Henty shipped a load of southern pine pulp to Canada, where it was made into newsprint. By the end of the decade, the viability of making newsprint and other grades of paper from southern pine was established. Economic conditions, which had halted southern pulp and paper mill development in the early 1930s, improved so that new mills, such as the Crossett Paper Mill (built as an operation of the Crossett Lumber Company), were either opened or planned, relying on copious supplies of young southern pine pulp. Thus the ugly ducklings of southern forests, the trees deemed too small to harvest, became if not quite swans, then at least of commercial interest. Replanting could be undertaken with a relatively close harvest event horizon.[15]

◊ ◊ ◊

While industrial evolution provided something to do with the trees that were once dismissed as useless, Arkansas's pine (and for that matter, their deciduous cousins) began a period of substantial recovery. To some degree, the recovery began with the designation of some 1.1 million acres of Ozark and Ouachita woodlands as national forests in 1907 and 1908. The newly created National Forest Service bore the charge of protecting these tracts from fire, unlawful trespass, and timber theft. The Forest Service was not alone in attempting to apply principles of scientific forestry to managing timber resources. A handful of lumber companies began taking steps in the 1920s and even earlier to ensure that there would be timber to harvest decades into the future. As others cut and ran, these outfits experimented with fire protection, selective cutting, and the encouragement of natural reseeding. Thus, even as the Big Cut played out, the roots of Arkansas's forest recovery were already established.

And after 1930, the pace accelerated. The Arkansas Forestry Commission, created in that year, worked to extend fire protection to non-federal forest tracts statewide. Within a few years, crews of young workers of the Civilian Conservation Corps (CCC) would go into the woods, blazing and improving roads, building recreation facilities in the national forests, and planting seedlings on thousands of acres of federal land. The course of

---

14   Lawrence Earley, *Looking for Longleaf: The Fall and Rise of an American Forest* (Chapel Hill: University of North Carolina Press, 2004), 185-187.
15   Ibid., 187.

forest recovery was also helped by the downturn in construction occasioned by the Depression: fewer houses being built meant fewer lumber-grade trees being cut down. Thus, by 1939, the optimism expressed by the designation of the pine as Arkansas's state tree was justified. A full study of the forests' conditions would not be attempted until 1947–1951, but enough anecdotal evidence was there to justify Boyd Tackett's tribute to one of the state's few renewable resources.[16]

The question of what sort of pine was designated by House Concurrent Resolution 2 is seldom raised, perhaps because most Arkansans assume that a southern pine is a southern pine is a southern pine; Tackett's resolution said "pine tree" but did not specify a species. Various sources identify particular species as "the" official tree, but the resolution and the section of the Arkansas Code (Title 1, Chapter 4, Section 1-4-119, for the curious) enshrining the designation are more generous and inclusive: if it's a pine, it's fine. And official.

Four species of pine are considered native to Arkansas: the shortleaf pine, the loblolly pine, the slash or Cuban pine, and the longleaf pine. The shortleaf, or *Pinus echinata*, is known by an assortment of nicknames: shortleaf yellow pine, southern yellow pine, yellow pine, shortstraw pine, Arkansas pine, and old field pine. Its bark is rough and broken into irregular patches that flake off and reveal the redder young bark beneath. Needles are short, hence the name shortleaf pine. This tree has the distinction of being classed as an endangered species—in Illinois.[17]

The loblolly (*Pinus taeda*) is perhaps the most often identified as the official state tree—perhaps because its name, which is hard to say without smiling.[18] It goes by several other local nicknames, including bull pine, rosemary pine, old field pine, shortleaf pine, North Carolina pine, and, thankfully, Arkansas pine. Given a good head start, a loblolly will grow to a height of fifty feet in its first twenty years, and mature trees have both a deep tap root and a strong lateral root system, making them resistant to blowdown. It is considered the leading commercial tree of the Southeast and the most common pine in Arkansas forests.[19]

The slash or Cuban pine (*Pinus elliotti*) is less common in Arkansas than the loblolly or shortleaf pine, but some stands can be found in the South; it is more common in our neighbor states of Mississippi, Louisiana, and Texas. Its needles or leaves are slightly longer than the loblolly's. Slash pine excels in the production of sticky stuff; it is the preferred pine species for naval stores (turpentine, pine tar, and rosin) made from the resin. The

16   And the evidence of the Southern Forest Experiment Station's 1953 study of Arkansas forests was impressive. Based on field work conducted from 1947 into 1951, it revealed that yearly pine growth exceeded removals by 13 percent; hardwoods' growth exceeded losses by some 63 percent, perhaps reflecting the smaller market demand for hardwood. It had been found that despite its low resin levels, hardwood made inferior pulp due to its generally shorter fibers (Gray, "Arkansas Forest History"); see also Phillip R. Wheeler, *Forest Survey Release No 71: Forest Statistics for Arkansas* (New Orleans, LA: U.S. Department of Agriculture, Southern Forest Experiment Station, 1953). http://www.srs.fs.usda.gov/pubs/fsr/fsrs/fsrs-071.pdf (accessed August 14, 2015).

17   "Shortleaf Pine." U.S. Department of Agriculture Natural Resources Conservation Service Plants Database. http://plants.usda.gov/core/profile?symbol=PIEC2 (accessed August 14, 2015).

18   The derivation of the term is curious; in English mariners' argot, a loblolly is a thick porridge or soup cooked in a pot. The word came ashore in the southern colonies, used to describe mud-holes or mires—in general, soft, wet ground. Thus, the pine that grew in or around such wet places was awarded the name.

19   "Loblolly Pine." U.S. Department of Agriculture Natural Resources Conservation Service Plants Database. http://plants.usda.gov/core/profile?symbol=PITA (accessed August 15, 2015).

The Iron Mountain Line offers inducements for relocation, ca. 1878.

strong, heavy wood also makes it valuable for other timber products, such as pulpwood (if harvested early), railroad ties, poles, pilings, and plywood veneer.[20]

Longleaf (*Pinus palustris* or *australis*) is the aristocrat of the southern pines but is not usually associated with Arkansas: it was the characteristic pine of the coastal forests from Virginia to Florida and west as far as Louisiana, extending in a band about 150 miles wide inward from the coast. There have been claims made that the longleaf was native to some parts of southern Arkansas but, if so, it has since become rare; once logged out (as it was in much of the South), its shade intolerance and slow natural reproduction rate mean that it will usually be displaced by faster-growing pines (such as the opportunistic, assertive loblollies[21]). In recent years, however, foresters and conservationists in southern states have fostered a comeback for longleaf. Across the southeastern United States, longleaf forests once covered as much as 87 million acres; today, the extent is between 5 and 10 million. Maybe this number will increase and, just maybe, once again overlap into Arkansas.[22]

◇ ◇ ◇

In 1909, the peak year of the Big Cut, the lumber industry was the largest single employer of factory wage earners in Arkansas. Its employment footprint is

---

20   "Slash Pine." U.S. Department of Agriculture Natural Resources Conservation Service Plants Database. http://plants.usda.gov/core/profile?symbol=PIEL (accessed August 15, 2015).

21   Not to be confused with *Loblollies*, a gourmet frozen treat worthy of Euell Gibbons himself, featuring flavors based on ripe Arkansas fruits and berries, their sweetness tempered by a delicate hint of gum turpentine from select second-growth southern conifers, coming soon to a gourmet grocery near you. Not.

22   "Longleaf Pine." U.S. Department of Agriculture Natural Resources Conservation Service Plants Database. http://plants.usda.gov/core/profile?symbol=PIPA2 (accessed June 20, 2015).

no longer so huge, but the state tree remains a mainstay of the state economy and a dominant feature of its landscape as well. A 2005 survey revealed the loblolly to be the most populous tree in Arkansas, with an estimated 171.1 million units; the shortleaf was runner-up with a mere 98.2 million units. In 2014, Arkansas forests yielded 5,428,916 tons of pine pulpwood, 6,918,917 tons of pine sawtimber (that is, destined to be made into lumber), and 2,404,656 tons of "other pine timber" (destined to be chipped and made into OSB, sliced for plywood veneer, or made into utility poles) valued (as delivered to the mills) at $532,657,224.[23] Virtually all aspects of wood product production are represented in Arkansas—from chemicals to paper (kraft, tissue, etc.) to manufactured wood including plywood, to, yes, building timber. A Crossett community history website claims that the first plywood made from southern pine was produced at the Crossett Lumber plant, which was purchased by Georgia-Pacific, a major national wood products corporation, in 1962; the plywood plant is currently not in operation.

Numbers are one thing—forests are something else. The extent of natural-origin pine forests in Arkansas has declined in recent decades, but the acres of pine plantations, mainly planted in loblolly pine, have increased, from 55,000 acres in the early 1950s to over 2.9 million acres in 2005.[24] These plantations are efficient wood factories, planted and maintained to be harvested every twenty-five to thirty-five years. The aesthetics and environmental desirability of such even-aged tree farms are open to debate, but their efficiency has been demonstrated. Mills will have their trees, and these tree-factories will supply them.

Once, as much as 95 percent of the place that became Arkansas was forested; today, that figure remains above 50 percent.[25] Although great clearings have been made for roads, farms, and settlements, it is still possible to turn off of a road running through a national forest, or a rural stretch of second-growth piney woods, and be confronted by the descendants (functional and spiritual, if not genetic) of the forest sentinels that met de Soto and his column. It takes little time to hike to the top of a forested ridge, find a spot of higher ground, and then look around, seeking the horizon. The modern eye will be drawn to communications towers, lines indicating roads cut through the tree stands, or other innovations, but with a little work, or possibly removal of one's glasses, these visual irritants can shrink in significance. Ignoring the intrusions (well worth the try) reveals the contours and textures that have marked Arkansas's hills and plains for millennia. With a little more luck, it is just possible to find spot where cellular service weakens, or even drops out altogether, giving the observer the chance to drink in the forests extending for miles and, maybe, feel a little kinship with those men of the Extremadura, nearly five centuries gone, who sailed so far from home upon this ocean of trees.

23   Figures derived from calendar year 2014 forest products severance tax figures published by the Arkansas Forestry Commission and furnished courtesy of Professor Matthew Pelkki of UA–Monticello School of Forest Resources (personal communication, 2015).

24   Crossett Public Library. http://www.crossettlibrary.com/aboutus/crossett-public-library-crossett-history (accessed August 15, 2015); Georgia-Pacific corporate website. http://www.gp.com/Company/Company-Overview/Locations/Crossett (accessed August 15, 2015).

25   J. F. Rosson and A. K. Rose, "Arkansas's Forests, 2005," General Technical Report SRS-166, (Asheville, NC: U.S. Department of Agriculture, United States Forest Service, Southern Research Station, 2005), cited in Don C. Bragg, "A Brief History of Forests and Tree Planting In Arkansas," *Tree Planters' Notes* 55, no. 1 (2012): 15. http://www.rngr.net/publications/tpn/55-1 (accessed August 15, 2015).

For further reading:

Balogh, George. "Forest Management and Conservation." *Encyclopedia of Arkansas History & Culture.* http://www. encyclopediaofarkansas.net/encyclopedia/entry-detail.aspx?search=1&entryID=5158 (accessed August 15, 2015)

———. "Timber Industry." *Encyclopedia of Arkansas History & Culture.* http://www.encyclopediaofarkansas.net/encyclopedia/entry-detail.aspx?search=1&entryID=2143 (accessed August 15, 2015).

Daniels, Jonathan. *The Forest Is the Future.* New York: International Paper Company, 1957.

Earley, Lawrence. *Looking for Longleaf: The Fall and Rise of an American Forest.* Chapel Hill: University of North Carolina Press, 2004.

Gray, John. "Arkansas Forest History (1993)." Arkansas Forestry Association. http://www.arkforests.org/?page=foresthistory (accessed August 15, 2015).

Smith, David C. *History of Papermaking in the United States, 1691–1969.* New York: Lockwood, 1971.

Ware, David. "Official State Tree, a.k.a: Pine Tree." *Encyclopedia of Arkansas History & Culture.* http://www. encyclopediaofarkansas.net/encyclopedia/entry-detail.aspx?entryID=3139 (accessed August 15, 2015).

CHAPTER 6: STATE GEM

Or, the Right (Very Hard) Stuff

Diamond, composed of densely packed carbon, is the hardest naturally occurring substance on earth. It is prized when faceted and polished into a gemstone, but it has unique physical and chemical properties—aside from its brilliance and "fire"—that make it important to industrialized society. Pulverized industrial-grade diamonds are used to cut and polish gem-grade stones. Other uses include surgical blades, glass cutting and engraving tools, wiredrawing dies, metal-cutting tools, and drill bits.

Like almost any other imaginable substance, it can also be pressed into service as a symbol, and so it was, on February 22, 1967, when Governor Winthrop Rockefeller signed Act 128, an omnibus measure designating the diamond as the state gem.[1] The measure, introduced in the Senate by Robert Harvey, J. Hugh Lookadoo, and Olen Hendrix, called attention to Arkansas's status as one of the few places in North America where diamonds are present—and the only such place where tourists may hunt for them.[2]

[1]   The same measure designated quartz crystal as the state mineral and bauxite as the official state rock. It would fall to a later generation to designate the official state dirt.

[2]   In 1967, diamonds were rumored to have been found in several North American locales but up to that point, only Arkansas had proven its potential. In 1976, deposits of diamondiferous kimberlite were found along the Wyoming-Colorado border, north of Fort Collins. During the 1990s, two of these were developed as the Kelsey Lake Diamond Mine; significant quantities of diamonds were recovered, but the operation was closed in 2001 and fully reclaimed by 2006. Other sites either containing diamonds or the potential for them have been located in Alaska, Montana, and Minnesota, and several diamond mines operate or have operated in northern Ontario, Quebec, Nunavut, and the Northwest Territory of Canada.

◇ ◇ ◇

Diamonds were not always diamonds. Or, at least, that was not their "birth name." In India, where the stones were first mined and used, the Sanskrit terms for them were *vajra*, meaning thunderbolt, and *indrayudha*, or Indra's sword (or weapon). Indra was a warrior god of the Vedic scriptures, the counterpart of the Germanic Wotan, Norse Odin, Greek Zeus, and Roman Jupiter. Indra encompassed and controlled the universe, balancing the earth in the palm of his hand and playing with it as pleased him; he created rivers and streams by shaping the mountains and valleys with his sacred axe.[3] He rode upon a white elephant, brought rain as god of the thunderbolt, and was the great warrior who conquered the *asuras*, or anti-gods, and defeated scores of fearsome opponents with his sword made of thunderbolts.

◇ ◇ ◇

The defining quality of the diamond, its hardness, is the source of its name in western society. As examples of "Indra's sword" appeared in the Levant, then Mediterranean Europe, they acquired a new name derived from the Greek *adamao*, which may be translated as "I tame" or "I subdue." The adjective *adamas* was used to describe the hardest substance known, the invincible, one that could subdue any other. From this root issued both "adamant" (meaning hard or unyielding) and diamond, the name of the unyielding gem.

A few diamonds found their way to the Mediterranean during ancient times. These were almost certainly Indian stones, carried across the long overland trade routes of central Asia and the Levant. This possibility is supported by Pliny the Elder, writing before 79 C.E. He described six types of diamonds, one of which he specifically identified as coming from the subcontinent.[4] Later Roman authors noted that the *adamas* was found in the sands of various Indian rivers.

Diamonds (as distinct from crystals) remained rare curiosities for centuries. With the collapse of the Roman and Byzantine empires, the paths over which the early-arriving gems had been carried fell into disuse. Some writers have also suggested that diamonds' association with Eastern mysticism and polytheism tarnished them in the eyes of the leaders of the ascendant Christian Church and its adherents.[5] The Black Death and other factors conspired to keep Europe's contact and trade with Asia minimal, hence, little importation of gems. During the thirteenth century, however, the wide extent and relative stability of Mongol rule by the family of Genghis Khan—what is sometimes called the "Pax Mongolica," extending at one point from the Pacific Ocean as far west as the Black Sea—created conditions favorable to trade between the two. Trade between Europe and Asia then flowered; it was encouraged, dominated, and manipulated by the great Italian city-states, particularly

---

3   Indra also had a notable soft side. Like his counterparts in other cultures, he was virile and prone to wandering from the marital straight and narrow when the opportunity arose, sometimes disguising himself either to lull his amorous targets or to evade the wrath of his consort Indrāni. Sometimes, though, Indra incurred a heavy price for his amorous adventures: he was once hacked to bits by an outraged husband, so much so that the other gods struggled to put him back together again. While reassembling Indra, they found that he had been not only dismembered but also demembered; they completed him using the phallus of a ram, presaging the later therapeutic surgeries of sometime Arkansas resident and eclectic clinician Dr. John Brinkley.

4   This observation is credited to Pliny the Elder but comes to us through the work of his nephew, Pliny the Younger, who edited and published the final twenty-seven volumes of his late uncle's magnum opus, the *Natural Histories*. Pliny the Elder managed to issue the first ten books before his untimely death associated with the eruption of Vesuvius in 79 C.E. His bottomless curiosity and love of scholarship were equaled only by his ill-timed desire to witness the volcanic eruption from a close vantage point.

5   Although, to be fair, it should be noted that similar associations did not seem to bring ecclesiastical disfavor upon gold or silver.

Venice. Goods traveled overland via central Asia and the great Silk Road, or else by the arduous water route, south through the Gulf of Suez, around the horn of Persia, then along the Indian coast, with connections to the Spice Isles beyond. In the context of this trade, Indian diamonds began to once more find their way west. These were mostly smallish stones, so rather than being used as the central ornaments of jewelry, they were used as accents, such as complementing pearls in gold settings. The stones may have been small, but they were rare, hence highly valued. Louis IX of France (1214–1270) issued a royal decree reserving diamonds for the king—that is, for himself.

This reservation could not last: demand drove sources of supply. Within 100 years, diamonds appeared in royal jewelry of both men and women, then among the greater European aristocracy, with the wealthy merchant class showing the occasional diamond by the seventeenth century. As more diamonds reached Europe, demand for them continued to increase and so did the size of gems reaching Europe. There were not enough to saturate the market, and their brilliance and hardness made those who could afford them want more (and ever larger) ones. Another factor in their popularity (as well as the demand for larger stones) was the development of faceting, which enhanced the gems' brilliance and fire. But this came at the expense of size. To end up with a gem of a respectable size, a larger rough stone was necessary. During the late sixteenth and early seventeenth centuries, European diamond cutters refined techniques of polishing, sawing, grinding, and cleaving to create the ancestors of today's rose, brilliant, and marquise patterns.[6]

For decades, even centuries after their introduction into the West, the supply of diamonds for Europe was limited by the nature of trade between Europe and India. It was a hybrid route, partially on water and much of it running overland through Arabic territories and the old Levant, through expanses where rough terrain, aridity, and brigands kept the cost of transporting goods high. After 1400 or so, the route became less safe than in decades past, as the Pax Mongolica foundered. Change was in the cards, however. In 1499, Portuguese mariner Vasco de Gama pioneered a sea route to India and East Asia, rounding Africa's Cape of Good Hope. The new route was long and hazardous, but it nevertheless provided Europe with a way to avoid the overland impediment to trade. Thus, more diamonds could be shipped—and market demands encouraged supplying ever larger examples. The result was that by the dawn of the eighteenth century, the Indian diamond mines found it hard to supply enough large, rough stones to meet European demands.

The developing scarcity of large Indian stones coincided, however, with the development of a new source: the Portuguese New World colony of Brazil, in an area which subsequently was named after its product: Diamantina. Here, the crystalline thunderbolts were discovered in alluvial deposits around 1725. By 1730, a steady stream of rough stones had entered the European market, while prospectors in Brazil sought—and found—new diamond deposits throughout the rest of the century, greatly increasing the world supply of diamonds. The new deposits yielded enough stones so that the prices of rough diamonds dropped by the late eighteenth century to about a third of what they had been before the Diamantina discoveries. This trend would continue as late as the 1860s, when the Brazilian diamond deposits began to exhibit the first signs of their depletion.

---

6   The earliest Western diamond-cutting industry was located in Venice, the great city-state port through which much of Europe's trade with Asia passed, appearing sometime after 1330. The trade spread with demand; by the late fourteenth century, the diamond trade route went to Bruges and Paris, later centering upon Antwerp, which remains a center of diamond cutting and trading.

Over time, the combination of lower prices and increased availability brought about a certain "democratization" of diamonds. Once, they had been the province of the royal, the noble, or (at least) the very rich; by the end of the eighteenth century, however, a new economic sector was on the rise: the prosperous merchants and professionals who would make up what we call the "middle class." These individuals had money enough to spend on little luxuries. Depressed diamond prices offered them something literally durable in which to invest their pocket change. This is not to say that great, showy diamonds were for everyone or anyone; high-quality diamonds, particularly of large size, remained relatively scarce.[7]

Two events of the second half of the century dramatically transformed the traditional diamond trade. The first was the discovery, in 1867, of rich diamond deposits in South Africa, the richest ones ever discovered. In 1871, the world's production of diamonds topped one million carats for the first time—with the majority of this carat weight made up of South African stones. This opened up the dizzying prospect that there might be mined or discovered a large enough quantity of diamonds so that almost anyone could afford to own one. The other event, or perhaps "development" is the better term, was the creation of an integrated production and marketing system which would in time control the entire output of the South African mines and, effectively, control world prices and supply of diamonds. The emergence of this cartel meant that diamond prices would be maintained by controlling how many went to market. Manufactured, rather than real, scarcity would ensure that both demand and price would remain high.[8]

Arkansas's diamond story unfolded within the same universe as that of DeBeers and South Africa, with their cartels and blood diamonds, but, for the most part, it remained isolated from the vagaries of world markets and demand. The state's diamond-bearing soils are confined to the southwestern portion of the state. Diamonds are recovered from the Prairie Creek diamondiferous pipe, a roughly triangular surface outcrop exposed over thirty-seven acres situated two and a half miles southeast of Murfreesboro in Pike County. The site is a volcanic pipe—a deep, tapered vent of a long-dormant volcano—formed during the Cretaceous period[9] by a series of gaseous explosions, as were several other pipes nearby. The pipe is filled with what was long known as "peridotite," a coarse-grained igneous rock. Geologists first noticed the site as early as 1842 but seem to have not recognized its diamond-bearing potential. This changed, however, in light of the South African discoveries

---

7   Then, as now, a premium was placed on the diamond's clarity and color. The most highly prized were stones of so-called "first water" quality—that is, stones whose visual purity rivalled that of the clearest water. Stones falling short of this standard but still mainly clear were described as being of second or third waters, until they could be described as being colored. This manner of description dates back at least to the fifteenth century.

8   The story of the growth of the world's diamond trade and its central player, DeBeers Consolidated Mines, is sketched in many academic and journalistic accounts, as well as in the promotional literature and journalism issued by or with the assistance of the diamond industry itself. Such literature tends to cast a romantic veil over what was an enervating saga of hard work, power politics, and cutthroat competition. The saga of Cecil John Rhodes, English expatriate, enthusiastic imperialist, and the central figure in the organization of DeBeers Consolidated Mines, was travestied in 1975's *Cecil*, a musical comedy penned as a student work by latter-day novelist Don Winslow.

9   The Cretaceous, the name deriving from the Latin "creta" (chalk), is a geologic period that ranged from about 145 to 66 million years ago. In the geologic timescale, the Cretaceous follows the Jurassic Period and is followed by the Paleogene Period of the Cenozoic Era. The Cretaceous was a relatively warm period. Dinosaurs dominated the land, while new groups of mammals and birds, as well as flowering plants, appeared. The Cretaceous ended with a large mass extinction, the Cretaceous–Paleogene extinction event, in which many animal groups—including non-avian dinosaurs, pterosaurs, and large marine reptiles—died out, leaving things mainly to the mammals to sort out.

of the 1870s. Previously, diamonds had been recovered only from alluvial deposits such as stream beds, but in Africa, they were discovered in volcanic pipes filled with varieties of peridotite, renamed "kimberlite" in honor of the Kimberley districts where they were found. Thus, geologists around the globe had reason to re-examine such features wherever they occurred.

In 1889, Arkansas state geologist John Casper Branner visited the Pike County site and carefully mapped the extent of what appeared to be peridotite deposits. Chemist Richard Brackett analyzed soil and rock samples from the field, confirming that the pipes were peridotite or kimberlite; this conclusion was included in their published report. Branner later claimed to have spent several hours on his hands and knees during his inspection visit looking for diamonds but apparently found none. He later explained that he had refrained from booming the diamond-bearing potential of the Pike County site because he did not want to set off an uncontrollable mining stampede in the area, a story which in hindsight seems both a little far-fetched and, yet, evidencing a prudent move. In the late 1880s, rumors of gold strikes had brought many prospectors and would-be mining barons to western Arkansas.[10] Possibly another influx of such impecunious enthusiasts was averted by Branner's circumspection.

The potential was identified but at least understated, and the Murfreesboro pipes became farm land. In 1905, some 243 acres of land, including much of the exposed surface of the Prairie Creek pipe, was sold to John W. and Sarah Huddleston. According to his biographer, Huddleston's intention was to farm part of the property and improve, then subdivide and sell, the remaining land, establishing himself as a small-holding developer in the same mold as John "Johnny Appleseed" Chapman of an earlier generation.[11]

Huddleston was also, apparently, an "avid outdoorsman and prospector," so was presumably open to the possibility of his land holding some profitable surprises. The traditional "discovery story" holds that on or about August 1, 1906, Huddleston took a walk across his farmland. One may imagine him walking along, his feet occasionally scuffing soil to one side or another, displaying the characteristic gait of the veteran surface-picker. His biographer notes that while he walked along a public road that ran through his property, he noticed a couple of crystals which he picked up and later had evaluated. This may seem an implausible story, particularly given that Branner, an experienced geologist and prospector, had claimed to have found no sign of diamonds during his energetic inspection of 1889, but Huddleston had a couple of factors working in his favor. First, his land had presumably been tilled, one

Spot where the first diamond was found in Arkansas; Murfreesboro (Pike County), ca. 1920.

---

10   Or, he may have simply been embarrassed. In any event, it is clear that the stones "did not know him."
11   See chapter on the state's floral emblem.

time if not several; this act alone would tend to bring up subsurface features, including, possibly, diamonds.[12] Second, Huddleston was walking along a public road. This was almost certainly a dirt road, bladed across his land and built up by taking material from the roadside and piling it onto the road surface, then leveling it but leaving trenches, or "borrow ditches," alongside. Thus, by walking along the road, Huddleston was able to eye the most disturbed part of his property—the place most likely to exhibit any geological or gemological curiosities.

John Huddleston and Samuel Reyburn

Huddleston did not run into Murfreesboro shouting "Eureka!" Instead, he apparently sent the crystals to Charles Stifft, a Little Rock jeweler of good repute, asking for an evaluation. Stifft sent them along to a New York gemologist who confirmed that the crystals were in fact "the true gem"—fragments of Indra's sword had cropped up in Pike County. In September, the news caused some commotion, and Huddleston signed a lease-purchase agreement with would-be mining magnates. He received $360 in cash for a six-month option, with a purchase price of $36,000 dollars.

At this point in the story, Huddleston slips not out of the picture but "over to the side"; he remained in the area, buying and selling real estate and paying frequent visits to his former property, which had been optioned by a group of Little Rock businessmen led by Samuel W. Reyburn, a banker and lawyer. Sam Reyburn and his partners also sought and secured options on properties adjoining Huddleston's, securing control of all the formation except a few acres at the northeast corner.

The Reyburn syndicate began digging for diamonds on the southeast side of the formation and soon found diamonds at the surface, carried by erosion and concentrated in a layer of black gumbo (or muck, to you) averaging about one foot thick and extending at places to four feet. These were the easiest "pickings"; the gumbo proved to be very productive. The mining engineers kept trying, however, to find diamonds in the Prairie Creek kimberlite, not just in the runoff layer. The prospects seemed good that the Arkansas pipes could equal the productivity of the South African diamond reefs and so several groups of speculators/investors poured money into finding the elusive mother lode, the diamond-bearing matrix presumed to be hiding in the peridotite. These hopes created a modest diamond "boom" that echoed far beyond Pike County—the 1913 design of the Arkansas state flag included a horizontally oriented rhombus or stylized diamond shape inspired by the Prairie Creek pipe's bounty.

Ventures such as the American Diamond Mining Company, the Kimberlite Diamond Mining and Washing

---

12   The diamond-hunting fields of the Crater of Diamonds State Park are periodically plowed.

PROSP CTING   OR DIAMOND   IKE COUNTY   A K

Company, and the Ozark Diamond Mining Company (reorganized in 1909 as the Ozark Diamond Mines Corporation[13]) poured money and other things into the Pike County diggings but with modest success.[14] Even the Reyburn syndicate, which finally reorganized as the Arkansas Diamond Company (ADC), met very modest success: the highest recorded yield from the kimberlite on the southeast slope came from 482 loads washed in 1909: an average of two carats per 100 loads, or only about one-sixth of the average needed for minimal commercial production. By the end of 1925, the Arkansas Diamond Company had halted its activities.[15] Three years later, a new group of Arkansas investors took over the operation, then leased it to yet another group. None of these measures found much success in the pipe. In 1932, even surface mining came to an end. An expected demand for industrial diamonds during World War II failed to revive the field, and the development in the 1950s of man-made diamonds suitable for industrial purposes probably sealed the fate of Arkansas's prospects as a diamond-mining powerhouse.[16]

This did not preclude a different sort of development. Within a few years of the field's discovery, land ownership had devolved to a pair of competing companies: the ADC and the Ozark Diamond Mines Corporation. From 1909 forward, these companies operated under the constraints of cash shortages, poor markets, poor management, lawsuits, and, possibly, sabotage. They did not, however, control the entire surface of the Prairie Creek pipe. During the 1930s, the Mauney family, which owned one corner of the diamond pipe, operated a modest "you dig 'em" operation, selling ice creams to amateur prospectors. After World War II, the remaining failed commercial mining operations followed suit, opening competing tourist attractions, the "Diamond Preserve of the United States," and, more homey-sounding "Big Mine."

---

13   The proprietors were seemingly oblivious to the fact that the diggings were on the southern edge of the Ouachita, rather than Ozark, Mountains.
14   Enhanced production efforts included the introduction of hydraulic excavation, in which workers used high-pressure water jets to break down the soil and flush material through sluice boxes, where diamonds could be recovered. This technique was first employed at Prairie Creek in 1914.
15   See the next footnote for discussion of a possible contributing factor.
16   Rumors have surfaced over the decades suggesting that the failure of the Arkansas diamond diggings to become a second Kimberley was due to the sinister machinations of the international diamond cartel. According to a wartime Justice Department investigation, after failing to gain control of the area in 1910, the London-based Diamond Syndicate allegedly worked to downplay the mine's potential and to sabotage production; in 1919, a small commercial diamond-washing plant was destroyed by fire, inspiring talk of conspiracy. During World War II, the Justice Department alleged that a 1921 closed-door deal between Sam Reyburn and other principals of the Arkansas Diamond Corporation and Sir Ernest Oppenheimer of the international diamond syndicate, brokered by the J. P. Morgan firm, had led to the Arkansas mines being shut down. See Edward Jay Epstein, *The Rise and Fall of Diamonds: The Shattering of a Brilliant Illusion* (New York: Simon and Schuster, 1982).

These operations combined in the early 1950s to operate as a single private prospector's paradise, the "Crater of Diamonds." For a small fee, visitors could indulge in a day's good, dirty fun, keeping any diamonds they found. In 1969, General Earth Minerals of Dallas, Texas, bought both operations but continued to operate the tourist attraction as "Crater of Diamonds." Ultimately, the volcanic pipe and some surrounding acreage became Crater of Diamonds State Park in 1972 when the state bought the property for $750,000. The possibility of unearthing gem-quality stones has inspired a steady draw of visitors to this unorthodox attraction: nearly 3.4 million guests visited the park from 1972 to 2014. The enduring popularity of this attraction was memorialized in the 2003 Arkansas commemorative state quarter, which bore a representation of a diamond, depicted in a side view of a round brilliant cut.

◇ ◇ ◇

John Huddleston, the "Diamond King" of Arkansas, lived out the rest of his life not far from the Prairie Creek diamond field. Legends surrounded him, suggesting that he had been cheated by the Reyburn syndicate and that he died a pauper—but in reality he fared at least as well, and perhaps better, than most who sought to make Arkansas a diamond giant. Huddleston invested his profits from the sale of the Prairie Creek property in real estate. In 1908, Huddleston, his wife, and their five daughters moved to nearby Arkadelphia, so that the girls could enjoy life in the small city. And enjoy it they did—for they were comfortably well off by the standards of the time. But fate is no respecter of comfort. In 1917, Sarah Huddleston died, followed in the next year by the couple's youngest daughter.

Group of diamond miners soon after the discovery in 1906 Murfreesboro, Arkansas

Huddleston soon moved home to Murfreesboro, where he looked after his real estate holdings and enjoyed his grandchildren. A second marriage, however, led to financial hardship—and the onset of the Depression made matters worse. By the mid-1930s, Huddleston had disposed of his properties, except his Murfreesboro home. He farmed a little and ran a secondhand store from his home on Kelly Street. He died at home on November 12, 1941, after a brief illness and was buried in a small cemetery three miles south of the diamond field.

His modest fortunes at the end of life might lead some to question whether or not he was a success, but chances are that Huddleston himself would have made few complaints. He made more money off his diamonds than most; he was treated fairly, invested prudently, and, for a long stretch, did well with those investments. Like many, Huddleston was cleaned out thanks to the Great Depression but in the end died at home, with his own roof sheltering him, leaving behind a good reputation as well as an example of luck that many have sought to emulate.

And what hath John wrought?

Recovery figures are incomplete, but an estimated 110,000 diamonds, thought to average 0.25 carats, have been recovered from the Prairie Creek pipe by commercial efforts and tourists. Since the site became a state park, the state has maintained records of the number of diamonds discovered and reported. Between the years 1972 and 2014, 31,476 diamonds weighing a total of 6294.20 carats were reported. The largest known stone discovered and reported during this period remains a 16.37-carat white diamond unearthed in 1975 by a Texan, though in 1923, a diamond weighing 40.23 carats had been unearthed.

On 362 days out of the year, the park is open to prospecting. And make no mistake about it: Crater of Diamonds is a park. It features campsites, a café, wildlife viewing opportunities, and even a water park, offering summer visitors a cool recuperation from a day's hot work of digging, sifting, and washing. You may rent some simple equipment—a folding shovel, a hand screen, and a plastic bucket—and go to work mucking through the soil (reclassified in the 1980s as lamproite[17]), looking for a personal gem. On a good day, you may look out at scores of hopefuls scattered across the thirty-seven-acre diamond field, each hoping to catch a little of John Huddleston's luck. They stand, feet planted in earth dry or muddy, tired and often hot but sustained by the allure of possibilities. In any shovelful of earth, after all, may lay a crystal thunderbolt, a precious shard of the sword of Indra.

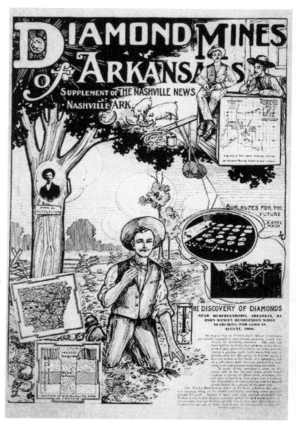

Diamond fever hits the local press. Nashville, Arkansas, newspaper supplement, ca. 1911.

---

17   From early days, the Prairie Creek pipe was described as either peridotite or kimberlite. In the 1920s, however, Swiss mineralogist Paul Niggli first introduced the term "lamproite" in his mineral crystal classification; "lampro" is from a Greek word meaning "glistening" and refers to the mica crystals that are found in this type of volcanic rock. Lamproites generally contain a higher level of potassium than kimberlites and are deposited in different patterns. By 1984, the Prairie Creek deposits were reclassified as lamproites.

For further reading:

Acts of Arkansas, 1907.

Arkansas Department of Parks and Tourism. Crater of Diamonds State Park. http://www.craterofdiamondsstatepark.com/ (accessed July 9, 2015).

Banks, Dean. "Diamond Mining." *Encyclopedia of Arkansas History & Culture*. http://www.encyclopediaofarkansas.net/ encyclopedia/entry-detail.aspx?search=1&entryID=2146 (accessed July 9, 2015).

———. "John Huddleston, 1862–1941: The Man Behind the Myth of 'Diamond John.'" Pike County Archives and History Society. http://www.pcahs.com/JohnHuddleston/JohnHuddleston.pdf (accessed July 9, 2015).

Branner, J. C., and Brackett, R. N. "The Peridotite of Pike County, Arkansas." *American Journal of Science* 38 (1889): 50–59.

"Crater of Diamonds State Park." *Encyclopedia of Arkansas History & Culture*. http://www.encyclopediaofarkansas.net/ encyclopedia/entry-detail.aspx?search=1&entryID=11 (accessed July 9, 2015).

Epstein, Edward Jay. "Have You Ever Tried To Sell A Diamond?" *Atlantic* (February 1982). Online at http://www.theatlantic. com/magazine/archive/1982/02/have-you-ever-tried-to-sell-a-diamond/304575/ (accessed July 9, 2015).

———. *The Rise and Fall of Diamonds: The Shattering of a Brilliant Illusion*. New York: Simon and Schuster, 1982.

Flood, Gavin. *The Blackwell Companion to Hinduism*. Malden, MA: Blackwell, 2003.

Hart, Matthew. *Diamond: Journey to the Heart of an Obsession*. New York: Walker & Sons, 2001.

Howard, J. Michael. *Finding Diamonds in Arkansas!* Arkansas Geological Survey, 2007. Online at http://www.geology.ar.gov/ pdf/pamphlets/AGES%20BROCHURE-DIAMONDS%2011-13-07.pdf (accessed July 9, 2015).

Millar, H. A. *It Was Finders-Keepers at America's Only Diamond Mine*. New York: Carleton Press, 1976.

Ware, David. "Official State Gem, a.k.a. Diamond." *Encyclopedia of Arkansas History & Culture*. http://www. encyclopediaofarkansas.net/encyclopedia/entry-detail.aspx?search=1&entryID=3141 (accessed July 9, 2015).

Worthington, Glenn W. *A Thorough and Accurate History of Genuine Diamonds in Arkansas*. Murfreesboro, AR: Mid-America Prospecting, 2003.

Younger, Joan D. *The Book of Diamonds: Their History and Romance from Ancient India to Modern Times*. New York: Crown, 1965.

Zoellner, Tom. *The Heartless Stone: A Journey through the World of Diamonds, Deceit and Desire*. New York: Macmillan, 2007.

CHAPTER 7: STATE ROCK

Some that glisters may be pot-metal.

At the foot of a grassy slope just to the west of the Arkansas State Capitol, a boulder rests, largely unsought. It is accessible but hides in plain sight; a street swings by it, but no footpath encourages pedestrians to examine it. It is a low lump of rough-surfaced rock that rests on a small concrete pad. Few capitol employees notice it save to use it as a landmark, as in "my session parking spot's right by the little boulder" (which is just across the drive from a much larger and somewhat better-known boulder[1]). On non-rainy days, a handful of capitol visitors may seek out the boulder, guided by the grounds tour brochure procured from the information desk inside. It's likely that few are impressed by the low-key landmark, but if they have gone so far as to reach it, they may at least linger long enough to read an attached plaque. If they do, they will learn that the boulder was placed there in 1943 to commemorate the aluminum industry and its contributions to the war effort. The unassuming boulder is made of the rock that was Arkansas's

---

1   The better-known boulder is one recovered from Granite Mountain, south of Little Rock, and placed on the grounds behind the capitol in 1936 to commemorate the centennial of Arkansas statehood. Its slightly higher fame may stem from its concrete pad, which bears the signatures of two governors, including "father of the capitol," George Washington Donaghey; it also enjoys some slight renown, at least among rock hounds with senses of humor, because despite its name, it is not, in fact, a granite boulder. Instead, it is a good example of weathered syenite, an igneous rock similar to granite but one that incorporates more feldspar than granite, in which quartz (see chapter on the state mineral) is present.

connection to the industry: bauxite.[2]

◇ ◇ ◇

Bauxite, the most common ore of aluminum, was designated the official state rock of Arkansas in 1967. It is a sedimentary material composed primarily of one or more aluminum hydroxide minerals, plus mixtures of silica, iron oxide, titania, aluminum silicates, and other impurities in minor or trace amounts. Bauxite takes its name from the village Les Baux-de-Provence in southern France, where geologist Pierre Berthier first identified it in 1821. Berthier dubbed it "alumine hydratée de Beaux"; in 1847, Pierre Dufrenoy congealed the lengthy moniker somewhat, proposing that the ore be called "beauxite." Not until 1861 did yet another researcher further refract the name, acknowledging the district of the ore's origin, Les Baux.[3]

Although aluminum is the second-most-abundant metallic element in the world, it was only identified as such in the early nineteenth century. Aluminum is found in most rocks, clay, soil, and vegetation combined with oxygen and other elements; aluminum-bearing compounds have long been used by humans. Pottery was made from clays rich in hydrated silicate of aluminum, and ancient Middle Eastern civilizations used aluminum salts for the preparation of dyes and medicines. They are used to this day in indigestion tablets and toothpaste. It was only in 1807, however, that English chemist Humphrey Davy hypothesized the existence of the element, arguing that "alum" (hydrated potassium aluminum sulfate, used since classical antiquity as an astringent, as well as in dyeing and medicine and today most often encountered in "styptic pencils" sold to stop bleeding resulting from minor shaving mishaps) was the salt of an unknown metal which he said should be called "alumium." Davy could not coax this metal into view, but in 1825, Danish researcher Hans Christian Oersted managed to produce nodules of what by then had been renamed "aluminum" or "aluminium."[4]

For the next sixty years, aluminum remained a rare and exotic metal, as scientists determined its properties and worked toward methods of refining usable quantities of it, then finding uses for those quantities. It was employed as a semi-noble jewelry metal; aluminum place settings graced the table of French emperor Napoleon III.[5] In America, its best-known placement was as the 100-ounce pyramidic cap of the Washington Monument

---

2   Commonly pronounced "bow-k'zeit" in the United Kingdom and "box-ite" in America; apparently its earliest common pronunciation was the French "bow-zite" (corresponding to "Les Beaux," the alternate spelling of its place of origin), but the Anglo-American habit of making even the most silent of consonants count for something may have led to the articulation of the word at the stressed "x."

3   The name, it appears, was often rendered as "Les Beaux," a spelling which for unknown reasons seems to disappear in the first half of the nineteenth century. Go figure.

4   The usual United States–standard English spelling "aluminum" was in fact also coined by Sir Humphrey Davy, who thought it would be easier to pronounce than the curt "alumium." From this coinage descended "aluminium," a spelling preferred today in parts of the world once parts of the British Empire. The addition of the second "i" seems to have been the handiwork of his classically trained contemporaries, whose preference for the extra syllable and, presumably, a slightly more exquisite pronunciation ("ah-lyu-MIN-ee-oom" versus "uh-loo-mi-num") allowed the new metal to take its place alongside potassium, magnesium, and sodium—all of which had been either discovered or named by Davy. The short version was the only one listed in Noah Webster's dictionary of 1828 and while both continued in stateside use (scientists clinging to the "ium," with most others opting for the shorter form) through the end of the century, by 1900, the "ums," rather than the "i"s, had it. When the American Chemical Society finally embraced "aluminum" in 1925, it did no more than ratify the popular choice.

5   The price of the bright, light metal was roughly that of pure silver, a traditional precious metal. In the early 1880s, the price for both metals was around $1 per ounce. Aluminum was much more expensive to produce than silver and much less of it was in fact produced, which might have been expected to raise its price, but demand remained low, since it was still a curiosity rather than a metal of mass consumption. The invisible hand of the market kept a restraining finger or two on the price of alumin(i)um.

in the District of Columbia, cast by the Frishmuth Foundry of Philadelphia and installed on December 6, 1884. Aluminum was chosen for its electrical conductivity properties, as well as for its lightness and resistance to staining. This—the largest single aluminum casting created to that date—thrust the light metal into the public eye.[6]

In 1886, metallurgical experimenters in France and the United States almost simultaneously developed a smelting process which in its essentials has been used ever since: dissolving aluminum oxide in molten cryolite (itself an aluminum ore), then extracting the aluminum by electrolysis.[7] All that was needed was an aluminum oxide–rich source and one soon appeared. In 1888, Austrian Karl Bayer invented an improved process for making aluminum oxide from bauxite, that reddish rock found in the vicinity of Les Baux-de-Provence, the ancient hilltop town located in the Alpille mountains of southern France.[8] These inventions sealed the fate of aluminum as a precious metal—by 1890, its cost tumbled some 80 percent from its earlier perch.

With aluminum readily available, it only remained to find something to do with it—and plenty of ideas already existed. As early as the 1850s, aluminum had been touted as a material for cookware; in 1856, Charles Dickens had predicted, "Aluminium may probably send tin to the right about face, [and] drive copper saucepans into penal servitude." In 1865, Jules Verne spun a tale of a space capsule, made of aluminum, shot from Earth to the moon. As the metal's price tumbled, it was introduced as a substitute for copper and brass; its electrical conductivity made it a useful material for power transmission. Its high ratio of strength to weight ensured that it would be a fundamental material of aeronautics. In 1910, aluminum cooking pots were joined in the kitchen by aluminum foil, effectively guaranteeing a future full of leftovers for many, many households.[9]

With the aluminum boom in prospect, geologists sought ample deposits of the now-valuable bauxite ore—and Arkansas proved capable of supplying the needful. Bauxite had been described as early as 1842, in a deposit in the Granite Mountain area of Pulaski County. This find lay largely unremarked on until, in 1887, state geologist John Casper Branner identified a sample collected in southern Pulaski County as the aluminum ore.[10]

The first attempts to exploit Arkansas bauxite commercially began in 1896, when twenty tons of ore were

---

6   It also ran the risk of providing the popular press with a government procurement scandal along the lines of the overpriced tools and toilet seats revealed in twentieth-century investigations. The Frishmuth Foundry, the only commercial aluminum reduction plant in the nation, bid a price of $75 to create the cap; their contract admonished them "but should that cost be necessarily and unavoidably exceeded in producing a perfect piece of workmanship, the account shall be submitted setting forth that fact." On November 12, 1884, foundry owner William Frishmuth informed the monument's superintendent that "After hard work and disappointments, I have just cast a perfect pyramid of pure aluminum made of South Carolina Corundum…. Cost of pyramid more than calculated." The bill was in fact for $256.10; after some stern words and a careful audit, a final price of $225 was agreed upon.

7   This process has nothing to do with electrolytic hair removal but sounds positively hair-raising to a non-adept.

8   Les Baux-de-Provence, a village of the Bouches de Rhône *département* of the province of Provence, is located on a high plateau and has been continuously occupied since prehistoric times. Its exploitable deposits of bauxite were exhausted in the early twentieth century.

9   Engineer and culinary historian John Ragsdale notes that an aluminum Dutch oven was sold as early as 1889, bringing relief to the legions of draft animals expected to haul the useful but weighty utensils into the woods on camping and hunting excursions. See chapter on Dutch ovens.

10   Branner published his findings in 1891, mining them for a subsequent publication in 1897. The sample had been brought to him by Ed Weigel of Little Rock; it was being used to surface the road between the capital city and Sweet Home, the location of the Arkansas Confederate Home, whose original building would later be demolished in order to facilitate bauxite mining.

shipped to out-of-state refractories. By 1899, that figure soared to over 5,000 tons.[11] The industry remained centered in Pulaski and Saline Counties throughout its history; early mines were operated by the General Bauxite Company and also by Pittsburgh Reduction Company, which purchased tracts of land in Pulaski and Saline Counties. Ultimately, the Pittsburgh company bought out the local producers of the ore, including General Bauxite. Pittsburgh Reduction would go on to incorporate as the Aluminum Company of America (known after 1945 as Alcoa).

As bauxite mining boomed, the district attracted a population, centered in the quintessential company town called—what else?—Bauxite. The town was at the center of workers' camps and provided services for them, including stores, a post office, medical care, and schools. It was not an incorporated municipality but rather an Aluminum Company of America operation. Throughout its decades of existence as such, Bauxite was noted for the high level of services it supplied mine and plant workers and their families.

Arkansas's bauxite deposits proved to be the largest commercially exploitable deposits in the nation. Throughout most of the twentieth century, Arkansas remained the nation's major bauxite producer, providing about 90 percent of all domestic tonnage mined. During World War I, production of the ore rose rapidly, growing from 195,247 long tons in 1914 to 562,892 long tons by war's end in 1918. Around the company town of Bauxite, workers' camps sprang up, with names such as Africa Camp, Italy Camp, and Mexico Camp denoting the dominant national or ethnic group in each one.

During the interwar years, thanks to innovations in refining, the availability of aluminum increased while its price declined; this led to increased use of the refined metal in such industries as construction, transportation, and the production of household goods. At the same time, Arkansas bauxite production fluctuated according to market demands for aluminum and the development of new sources of high-grade bauxite in South America and the Caribbean. The Great Depression of the 1930s further depressed production. By the mid-1930s, annual output of Arkansas

Three views of a booming business: postcards ca. 1906–1911.

---

11   This and subsequent tonnage figures are reckoned in "long tons," a unit equal to 2,240 lbs., used in production reporting by the Arkansas Geological Survey.

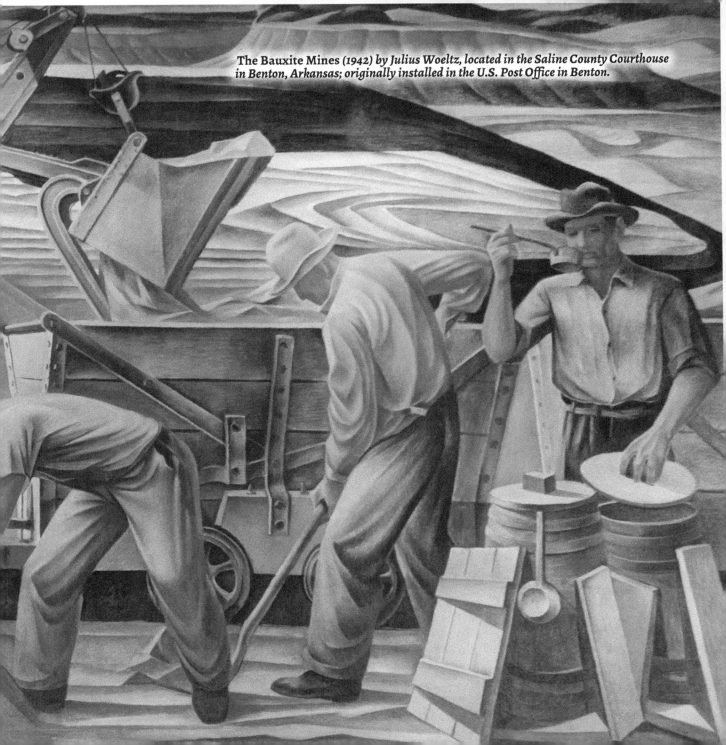

The Bauxite Mines (1942) by Julius Woeltz, located in the Saline County Courthouse in Benton, Arkansas; originally installed in the U.S. Post Office in Benton.

bauxite was barely one-tenth of what it had been in 1918. Notably, Alcoa continued to treat its employees well, providing free vegetables from community garden fields, reducing rents, and maintaining free utilities.

Loading cars with bauxite, ca. 1912.

The onset of World War II brought a revival of the industry. In the early stages of the war, ships carrying bauxite to the United States suffered high losses to enemy submarines. To keep defense plants producing, domestic production needed to equal and surpass what had been recently imported. The tonnage of bauxite mined in Arkansas quickly increased to meet wartime demands for aluminum, which was especially critical to the military aircraft industry. Triple shifts kept production running around the clock and necessitated importation of miners and mill workers from across the country. Between six and seven thousand workers, plus their families, made the Bauxite district boom; camps abandoned in the post–World War I slump were reopened and new housing was built at nearby Pine Haven. A new refinery was built at Hurricane Creek by Reynolds Metals. In 1942, the federal government took steps to build a strategic reserve stockpile of Arkansas bauxite; the first contract was let to Reynolds Mining, a subsidiary of Reynolds Metals. Smaller operators were initially encouraged by this initiative, but they eventually were bought out or crowded out by the area's two major players, Reynolds and Alcoa. In 1943, a total of 6,036,490 long tons of bauxite was mined for refining, which marked the industry's apex.

From this high point, however, Arkansas's bauxite bonanza cooled. After 1943, the strategic reserve program for bauxite was phased out; as shipping conditions improved, imported bauxite from South America returned to U.S. plants, reducing demand for the lower-concentration domestic ore. In 1944, Arkansas production fell to 2,695,317 long tons, and it was not until 1970 that production again exceeded two million long tons.

In 1967, the Arkansas General Assembly acknowledged the industry's significance by designating bauxite as the official state rock. This designation was contained in an omnibus measure, Act 128, which also honored diamonds (official state gem) and quartz crystals (official state mineral). Act 128 was introduced as Senate Bill 143 by Senators J. Hugh Lookadoo, Robert Harvey, and Olen Hendrix. None of these senators represented major mining districts; rather, they asserted that it was essential that the General Assembly immediately designate a state gem, mineral, and rock in order that various interested clubs and individuals in Arkansas could trade them. Thus, the legislation contained an emergency clause, ensuring immediate effect.

The emergency clause might almost have been interpreted as a sign that the legislature and the state's "friends of bauxite" knew that time was not on their side; by the time Act 128 became law, the cloudy future of the bauxite and aluminum industry in Arkansas could be foretold. Because of changing domestic and world economic conditions, the market share of Arkansas bauxite stumbled. Production fluctuated during the 1960s, but the trend was mainly downward. In 1967, the year of bauxite's designation as the state rock, Alcoa informed those who remained in Bauxite that the unincorporated town would be abolished in 1969; company-provided services would be eliminated and facilities either sold or abandoned. Mining continued, but miners and their families were now forced to either move to nearby Benton or Alexander, or consider other options. The town of Bauxite almost disappeared, but ultimately, the "other" option was pursued. In 1973, it incorporated, combining with the adjacent settlement of West Bauxite. Since 1980, its population has remained stable, between 400 and 500 residents.[12]

The year 1982 was a milestone, of sorts: it marked the last year in which Arkansas bauxite was mined for metal production. After this, Alcoa and Reynolds mainly focused their activities on reclamation of surface-mined lands. It did not, however, quite signal the end of the bauxite mining business. Small tonnages continued to be mined and used in the production of alumina-based materials, including chemicals and abrasives, into the 1990s. More recently, demand for a bauxite derivative has come from another quarter: the oil and natural gas production industry. Sintered bauxite is prized as a proppant used in hydraulic fracturing, commonly referred to as "fracking." A proppant is a solid material, typically treated sand or man-made ceramic, designed to keep an induced hydraulic fracture open during or following a fracturing treatment. It is added to fracking fluid which may vary in composition depending on the type of fracturing used. Sintered bauxite produces spherical grains that are lightweight, consistent in size, and strong—able to resist geologic pressures. Beginning in 1996, quantities of bauxite were shipped from central Arkansas to the Fort Smith plant of Saint-Gobain Proppants, a subsidiary of the France-based Saint-Gobain, S.A., a multinational organization specializing in construction and high-performance industrial materials.

Encouraged by an upswing in the fracturing industry, Saint-Gobain expanded production, building a new facility in Saline County close to the bauxite source, which opened in 2012. By the end of 2014, however, lower oil and gas prices dictated a downturn in proppant production. In January 2015, Fort Smith's Saint-Gobain plant was closed on an interim basis, resulting in the layoff of 120 employees. This followed the November 2014 closing of a competing proppant operation in nearby Van Buren. Saint-Gobain's Saline County plant, however, capable of producing over 147,000 tons of proppant annually, remained open.

If you seek the state rock, or at least evidence of it, look around you. It is hard to imagine a world bereft of the light-metal technologies that entered the market only with abundant, cheap quantities of aluminum. Both

---

12   One highlight of modern-day Bauxite is the Bauxite Historical Association's museum, located in the former Bauxite Community Hall, built by Alcoa in 1925 and maintained by the company until 1986.

Dickens and Jules Verne were proved prophetic. The feat of aeronautics was made possible by alloy components, airframes, and coverings, and anyone who cooks revels in the convenience of aluminum cooking pots. Even the Dutch oven, the near-sacred touchstone of primitive camping and cuisine, is available in a lightweight cast-aluminum version and in several sizes. The aluminum tool or pot or foil you may lay your hands on almost certainly was made of metal whose ore came from far off places, but thanks to the high recyclability of aluminum, there's at least a chance that a little Arkansas-sourced aluminum is part of its DNA.

Or, a trip to the source may be in order. If you are traveling along I-30, turn south at the Reynolds Road exit. Proceed through the heart of Bryant, past the home improvement stores and a clutch of fast food and convenience stores, past the handsome new high school and over the train tracks, then south on Reynolds/Highway 183. Just before you reach Tom Road, you will cross over from Bryant to Bauxite. Travel along 183, which turns into Benton Highway. Turn south again at School Street—note, on the right, a sign slightly overgrown in weeds boasting of the Bauxite Miners high school football team. Keep going until the signs for the Historical Association museum appear. Along the way, search for landscape that looks as though it is the product of some heroic-scale model railroader who has mastered the art of applying vegetation but who has not quite the knack for smoothing out ground contours. After reaching such a spot, pull over; it may well be a reclaimed area, one of the Reynolds or Alcoa surface mines that proved such a mainstay of the American war machine some seven decades ago. Look down, and if you see a piece of gravel exhibiting some round nodes, chances are that you will have found your own specimen of the state rock, not as large as the boulder located behind the State Capitol but worthy of at least a downsized version of the encomium found on the boulder's plaque:

THIS BAUXITE BOULDER OF HIGH QUALITY ALUMINUM-BEARING ORE WAS PLACED MARCH 1943 TO SYMBOLIZE ARKANSAS'S CONTRIBUTION TO WORLD WAR II. THE BOULDER WEIGHS NEARLY TWENTY TONS. IT WAS BROUGHT FROM THE DULIN BAUXITE MINE NEAR SWEET HOME, PULASKI COUNTY. THE STATE OF ARKANSAS IS FURNISHING OVER 98 PERCENT OF ALL BAUXITE MINED IN THE UNITED STATES FOR ALUMINUM PRODUCTION.

THIS TABLET IS MADE OF ALUMINUM MANUFACTURED FROM THIS TYPE OF ORE.

**HOMER M. ADKINS, GOVERNOR
C. G. HALL, SECRETARY OF STATE.**

For further reading:

Aluminum Association. http://www.aluminum.org/aluminum-advantage/history-aluminum (accessed August 16, 2015).

Bachus, Gordon Scott. "Background and Early History of a Company Town: Bauxite, Arkansas." *Arkansas Historical Quarterly* 27 (Winter 1968): 330–357.

Bramlette, M. N. *Geology of the Arkansas Bauxite Region*. Little Rock: Arkansas Geological Survey, 1936.

Bryan, Wayne. "Yesteryear When Bauxite was Booming." *Arkansas Democrat-Gazette*, Trilakes Edition, August 1, 2013. http://www.arkansasonline.com/news/2013/aug/01/yesteryear-when-bauxite-was-booming/?f=trilakes (accessed August 16, 2015).

Harrington, Laura. "Bauxite (Saline County)." *Encyclopedia of Arkansas History & Culture*. http://www.encyclopediaofarkansas.net/encyclopedia/entry-detail.aspx?entryID=382 (accessed August 16, 2015).

Howard, J. Michael. "Bauxite Mining." *Encyclopedia of Arkansas History & Culture*. http://www.encyclopediaofarkansas.net/encyclopedia/entry-detail.aspx?entryID=2145 (accessed August 16, 2015).

Ware, David. "Official State Rock, a.k.a. Bauxite." *Encyclopedia of Arkansas History & Culture*. http://www.encyclopediaofarkansas.net/encyclopedia/entry-detail.aspx?entryID=3143 (accessed August 16, 2015).

CHAPTER 8:
STATE MINERAL

A Gem-ish, Slightly Less Adamant

Imagine traveling southwest out of Little Rock, headed for the grand old resort of Hot Springs. You might take the old Stagecoach Road, but a more likely bet is U.S. 70/270. Stop for a snack in Benton at the Kream Kastle Drive Inn, a little ways east of Ten Mile Church, then proceed on. Before reaching the outskirts of the Spa City, you will probably notice one or two rock shops, small operations characterized by trestle tables out in front, each loaded down with tinted crystals and crystal clumps and round things which, if carefully split, promise miniature wonderlands. You might be tempted, but lunch at the Pancake Shop on Central—buckwheat and blueberry pancakes—awaits, and for now, at least, you're traveling light.

Thread the needle through Hot Springs and back onto 270. Head west, pass through the Crystal Springs District, going into the southern edge of the Ouachita Mountains. Camp Clearfork is on the left—a onetime Civilian Conservation Corps (CCC) project—but the road goes on. Cross Shangri-La Road, a gravel track just east of a south-lying finger of Lake Ouachita, ignoring the sign for a rock shop. Continue on, and in a few minutes more, the welcome signs will hove into view for Mount Ida, rock-hound heaven and what may be the spiritual home of Arkansas's designated state mineral: crystal quartz.

As part of the omnibus measure signed by Governor Winthrop Rockefeller on February 22, 1967, quartz crystal was declared the state mineral. The measure was introduced as a nod to Arkansas rock and mineral collectors and clubs; the text of the bill asserted that passage was essential in order that Arkansas gemologists, mineralogists, rock hounds, and other hobbyists might trade officially designated state gems, rocks, and minerals with like-minded enthusiasts in other states. Act 128 helped draw attention to the distinctive quartz crystals mined in the central Ouachita Mountains, long prized by collectors and also of economic value, particularly in the electronics industry.

◇ ◇ ◇

Quartz is the second-most-abundant mineral in the earth's continental crust, edged out for first place only by feldspar. Quartz is made of silicon and oxygen; its "formal" name is silicon dioxide (SiO_2), 46.7% silica, 53.3% oxygen. This mixture turns crystalline when it is heated above 573° C (1063.4° F); the general rule is that the higher the temperature, the larger or coarser the crystals. Such temperatures would, of course, be encountered during periods of intense, fundamental geologic activity. In Arkansas, the era of quartz crystal formation is believed to have occurred late during the formation of the Ouachita range, some 250–280 million years ago.

While the majority of quartz crystallizes from molten magma, much of it chemically precipitates from hot hydrothermal veins, sometimes with ore minerals like gold, silver, and copper; in such cases, the quartz is considered *gangue* or worthless rock.[1] Large crystals of quartz are found in magmatic pegmatites (igneous rock clusters made up almost entirely of crystals). Well-formed crystals may reach several meters in length and weigh hundreds of kilograms.[2]

The Exceptionally Large and Important Additions to our stock during October have been a rare treat to mineral collectors. Not for a long time have so many extra fine minerals been offered for sale.

ARKANSAS QUARTZ. On Mr. English's recent visit to Hot Springs we secured probably the largest and finest collection of Quartz ever sent to New York. Wonderful museum groups of large, stout crystals; delicate little groups of needle-like crystals; limpid and also ferruginous crystals; phantoms and enclosures of chlorite, manganese, etc.; twisted crystals; distorted and modified crystals; a thousand choice crystals and groups from which to choose, at 5c. to $50.00. Truly **grand** is our display!

Arkansas crystals hit the Big Apple, ca. 1880.

◇ ◇ ◇

Some haziness attends the origin of the name "quartz." An etymologic dictionary suggests that it is derived from the German word *quarz* and its Middle High German ancestor *twarc*, which probably originated in Slavic (it seems an etymological kissing cousin to the Czech *tvrdý*, meaning hard, which surfaces in Polish dialect as *twardy*).[3] The things we call quartz crystals were simply styled "crystal" (following the lead of Greek and Roman natural philosophers) until well into the eighteenth century. The first reference to a substance dubbed "quertz" is found in a treatise on ores and minerals, *Ein Nutzlich Bergbuchlein*, first issued in 1505. The reference is to a milky stone, not a clear crystal,

---

1   The term is French but derived from the German *gang*, meaning vein or course. It is usually pronounced as "gang" or "gong," but this writer has heard student attempts ranging from "gangway" to "ganja."

2   This explanation of the genesis of quartz is at variance with the theories advanced by Roman naturalist Pliny the Elder, who believed quartz to be water ice, permanently frozen after great lengths of time. (The word "crystal" comes from the Greek word κρύσταλλος, "ice.") He supported this idea by saying that quartz occurred near glaciers in the Alps but not on volcanic mountains.

3   Czech miners, however, historically called quartz "kremen," though they knew that the stuff was pretty tvrdy.

which was broken up and removed as spoil or *gangue* (see footnote 1, above) from silver mines in Saxony; it was styled *querkluftertz*, a word surely ripe for condensing, meaning a cross-vein ore. As late as the mid-eighteenth century, the term largely remained a Saxon usage; not until 1784 did chemical analysis demonstrate that clear crystal and the milky or cloudy waste-rock were two flavors of the same silicate formula. Thus, by the time of Arkansas's establishment, the question of what to call the stuff had been at least somewhat settled.

◊ ◊ ◊

Quartz may be divided into two gross classifications. The second of these is further divisible into a pair of sub-classes. The first gross classification is the macrocrystalline, what one has in mind when speaking of the state mineral. Quartz often appears in large, well-formed, and sometimes regular crystals or crystal "crusts." The purest silicon dioxide forms clear crystals. The addition of various impurities can produce colored, milky, or smoky crystals such as citrine, rose quartz, amethyst, smoky quartz, or milky quartz.

The ideal quartz crystal shape is a six-sided prism terminating with six-sided pyramids at each end. In the real world, however, quartz crystals are often twinned, distorted, or so intergrown with adjacent crystals of quartz or other minerals as to show only part of this shape, or to lack obvious crystal faces altogether, thus taking on the appearance of a massive lump. Well-formed crystals typically form in a bed of source minerals from which they grow into a void; thus only one termination pyramid is present. However, double-terminated crystals can occur where they develop freely without attachment, for instance within a matrix of gypsum (calcium carbonate). A quartz geode is formed in an approximately spherical void, which becomes lined with a bed of crystals pointing inward, toward one another.

The second gross classification is termed microcrystalline or cryptocrystalline in which crystals are microscopically small and arranged in slender "fibers" or parallel bands. These include the chalcedonies, long favored by stone carvers, as well as other opaque gemstone varieties of quartz or mixed rocks containing quartz, often exhibiting contrasting bands or patterns of color. Such semiprecious stones, including agate, sard, onyx, carnelian, heliotrope, and jasper, are variously colored, smooth, and often translucent. These are the stones of art: in archaic and historic Europe and the Middle East, different varieties of quartz were favored for jewelry and hardstone carving. Quartz was also used in ancient Ireland (in Irish Gaelic, quartz is styled *grian cloch*, which means "stone of the sun") and in other countries for stone tools. Both microcrystalline quartz

James A. Bauer of Hot Springs (Garland County), 1958. Bauer operated the Quartz Crystal Cave, a museum where he displayed hundreds of specimens of Arkansas quartz.

and rock crystal were knapped[4] as part of the lithic technology of the prehistoric peoples.

This microcrystalline class also includes a plainer but useful sub-class: cherts, flint, and jasper. These are quartzes of a workaday persuasion. In centuries past, they provided the keen knapped edges of aboriginal tools and the spark of conquerors', setters', and soldiers' flintlocks. These are the plain cousins of the shiny chalcedonies, but they share the essential chemical base: microscopic crystals of silicon dioxide.

QUARTZ CRYSTAL CAVE & MUSEUM
435 Whittington Ave.

Hot Springs National Park, Arkansas

Quartz is reckoned to make up nearly a quarter of the earth's surface, yet there exist few known locales exhibiting enough high-quality rock crystal to support commercial mining. Good-quality colorless crystals have been found near Little Falls, New York, and at Lyndhurst, Ontario. Smoky quartz crystals have been found in the high Rockies and the European Alps, and amethyst in Maine, Pennsylvania, and North Carolina. The largest discovered deposits are in Brazil, where quartz has been mined in the states of Minas Gerais,[5] Goiás, and Bahia. Another source is the island of Madagascar, lying off the east coast of Africa.

Another source is in the heart of Arkansas. The crystals are produced from veins in sandstone and shale. The quartz belt is about thirty to forty miles wide, extending southwest from near Little Rock into eastern Oklahoma. Arkansas quartz crystals are usually milky in appearance because of pockets of impurities, but many individual crystals have colorless, almost clear, terminations. On large "plates" of crystals, the individual crystals are often short, but it is not unusual for smaller crystals to be six times as long as they are thick, or more. These slender points are often used in making earrings and pendants.

◇ ◇ ◇

Apart from its ornamental qualities, rock crystal proved interesting to nineteenth-century French scientists Jacques and Pierre Curie, who in 1880 first observed quartz crystals' piezoelectric properties. Piezoelectricity is the electric charge that accumulates in certain solid materials (such as crystals, some ceramics, and even

---

4   Knapping refers to the shaping of stones by hitting, hammering, or chipping. In this context, it refers to producing stone tools by lithic reduction—that is, chipping away what is <u>not</u> wanted in order to end up with what <u>is</u>. Successful knapping yields sharp stone tools and lithic scatter—debris left behind to distract and beguile cultural resource survey workers.

5   The name of this province means, appropriately enough, "various (or general) mines." Minas Gerais is the site of Brazil's most extensive gold, silver, and diamond mining, plus its richest deposits of bauxite, graphite, and iron ore—and, of course, quartz.

biological matter) in response to applied mechanical stress.[6] For a time, the Curie brothers' discovery remained a laboratory curiosity, but researchers who followed the Curies explored and better defined the crystal structures that exhibited the quality of piezoelectricity. This work led to the 1910 publication of Woldemar Voigt's *Lehrbuch der Kristallphysik* (*Textbook on Crystal Physics*), which described some twenty natural crystal classes capable of piezoelectricity.

The first practical application for piezoelectric devices emerged during World War I. In France, physicist Paul Langevin and coworkers developed an ultrasonic submarine detector. The detector consisted of an ultrasound-generating device or transducer made of thin quartz crystals—carefully glued between two steel plates—and a sensitive hydrophone to detect the returned echo. By emitting a high-frequency pulse from the transducer, and then measuring the amount of time it took to hear an echo from the sound waves bouncing off an object, one could calculate the distance to that object. The name given to this system was sonar.

The success of this project created interest in piezoelectric devices. Over the next few decades, new materials and new applications for those materials were explored and developed, as piezoelectric devices found homes in many fields. Ceramic phonograph cartridges simplified player design, were cheap and accurate, and made high-fidelity record players practicable and affordable. Piezoelectricity was also found useful in generation of high voltages, electronic frequency generation, and even ultrafine focusing of optical assemblies. Piezoelectricity also acted as the ignition source for cigarette lighters, push-start gas grills, water heaters, cooking stoves, and, of course, as the micro-vibrating heart of quartz timepieces, presaged by Walter Marrison's quartz oscillator clock of 1927.[7] The regularity of these vibrations or oscillations made crystals essential in radio transmitters and receivers and, later, microprocessors. Thus, by the second half of the twentieth century, semiprecious gems had been harnessed to technology and the world economy.

Arkansas's pre–European contact native populations may have had no interest in oscillation, but they made use of quartz, both crystal and opaque, for weapons and tools. A quartz arrowhead estimated to be over 11,000 years old was discovered at a Garland County site. Farther to the east, the Plum Bayou people, an Archaic-period mound-building culture, fashioned projectile points and tools out of clear quartz. This activity continued into the historical period. In 1541, the de Soto expedition observed Native Americans chipping tools and projectile points from Ouachita quartz along the path of their slog through today's Arkansas. Early visitors to the Ouachitas, including members of the Hunter-Dunbar Expedition of 1804 and Henry Schoolcraft, a geographer, geologist, and ethnographer who passed through Arkansas in 1818–19, mentioned the abundance of quartz crystal.

During the nineteenth century, as health-seekers and other travelers became more common in the Ouachitas, the fame of the area's striking quartz crystals grew. In 1859, David Dale Owen reported that crystals were widely sold as curios to health-seekers taking the waters at Hot Springs. Some of the earliest crystal mining

---

6   The word piezoelectricity means "electricity from pressure." The phenomenon is also reversible: When a substance that demonstrates the piezoelectric effect is placed into an electrical field, its dimensions will slightly change. Electrify it, and doth it not vibrate? Squeeze it, and doth it not spark? It doth.

7   Marrison, a Bell Laboratories researcher, should not be confused with Walter Morrison, inventor of the Frisbee™ flying disc.

took place in the Crystal Range of Montgomery County, but, by 1900, quartz was also recovered from deposits in Garland and Saline Counties. Early crystal hunters were largely free to seek the stones where they wished, whether on timber sales or federal lands; few quartz miners bothered to file claims. Crystal prospecting was a simple matter that required a minimum of equipment, usually nothing more elaborate than a miner's pick and a bent iron "scratcher" bar, used to pry up loose crystals.

In the 1930s, a few individuals began to seek and extract crystal in a more orderly, businesslike way. These individuals followed the lead of Ocus Stanley (1909–1989), a Mount Ida native who, in about 1930, took out a mineral lease on lands on Mount Fisher, southeast of Mount Ida. Stanley is credited with establishing Mount Ida's first rock shop and, by example, stimulating the quartz-mining business.

Henry Schoolcraft: geographer and rockhounding Arkansas traveler.

By the time Stanley entered the Ouachita quartz diggings on a business basis, a second, more general, application for piezoelectric quartz had emerged: communications equipment. A radio station will transmit a signal at a particular frequency; a telephone call, whether it is transmitted over copper wire, optical fiber, or through the air as a cellular call, is transmitted by modulating a carrier wave that has a specific frequency. By 1920, researchers incorporated quartz crystal resonators into electrical circuits to produce stable frequencies. During the 1920s, quartz crystal oscillators and filters (devices allowing receiving instruments to exclude undesired frequencies) became standard parts of both radio and telephonic communication.

The production of quartz resonators and devices that incorporated them increased in the 1930s and, particularly, as World War II approached. Modern military planning relied on radio communications; any radio communication device depended on quartz. War-production demand for large, clear, single crystals of quartz for use in making quartz oscillator plates for radio frequency control emphasized the strategic importance of this industrial mineral, which in prewar years had been obtained mostly from Brazil. This supply, like that of bauxite, was considered susceptible to enemy attack and destruction. Accordingly, the national government became interested in the domestic location and extraction of this strategic non-metal mineral.

The search for radio-quality quartz in the United States during the war was stimulated by the War Production Board, the Metals Reserve Company, the U.S. Geological Survey, and numerous private concerns. For a time, Arkansas and other quartz districts around the nation enjoyed a minor quartz boom. The Arkansas diggings produced the greatest number of usable crystals, followed by California, western North Carolina, and southwestern Virginia. A mine was placed under federal supervision in Jessieville in Garland County, as was one in Saline County. A quartz-buying operation was established in Hot Springs in 1943; about 75 percent of the oscillator quartz mined in the district during this year, more than 4,000 pounds, was tested at this station. Quickly, however, the boom quieted. Although Arkansas produced crystals of good quality, geologists concluded that the longterm prospects for significant tonnage production were not good. Additionally, the predicted interruption of supplies from Brazil did not fully materialize; as with bauxite, supplies of high-quality crystals from Brazil made the lower-grade domestic product less attractive.

The market remained strong through the end of the war, but the availability of crystal from Brazil and other sources—coupled with the postwar development of techniques for creating cultured, or synthetic, crystals—effectively depressed industrial demand for Arkansas crystals. The local market became once again driven by tourist and collector demands.

Some industrial potential, however, remained. In the 1960s, a Japanese firm acquired control of a Garland County crystal mine with the intention of developing it as a source of the raw material for creating synthetic quartz crystals. During the 1980s, popular interest in crystals' possible metaphysical properties led to an upswing in demand. By the mid-1990s, this market section amounted to between 15 and 20 percent of total quartz-crystal sales. In addition, *lascas* (a non-electronic grade of quartz used as seed stock for creating synthetic quartz crystals), continued to be mined in Arkansas through 1997; in that year, the state's industrial quartz extraction was an estimated 450 tons. After 1997, however, industrial quartz crystal production in America drew upon stockpiled domestic and imported lascas supplies. This meant that demand for Arkansas crystals would be tied to jewelry, metaphysical, and collectors' or "specimen" markets.

Most of the quartz in the Ouachita Mountains occurs as milky veins. In addition to rock crystal and milky quartz, other varieties are present in this region. "Smoky" quartz occurs adjacent to igneous rocks near Magnet Cove in Hot Spring County; its dark color comes from defects in the crystal lattice caused by radioactivity that irradiated the crystal during or shortly after its formation during the heated Cretaceous era. Some natural smoky quartz has also been recovered from sites in Garland County, although much of the smoky quartz found in Arkansas rock shops is rock crystal that has been artificially irradiated. One sometimes finds quartz crystals with fluid inclusions (locally termed "bubble" quartz), or so-called "Herkimer Diamonds,"[8] regular double-ended crystals which form in Ouachita calcite veins. These weather away, leaving the crystals suspended in clay. Also found in the quartz belt is amethyst (purple or blue-violet quartz); this semiprecious stone occurs in Cretaceous igneous intrusive rocks, particularly in veins at the Crater of Diamonds State Park in Pike County, and as veins located in northern Saline County.

Today, several commercial crystal mines in Arkansas allow paying

Hydrothermal vein quartz (SiO_2) intruding quartzose sandstone from the Coleman Quartz Mine.

---

8   This name derives from double-terminated quartz crystals discovered in the late eighteenth century in and around Herkimer County, New York, and the Mohawk River Valley. Because the first discovery sites were in the village of Middleville and in the city of Little Falls, respectively, the crystals are also known as Middleville or Little Falls diamonds.

collectors to hunt for specimens. Rockhounding also continues on both private and public land. Although in the past some quartz was dug underground, today's quartz crystal mines are open-pit operations that will usually rent the basic hand equipment required.

Mount Ida is the center of this activity. A recent guidebook listed eight active dig-it-yourself operations in and around the little mountain town. Mount Ida also is home to several rock shops and, each October, the Quartz Crystal, Quilts, and Crafts Festival and the World Championship Quartz Crystal Dig, in which amateur diggers compete for modest cash prizes and the honor of unearthing the Best Cluster and Best Point.

For further reading:

Howard, Darcy, and Mike Howard. *Collecting Crystals: The Guide to Quartz in Arkansas*. Little Rock: A & I Studio Press, 2000.

———. Rockhounding Arkansas. http://www.rockhoundingar.com (accessed August 14, 2015).

McMillan, Allen. "Quartz Mining." *Encyclopedia of Arkansas History & Culture*. http://www.encyclopediaofarkansas.net/encyclopedia/entry-detail.aspx?entryID=1173 (accessed August 14, 2015).

———. World Championship Quartz Crystal Dig. *Encyclopedia of Arkansas History & Culture*. http://www.encyclopediaofarkansas.net/encyclopedia/entry-detail.aspx?entryID=4414 (accessed August 14, 2015).

McWhan, Dennis. *Sand and Silicon: Science that Changed the World*. New York: Oxford University Press, 2012.

Smith, Arthur E., Jr. *Collecting Arkansas Minerals: A Reference and Guide*. Little Rock: Ream Publications, 1996.

United States Department of the Interior, United States Geological Survey. *Mineral Commodity Summaries*, Quartz Crystal (industrial) and Gemstones Appendices, January 2015. Washington: Government Printing Office, 2015. http://minerals.usgs.gov/minerals/pubs/mcs/2015/mcs2015.pdf (accessed August 14, 2015).

CHAPTER 9: STATE INSECT

The Diligence of the Hive

The honeybee (*Apis mellifera*) is a social insect; that is, it lives in a society or community in which types of bees are assigned roles. Over centuries, even millennia, honeybees have been domesticated. Whereas they once lived in the widest variety of holes and crevices in walls, logs, and so forth, they have been cultivated by humans over the years and encouraged to live in man-made hives. This protects them and provides them with suitable environments for their characteristic activities: making wax, pollinating flowers and other plants, and producing honey.

Bees were once worshiped. The emperor Napoleon thought so highly of the honeybee that it was included on his imperial crest. In modern times, bees are still revered, valued, and respected. To date, fifteen states have honored the honeybee by designating it as one of their official symbols. Some states have paired the honeybee with a more aesthetically impressive or ornamental bug, such as the butterfly or the dragonfly—one for go and one for show, perhaps? Arkansas is one such state, having in 2009 adopted the Diana fritillary as the state's official butterfly. But in 1973, the symbolic spotlight rested upon the honeybee alone. In that year, the Sixty-Ninth General Assembly designated the honeybee as the state's official insect. Act 49, sponsored by Representative Tom Collier of Jackson County, extolled the bee's vital role in agriculture but mainly celebrated the insect's perceived virtues: diligence, ceaseless industry, defense of the home or hive, and productivity. These attributes, Collier's measure suggested, typified the "outstanding citizens of the state of Arkansas." Since then, fourteen other states have similarly honored the bee. In this, however, Arkansas was first.

◇ ◇ ◇

Honeybees are part of a large family or classification of insects known as the *hymenoptera*—this indicating that their wings are membranous, or somewhat translucent. About 20,000 varieties of bees have been identified, and relatives of honeybees include such disparate creatures as wasps, bumblebees, hornets, and ants.[1] True bees exhibit one characteristic that distinguishes them from their hymenopteran kin: while ants and wasps are carnivorous in at least one stage of their life cycle, bees always derive their nutrition from the pollen and nectar of flowers; they are models of the vegan lifestyle.[2]

As many as eleven distinct species of *Apis* honeybees have been identified; currently, seven are recognized, divided into forty-four subspecies. Each possesses genetic traits that are potentially desirable for beekeeping, such as honey production or heat tolerance. They may also possess others that are less desirable, such as susceptibility to disease or a testy defensive temperament. All of these families of honeybee are capable of successfully interbreeding, resulting in the prospect of myriad hybrid bees.

> ◇ ◇ ◇
>
> *How doth the little busy bee*
> *Improve each shining hour,*
> *And gather honey all the day*
> *From every shining flower!*
> *How skilfully she builds her cell!*
> *How neat she spreads the wax!*
> *And labours hard to store it well*
> *With the sweet food she makes.*
> —Isaac Watts
> ◇ ◇ ◇

The adult residents of any given hive fall into three divisions—or, rather, two groups and a fearless leader. The leader is, of course, the queen bee (the leader bee is always a female). She is the colony head, whose main job is to lay eggs, by the tens of thousands. A queen usually lives two or three years and may lay as many as 600,000 eggs during her reign. A colony or hive usually has only one queen, although before or just after a colony migration or "swarm," there may be younger queens—ladies in waiting, perhaps?—ready to emerge and replace her.

The second type of hive resident is the drone. These are the swarm's token males, who have big heads, seek out the warmest and best-sheltered spots in the hive, and go outside only on calm days, usually in the afternoon. The drones gather neither nectar nor pollen; their sole job is to fertilize the queen and this only a single time. After this brief romantic interlude, the drone either loses his genitalia inside the queen or is bitten; in either case, he scores once and then dies, having done what nature expects of him.

The third division, the worker bee, constitutes the group whose behavior gives bees their reputation for industriousness. These are infertile females—smaller than either the drones or the queen—that do most of the work within a hive. They gather pollen and nectar; their wings fan the hive to keep it cool in the summer heat; and they defend against all enemies, protecting the queen and her vital reproductive factory-work. They also construct the wax cells in which fertilized bee eggs are deposited, to be surrounded by condensed plant nectar or honey, then left to develop into larvae and, ultimately, become more worker bees.

---

1   Ants do not, by and large, exhibit membranous wings. But sexually active males and females do have wings, to the chagrin of nearby humans who think that marching ants at picnic grounds are nuisance enough, thank you.

2   Well, mostly. At times, when pollen and nectar are scant, or when human beekeepers have not provided sugary food for them, worker bees may kill and consume other bees' larvae, thereby both surviving and conserving the protein of their fellow workers and either modeling or inspiring human bureaucratic behavior (you decide which).

In some tropical zones of Africa, Australia, and the Americas, native stingless bees (*Apis meliponines*) are kept for honey and wax production. *Apis mellifera*, the so-called western or European honeybee, however, is the most common bee kept for both honey production and pollination around the world. Its origins are debated. Traditionally, it was believed to have first appeared in tropical east Africa, spreading north over the centuries. Recent research, however, suggests that the honeybees derive from an ancient lineage of cavity-nesting bees that arrived from Asia more than 300,000 years ago and rapidly spread across both Europe and Asia. The bees' ancestral home may be less significant than their diversification. Over centuries in isolation, different races or subspecies of *Apis mellifera* adapted to their specific regions, climates, and biomes, developing recognizable differences in behavior and appearance. The bees got around. And wherever they settled, they developed what was necessary to gain access to and make the best use of local resources.

"Honey hunting" from wild bees' nests was practiced throughout the ancient world. The honey was doubtless prized as one of the few things that you could gather that did not taste either bitter or dirty or bland or salty or, for that matter, burnt. A prehistoric cave drawing discovered in Spain in 1919 shows a human engaged in stealing some honey from a hive located in a hole in a cliff-wall, suggesting that hope (or, perhaps, optimism in the face of foreknowledge) has long been part of the human personality. The same drawing shows some rather large bees flying around the human, probably not in a very good mood, which brings to mind the Greek proverb, "If you love honey, do not fear the sting."[3]

Cave art, ca. 6000 B.C.E., from Arana Cave, near Bicorp, Spain, showing an at-risk honey gatherer.

---

3   The storied traditional last words of the young male—"Hey, watch this..."—also come to mind.

Bee veneration was a feature of Mediterranean cultures, particularly those of the Greeks and their predecessors. The high priestess of the oracular shrine of Delphi was, before Apollo took over the patronage of the shrine, referred to as a bee. On Crete, there existed a cult of the honey-goddess, Melissa by name; this was almost certainly connected to the tales of the upbringing of Zeus, child of Rhea and Cronus, who was nurtured by the nymphs Arastea and Io,[4] daughters of King Melisseus (Honey-man); little Zeus was nourished by honey and goat's milk.[5]

This all suggests that the ancient world understood there to be something sacred and mysterious about the work and produce of the bee. The Achaeans do not seem to have attempted to domesticate bees, but the Minoan civilizations of Crete began the process. On Crete, too, appeared the honey-wine known to us as mead. The conquering Achaeans took to the beverage with alacrity: Aristotle remarked, "When the honey is squeezed out of the combs an agreeable strong drink, like wine, is produced." Apollonius Rhodius (235 B.C.) related that the Argonauts kept vast stores of food and mead; the heroes grasped their kylixes or goblets with both hands, not forgetting to pour a cup of mead upon the sea before lifting anchors and shifting oars. It is telling that the Greek expression corresponding to the English "blind drunk" is "honey intoxicated." Beekeeping also flourished along the Nile. Honey was prized in ancient Egypt; barges loaded with swarms of honeybees went up and down the Nile by the season, "following the flowers."

As beekeeping methods spread, the beekeeping cultures worked out the grim details about how best to persuade their local bee swarms to stay in one region and "bee" useful. A first step in this was the provision of nesting space. Wild honeybees took refuge in any sort of recess—a crevice in a wall or cliff, a hollow tree, or perhaps an old discarded clay pot—but crafty sweet-hunters learned that a first step on the road to domestication was provision of a home. Some of the earliest artificial hives, or skeps, were nothing more than rolled cylinders of bark (in Abyssinia), straw houses (in France), conical baskets (France again), or man-hollowed tree trunks. A common early practice to encourage bees to take up residence in these man-provided hives was "tanging"—that is, making a great racket by hitting a metal pot or pan with a stick.[6]

◊ ◊ ◊

By the time of the age of exploration, the art/science of honey culture was well established in Europe, so it is no surprise that wherever Europeans went to claim and conquer, they seem to have brought and established colonies of *Apis mellifera*. In the 1600s, English colonists brought hive-loads of the *"apis of their eyes"* to Jamestown. The trip across may not have been pleasant (less so for their human shipmates than for the bees, one suspects), but the bees took to the forests and flora of the New World like, well, bees to flowers. Anticipating their human transporters' later political enthusiasms, colonies high-tailed it west, well in advance of settlement; as pioneers ploughed ever deeper into the woods, they often found advance colonies of the once-European bees thriving in the vastness of America's interior, displacing or hybridizing with the native bees. These first feral western honeybees were said to be prone to diseases and produced high-moisture, or "runny," honey. They

---

4   Their names are sometimes rendered as Amaltheia and Melissa; obviously, this naming business was sticky indeed.
5   Discussions of Potnia, the powerful bee queen and her priestesses who took the title of "Melissas," the bee-dependent origin stories of the Sa people of the Kalahari, as well as other heroic, sweet yarns must be deferred for the present.
6   In the interest of scholarly inquiry, your author has experimented with the tanging technique. Once. He will not repeat the experiment.

"Bee and Stag" silver coin from Ephesus, Ionia, ca. 390–325 B.C. Ephesus was a coastal Hellenic city located in present-day Turkey, settled in the 10th century B.C.E. by Attic and Ionian Greek colonists; it was known to the Apostle Paul. Ephesus used the bee on its coins since it was a producer of honey, so the bee advertised their most famous product. The city was also the location of the famous Temple of Artemis. Her priestesses were called "melissai" or the "honey bees" of the goddess. The stag, which adorns the reverse of this coin, is a symbol of Artemis, the goddess of the hunt; thus, this coin bore not one but two of the future symbols of Arkansas.

were easily excited but cold-resistant, hence they would last. In time, they would be bred with newly imported European stock, resulting in hardy, productive bee populations. Honeybees reached the eastern banks of the Mississippi and Missouri Rivers by 1809, and populations were reported in Arkansas within a decade.

For early Arkansawyers, honey represented both a source of nutrition and relief from the combination of blandness and saltiness that characterized the frontier diet. Even by the latter years of the nineteenth century, a bad fruit crop could mean that sweets were in short supply. One man born before the turn of the century later recalled, "Did you ever try eatin' fer two months without having something sweet? Well, that's what we had to do. It was bad."[7] For those who developed the skills of "honey robbing," the wealth of the hives provided a valued supplement to the diet.

Explorer Henry Schoolcraft, who traveled through Arkansas in 1819, noted that a trading keelboat that he encountered at the great fork of the White River carried with it beeswax collected by hunters and farmers living farther up the river. Schoolcraft also described the delight that Euro-American hunters took in finding honey: "The white hunters in this region, (and I am informed it is the same with the Indians), are passionately fond of wild honey, and whenever a tree containing it is found, it is the custom to assemble around it, and feast, even to a surfeit....When this scene of gluttony was ended, the dog also received his share, as the joint co-partner and sharer of the fatigues, dangers, and enjoyments of the chace [sic]."[8]

Honey-hunters would sometimes carry off more than the honey and beeswax; the swarms themselves could also be the prize. They were kept in homemade structures called gums, made by cutting three- to four-foot sections from hollow logs (often but not always sweetgum), burning the interior until the surface was slick, cutting one or two small inverted V's in the bottom as passageways for the bees, and covering the slanted top with a plank roof. A cross piece, nailed in the middle, provided a support for the honeycomb. Even after the practice evolved to using planks for the body of the skep, the name "gum" persisted, as did the practice of "tanging" to settle or attract bees to the new hive.[9]

By the time of Arkansas's statehood in 1836, honeybee populations were well-established in what was early dubbed "the bear state," honoring the vigorous ursine honey-grubbers of the piney woods. To the Euro-Americans, bees were part of the natural bounty given them to tap by a benevolent deity and their own exertions. To Native Americans, however, bees were something more: a foreshadowing. Novelist and historian Washington Irving, himself an early visitor to Arkansas, wrote in 1835:

It is surprising in what countless swarms the bees have overspread the Far West, within but a moderate number of years. The Indians consider them the harbinger of the white man, as the buffalo is of the red man; and say that, in proportion as the bee advances, the Indian and buffalo retire. They have been the heralds of civilization, steadfastly preceding it as it advanced from the Atlantic borders.[10]

7   Roy Edwin Thomas, *Authentic Ozarks Stories about Bee Huntin' and Stingin' Insects* (privately published, 1972), excerpted in Jeffrey K. Barnes, "Arkansas Arthropods in History and Folklore," online at http://www.uark.edu/ua/arthmuse/folk.html (accessed July 13, 2015).

8   Ibid.

9   T. C. Page. *Voices of Moccasin Creek* (Point Lookout, MO: School of the Ozarks Press, 1972).

10   Washington Irving, "A Bee Hunt," in *A Tour of the Prairies* (1835). Online at http://www.vcu.edu/engweb/eng372/irvingprairie.htm (accessed July 13, 2015). Irving also quotes a grizzled frontiersperson's testimony as to the relationship of bears to honey: "The bears is the knowingest varmint for finding out a bee tree in the world. They'll gnaw for days together at the trunk till they make a hole big enough to get in their paws, and then they'll haul out honey, bees and all."

In early Arkansas, the bee was esteemed for its products, particularly its honey. Moreover, bees enjoyed a reputation as a symbol of industry and utilitarian devotion to duty. The bees' community, the skep or beehive, became a sigil for not one but two states: Arkansas and Utah.

The beehive was incorporated into the design of the Arkansas territorial seal and was carried over into the design of the great seal of state in 1836. Since many of the early territorial and statehood leaders were members of Arkansas's early Masonic lodges,[11] the symbolism of the beehive would have been no mystery. An early "exposé" of freemasonry pointed out: "A bee has in all Ages and Nations been the Grand Hierogliphick of Masonry, because it excells all other living Creatures in the Contrivance and Commodiousness of its Habitation or combe."[12]

Masonic symbolic convention pointed to the beehive as a potent, positive symbol. An Arkansas Masonic officer wrote:

> The Bee Hive is an emblem of industry, and recommends the practice of that virtue to all created beings, from the highest seraph in heaven to the lowest reptile in the dust. It teaches us that we come into the world rational and intelligent beings, so we should ever be industrious ones; never sitting down content while our fellow creatures around us are in want, especially when it is in our power to relieve them without inconvenience to ourselves."[13]

Such inspiration may well have led Samuel Calhoun Roane to include the beehive in the state seal design; its pre-Christian symbolic and religious associations were probably considered less important than the example of communal industry made concrete in the representation of the straw skep or hive.

Interestingly, the beehive was also adopted by the pioneering colonists of the Church of Jesus Christ of Latter-Day Saints as a symbol for their great undertaking, Deseret or Utah. Nineteenth-century Mormon leaders consciously created symbols to buttress their community, the most persistent of which was the beehive. The origin of the beehive as a symbol was associated with Mormon scripture. The *Book of Mormon* noted that the Jaredites carried "with them Deseret, which, by interpretation, is a honey bee" (Ether 2:3).[14] The beehive was omnipresent as a symbol in early Utah history; it appeared as early as 1851 on the seal of the Territory of Utah. In 1881, an essay in *The Deseret News* of Salt Lake City made the explicit inspirational connection between the beehive and the evolving territory thus: "The hive and honey bees form our communal coat of arms....It is a significant representation of the industry, harmony, order and frugality of the people, and of the sweet results of their toil, union and intelligent cooperation." It was readopted on the state seal by the first state legislature in 1896.[15]

---

11   One such was the seal's credited designer, Samuel Calhoun Roane, who organized the first Masonic lodge in Arkansas in 1819.

12   Jonathan Swift, "Letter From the Grand Mistress" (ca. 1730), excerpted in Henry Sadler, *Masonic Reprints and Historical Revelations Including Original Notes and Additions* (London: 1898), excerpted in G.W. Bullamore, "The Beehive and Freemasonry," *Ars Quator Coronatorum* (1923), online at http:// freemasonry.bcy.ca/aqc/index.html (accessed July 13, 2015).

13   George Thornburgh, *Masonic Monitor of the Degrees of Entered Apprentice, Fellow Craft and Master Mason, together with the Ceremony of Installation, Laying Corner Stones, Dedications, Masonic Burial, Etc.* (Little Rock: 1903).

14   A number of scholars have pointed out connections and similarities between Mormon symbols and rituals and those of the Masonic lodges, of which some early LDS leaders were members.

15   Richard Oman, "Beehive Symbol." *Encyclopedia of Mormonism* (New York: Macmillan, 1992), 99.

◇ ◇ ◇

Bees were historically prized for their honey, as well as their beeswax, which served as a valuable polish, protectant, cosmetic, candlestuff, and even ingredient of various foods, particularly confections. During the nineteenth century, however, research revealed that the bees were responsible for much more—as they "got around," they pollinated. In the late 1700s, Joseph Gottlieb Kolreuter observed insect agency in the pollination of many flowers, generally classed as *Entomophilae*. Naturalists of the nineteenth century, building on Kolreuter's work, came gradually to understand and appreciate the work of bees and other pollinators, including birds, slugs, and bats.

Pollination is defined as the transfer of pollen, which contains the male gamete of a plant, from the anthers (where it is produced) to the stigma, the female part of the same or another plant of the same species. This process results in fertilization and reproduction of the plant. Wind pollinates grasses and many trees; birds and bats do the job for a few species of plants each, but insects pollinate the majority of plants—and of the insects, the honeybee is the most effective pollinator, responsible for "servicing" more than 80 percent of all cultivated crops. This includes many common fruits and vegetables, as well as nuts, herbs, spices, oilseed crops, forage, and ornamental plants. Honeybees thus add an estimated $15 billion or more to the U.S. economy each year in increased crop yields.

◇ ◇ ◇

Arkansas's beekeeping industry includes a small number of commercial beekeepers who manage large numbers of hives for pollination service and honey production, as well as an estimated 2,000 individuals and families who keep smaller numbers of hives either as hobbyists or as part-time beekeepers.

In 2013, the most recent year for which the USDA offers production statistics, Arkansas's 22,000 bee colonies produced approximately 1,320,000 pounds of

Jon Zawislak, extension bee specialist for the University of Arkansas System Division of Agriculture (right) shows students the queen bee of a colony that is about to be transferred to a new home.

honey, averaging 60 pounds per colony.[16] The price paid for Arkansas honey that year averaged $2.02 per pound, meaning that each colony might gross about $120 for its human owner. The profit might seem small, but there is a compensation: Beekeeping is one of the least regulated ways in which an Arkansan may strive to make money by selling an agricultural product to someone else.

In Arkansas, beekeeping is regulated by the Arkansas State Plant Board. The board seeks to protect honeybees so as to maintain viable populations for purposes of pollination. To this end, the board requires registration of all apiaries or bee-yards (that is, places wherein are found "kept bees").[17] Hobbyist beekeepers face few obstacles to selling their honey. Honey hobbyists (that is, producers of less than 500 gallons of honey per year for sale, which comes to just short of 6,000 pounds, or a lot of those little bear-shaped bottles) are not required to be inspected by the Arkansas Department of Health, although they may request such an inspection. These small producers may sell properly packaged and labeled honey directly to consumers at farmer's markets, from the site where the product is produced, or at county fairs and other special events. The honey must be labeled with the name and address of the business, list the common name of the product, and contain a list of ingredients ("Ingredients: Honey"). The label should also include the statement "This Product is Home-Produced" in 10-point type.[18]

A final, sweet consideration: Arkansas law characterizes honey as a farm product. As such, it is exempt from sales tax when sold directly from the place of its origin, including a beekeeper's home, a farmer's market, or even a roadside honey-and-lemonade stand.

In Arkansas, as in the rest of the nation, honeybee populations face a wide variety of challenges. Many have been with beekeepers for many decades, fighting off parasites or diseases. In recent years, however, a new specter has haunted the bee-yards: colony collapse disorder, or CCD. Beginning in the winter of 2006, beekeepers across the United States reported losses of 50 to 90 percent of their colonies. In many cases, the hives had appeared healthy and active within a few weeks of colony failure. Because the cause of death was undetermined, the term "colony collapse disorder" was coined to describe the situation.

CCD may not be a strictly new and distinct phenomenon. Large-scale bee die-offs have periodically occurred in the past. Older literature describes these situations as "spring dwindle disease," "fall dwindle," or "autumn collapse." In cases of CCD, however, the bee populations do not "dwindle"; instead, the adult population effectively disappears suddenly, within a few weeks or days. It leaves behind a healthy queen bee, few if any dead bees, combs full of honey and pollen, lots of healthy "brood" (babies on the way), and not enough "nurse" worker bees left to maintain the colony.

Many thousands of U.S. bee colonies have collapsed in recent years in some thirty-five states, including

16   "Honey." National Agricultural Statistics Service (NASS), Agricultural Statistics Board, United States Department of Agriculture (USDA), released March 20, 2015. http://www.usda.gov/nass/PUBS/TODAYRPT/hony0315.txt (accessed July 13, 2015).

17   Kept bees? I'm not making this up. It's right there in the plant board's apiary webpage: http://plantboard.arkansas.gov/PlantIndustry/Apiary/Documents/registrationProcess.pdf (accessed July 13, 2015). One wonders if the bees know that they are kept—and if they do, how do they retain their self-respect?

18   Arkansas Beekeepers Association. http://arbeekeepers.org/honey.html (accessed July 13, 2015).

Hydromel, or, Honey-wine, as made for the Queen

Take 18 quarts of spring-water, and one quart of honey; when the water is warm, put the honey into it. When it boileth up, skim it very well, and continue skimming it, as long as any scum will rise. Then put in one Race [root] of Ginger (sliced in thin slices), four Cloves, and a little sprig of green Rosemary. Let these boil in the Liquor so long, till in all it have boiled one hour. Then set it to cool, till it be blood-warm, and then put to it a spoonful of Ale-yest [yeast]. When it is worked up, put it into a vessel of a fit size; and after two or three days, bottle it up. You may drink it after six weeks, or two months. Thus was the Hydromel made that I gave the Queen, which was exceedingly liked by everybody.

The Closet of Sir Kenelm Digby, Knight, Opened (1699)

Arkansas. No single, definitive cause has been determined, but the bottom line is undeniable: Honeybees across the state and the nation are disappearing. Entomologists suspect that a convergence of factors—including historic and new bee diseases and parasites, a lack of genetic diversity among queen bees, the effects of pesticides and herbicides, and the alteration of traditional bee habitats by agriculture and climate change—may be responsible for the collapse phenomenon. This diversity of possible contributing causes complicates the search for a "prescription." U.S. Department of Agriculture recommendations amount to suggesting using fewer pesticides and planting more "pollinator-friendly" plants, thereby honoring and pleasing today's *Apis mellifera* as, doubtless, the ancient Cretans propitiated their beloved Melissas.[19]

For further reading:

"Arkansas Arthropods in History and Folklore." http://www.uark.edu/ua/arthmuse/folk.html (accessed July 17, 2015).

Arkansas Beekeepers Association. http://arbeekeepers.org/index.html (accessed July 17, 2015).

Downing, Laura. "Beekeeping." *Encyclopedia of Arkansas History & Culture.* http://www.encyclopediaofarkansas.net/encyclopedia/entry-detail.aspx?entryID=4449 (accessed July 17, 2015).

Graves, Robert. *The Greek Myths: the Complete and Definitive Edition.* London: Penguin, 2011.

Squire, David. *The Bee-Kind Garden.* Cambridge, UK: Green Books, 2011.

Ware, David. "Official State Insect, a.k.a. Honeybee." *Encyclopedia of Arkansas History & Culture.* http://www.encyclopediaofarkansas.net/encyclopedia/entry-detail.aspx?search=1&entryID=3144 (accessed July 17, 2015).

---

19   United States Department of Agriculture Agricultural Research Service, "Honey Bee Health and Colony Collapse Disorder." http://www.ars.usda.gov/News/docs.htm?docid=15572#bk (accessed July 13, 2015).

CHAPTER 10: STATE MUSICAL INSTRUMENT AND DANCE

—Or Lightning in the Air, Gingham on the Dance Floor

In 1985 and again in 1991, the Arkansas State Legislature designated elements of the state's traditional popular culture as official state symbols. On February 28, 1985, the legislature approved Act 277, designating the fiddle as the official musical instrument of the state of Arkansas, hailing its role as "a dominant musical instrument in the culture...of the people of Arkansas." Four years later, the square dance was made the official American folk dance of Arkansas.

On first glance, these measures might both seem to simply represent *pro forma* salutes to nostalgic culture memories, but this view discounts the life left in them. The violin, or fiddle, was indeed a constant element of Arkansas's folk culture since territorial or even colonial times, but it does not belong solely to the past: recent cohorts of fiddlers have both preserved the old musical traditions and incorporated new songs and styles, keeping the fiddle very much *au courant*. As for the square dance, it represents less a petrified folk tradition than a conscious movement that attempted to transform, then perpetuate traditional dance elements into a modern context. As such, it is an organized social activity that adopted for itself a stylized wardrobe referencing a mythical past as filtered through twentieth-century western films. Thus, square dancing can be dismissed as being far from "authentic" folk dancing (just as young fiddlers have sometimes been criticized for a lack of utter fidelity to tradition) but look again: Square dancing constitutes organized play, just as social dances served this purpose for decades and centuries, in early Arkansas and elsewhere. It is synthetic in the best sense but not just "made up"—it is a stylized, modernized continuation of an old tradition, and one that is, as often as not, accompanied by the piercing, insistent sound of a fiddle played hard.

The choice of the fiddle as the state's official musical instrument constituted an acknowledgment of the primacy of the vernacular violin in early American musical life. The words "fiddle" and "violin" describe the same instrument, the highest-pitched of the viol family of unfretted stringed instruments. The fiddle's design was effectively standardized by the mid-eighteenth century: a body shaped like an hourglass with a pronounced waist, an ovoid-arched fingerboard, four strings usually tuned in intervals of perfect fifths, an arched bridge or string support, and a wooden tailpiece or string anchor. This instrument is believed to have descended from the Byzantine *lira* or lyre; in its early forms, it was referred to interchangeably as *lira* or fiddle. It assumed its present form in the late seventeenth and early eighteenth centuries, in the hands of master violin makers working in and around the Italian cities of Brescia, Venice, and, most famously, Cremona.[1]

So, where did the name "fiddle" come from? The answer is, alas, almost as murky as the one explaining the origin of the "Dutch" oven. The etymology of "fiddle" is uncertain: the Germanic fiddle may derive from the same early Latin word *vitula* (stringed instrument) as do the French viol and Italian viola, or it may be natively Germanic. The name seems to be related to Icelandic *Fiðla* and also Old English *fiðele* (pronounced "fithele"). Variations include *fedele, fydyll,* and *fidel*. Exactly where the term fiddle came from, and its relation to "viol," may not be absolutely ascertainable, but it is clear, at least, that the term "fiddle" is at least as old as "violin" and, historically at least, was not considered a diminutive or slighting usage.

The violin sings, but the fiddle dances.

— Anonymous

Today, any violin, when used for playing vernacular or "folk" music, is apt to be termed a fiddle, but some subtle differences have crept in to distinguish the concert-hall instrument from that of the dance hall or front porch shivaree. Folk performers sometimes fit patent tuning pegs to the instruments, making them easier to retune during long, energetic performances; some also modify their instruments by flattening the bridge, making it easier to play double notes or chords, or by making a slightly thicker bridge top. Some prefer steel-core strings, others synthetic. Conversations with contemporary fiddlers reveal no single set of recommended modifications to the standard instrument, set up for classical playing. The distinction lies mainly in what's played, how it's played, and where it's played.

---

1   The "Violin" entry in the eleventh edition of the *Encyclopaedia Britannica* (1911) describes the beast with dry understatement: "A musical instrument consisting essentially of a resonant box of peculiar form, over which four strings of different thicknesses are stretched." Concerning the sound properties of the violin, *Britannica* sums things up neatly: "The acoustics of the violin are extremely complex, and notwithstanding many investigations by men of science…remain as a whole obscure." Robert William Frederic Harrison, "Violin," *Encyclopedia Britannica*, 11th ed. (New York: The Encyclopaedia Britannica Company, 1911), v. 28, pp. 102–107.

The violin or fiddle was perhaps the most commonly encountered musical instrument in the years of the United States' westward expansion. The fiddle's convenient size, robust construction,[2] and high volume, as well as the ease of rudimentary apprehension, made it well suited for carrying on long trips. Even the "musically challenged" could manage to scrape out the rhythms of sacred and secular melodies for family, community, and congregational gatherings.

And such gatherings often included dancing.

Visitors to early Arkansas recorded scenes of community celebrations which included cutting a rug, even if the "rug" was a plank or packed-earth floor. Observers such as Francois Perrin du Lac, Thomas Nuttall, and even Washington Irving all reported the dancing habits of the early Euro-Arkansans. James Miller, the first territorial governor, wrote of Arkansas Post that "they have one fiddler who can play but one tune." Some years later, German traveler and writer Friedrich Gerstäcker described a raucous July 4th event on the banks of the Fourche La Fave River which involved no fewer than three fiddlers.[3] Often, social square dances were held in private houses and were occasioned by the family needing community help with some kind of work, such as fencing or barn raising. One Ozarker participant recalled that:

> ◇ ◇ ◇
> *We consider that the man who can fiddle all through one of those Virginia reels without losing his grip, may be depended upon in any kind of emergency.*
> —Mark Twain, 1863
> ◇ ◇ ◇

> There was a time I was invited to more than twenty such log-rollings every spring...Altho...I was the only worker on my farm...I dared not decline such an invitation, because every year I was dependent upon the help of my neighbors myself....Dances followed log-rolling and house-raisings. Usually the orchestra consisted of only one fiddle.[4]

By the early twentieth century, such work-dances were less common than play-parties or socials, called for no purpose but to give participants a chance to pass a good time. These often involved traveling long distances to attend dances that would last into the wee hours of the morning. Many, possibly most, were family affairs, in which drinking and consequent quarreling were absent or at least rare. Nevertheless, such parties and the square dancing that went on at them were not viewed kindly by many churches, due both to the potential for alcohol consumption and a long-standing opposition of some sects to anything that might lead to licentious behavior.[5]

◇ ◇ ◇

---

2   The author once witnessed a dismaying incident in which an amateur-grade violin was inadvertently shot through the upper bout with a .32 pistol bullet. The owner, after ascertaining that the shot had not been meant as a comment on his musicianship, resumed playing. The tone and volume of the instrument remained adequate in the circumstances, although both improved after a luthier mended both holes.

3   Excerpted in: Nancy McDonough, *Garden Sass: A Catalogue of Arkansas Folkways* (New York: Coward, McCann & Geohegan, 1975), p. 189; see also Robert Cochran, "Arts, Culture, and Entertainment," *Encyclopedia of Arkansas History & Culture*. http://www.encyclopediaofarkansas.net/encyclopedia/entry-detail. aspx?entryID=386 (accessed July 17, 2015).

4   Drew Beisswenger and Gordon McCann, *Ozarks Fiddle Music* (Pacific, MO: Mel Bay Publications, 2008), 11.

5   Beisswenger, *Ozarks Fiddle Music*, 12; see also Hubert Halpert, "The Devil and the Fiddle," *Hoosier Folklore Bulletin* 2, no. 2 (December 1943), http://www. jstor.org/stable/27655458?seq=1#page_scan_tab_contents (accessed July 17, 2015) for some apropos Southern observations, collected in the early twentieth century, on dancing and fiddling and the Old Deluder.

What sort of dancing went on at such rustic balls and soirees? Witnesses and participants often simply said "square dancing" and let it go, but there was more going on than simple squares. Dances in the old Arkansas probably included gavottes, minuets, and *quadrilles*, French-derived dances involving four couples in a square. These all form the heart of today's square dancing, but the older dancing repertoire certainly also included dances derived from the ancestral homes of Arkansas's early settlers. Likely found in early Arkansas were country dancing, in which two rows of dances faced each other as couples (which descended from the English "longways" dances and were in their turn taken up by the French, who renamed them "contredanses"); set or circle dances; hornpipes, jigs, and reels; and even such innovations as the waltz. Dance forms that were fashionable in Europe found their way to the New World, and the dances of the elites on the coasts became the dances of the interior's folk—accompanied by the fiddle, sometimes some percussion instrument, and, in North America, a new phenomenon: the caller.

The caller—that is, a person who speaks cues or directions to the dances—is a distinctive characteristic of American folk dancing. Callers were already common by the early 1800s and noticed by European travelers, who thought the practice amusing and vulgar. After all, one was supposed to learn the steps of the most popular dances as part of one's cultured upbringing. The practice was considered less gauche than dangerous by dancing masters who traveled from town to town teaching steps and attendant etiquette, possibly because called dancing threatened the market for at least half of their repertoire.

On the other hand, dancing masters were few, particularly in the old Southwest, and isolated communities of setters would have their amusements. In such communities, there may have only been one or two people who knew how dances went, so calling, or shouting cues to the other dancers, would have constituted the fastest way to teach others and to get the party started. Often, the fiddler doubled as the caller, but the caller might well be one of the dancers. Over time, calling (like fiddling) developed into an art form. Callers learned to insert "patter"—encouragement, rhymes, and amphigory—into the dance instructions, both to maintain the tempo and to amuse the dancers. In this way, a good caller could supply the rhythm of the dance, even if the musician or musicians were not up to the task. He or she could also toss a surprise into a familiar dance by calling for an unexpected move, chasing away monotony and raising spirits. One historian of the square dance notes that called dances relieve dancers of the responsibility of constantly thinking ahead. But obviously a caller with a sense of humor could provide dancers with periodic reminders of the need to stay alert!

Along with the drum and possibly the military fife, the fiddle was one of the earliest, if not the earliest, European-style musical instruments to appear in Arkansas. Its association with Arkansas was made manifest in the humorous tale and song based on the legend of "The Arkansas Traveler." Popularized by—and possibly originating with—Arkansas politician and raconteur Sandy Faulkner, the story turned on a "city slicker" proving his mettle to a rural squatter by demonstrating skill on the fiddle; the result is an overwhelming outpouring of hospitality. The story was linked to a fiddle tune that bore the name "Arkansas Traveller" although it probably originated with Mexican-born Ohio fiddler Jose Tasso. The music appeared as early as 1847. The tale and the tune became celebrated nationwide; even as culture-conscious Arkansans sought to dispel the state's rural image, the tune remained popular both in live performances and recordings. It was the subject of a painting by Edward Payson Washbourne that, in the form of chromolithographs published by both Grozelier and Currier & Ives, hung in thousands of American households in the mid-nineteenth century. A second piece, left unfinished by Washbourne at his death, showed the squatter dancing to the "turn of the tune" played by the Traveler.

Dedication ceremony of monument to Sandy Faulkner at Mount Holly Cemetery in Little Rock, 1955.

By the end of the nineteenth century, other musical instruments were available and found in Arkansas—pianos, reed organs, concertinas, Spanish guitars, banjos, mandolins—but the fiddle remained popular. Part of its appeal must have been its availability. Native makers' instruments were praised and prized, but by the end of the century, violins in grades ranging from student to near-professional quality were available from such mail order concerns as Sears, Roebuck and Montgomery Ward.

The availability of these ready-made instruments did not prevent Arkansas craftsmen and craftswomen from trying their hands at making their own, however. One who did so to good effect was George Thomas Shrader, born in Tennessee in 1873 but raised in Bryant in Saline County. Shrader worked as a railroad conductor and sales clerk, but in the second decade of the twentieth century, he decided to try something new: fiddle making. In 1914, he began work on a pair of violins, carving native woods with simple hand tools. At the time, he had never seen a professional luthier (instrument maker) at work but, he explained, "I knew I could do it." He sent two violins to the Arkansas exhibit at the Panama Pacific Exposition in San Francisco in 1915 and received a silver medal for his work. A later example of Shrader's luthiery is preserved by the Arkansas

Fiddle made by George T. Shrader, from the Arkansas History Commission's collection.

History Commission. Their documentation indicates that it was carved with a pocket knife and a chisel from native sycamore and maple. Around the edge of the instrument are inlaid strips of maple and ebony. Unusually, Shrader chose to leave the instrument unpolished and unvarnished, the better to show the character of the wood. The inside of the instrument is signed in crayon, "Hand made by G. T. Shrader, Little Rock, Ark. 1919." An additional paper label repeats this information, adding "Complimentary to the State of Arkansas."[6]

Another Arkansas luthier of renown is Violet Hensley of Yellville, who has remained productive into her ninth decade. She made her first fiddle in 1932, at the age of fifteen, under the tutelage of her father. Since then, she has made more than seventy fiddles and one viola. She has also been an active and sought-after performer, collaborating with and mentoring younger fiddlers in the Ozark fiddling tradition.[7]

Trying to identify the distinctive features of Ozark fiddling is almost as frustrating as trying to sort out the etymology of "fiddle." Ethnomusicologists have pointed to so wide a variety of elements present on Ozark fiddling that it would be reasonable to conclude that while some general tendencies can be identified, no single, recognizable Ozark or Arkansas fiddling style exists. One writer notes that Ozark fiddlers prefer the standard EADG violin tuning, play more breakdowns than other types of tunes, and produce crisp, clean, single-note melody lines and few complex bowing patterns. Another observes that Ozarkers use fewer minor scales than fiddlers from other regions and that they incorporate relatively large numbers of tunes and techniques from French and African American musical traditions.[8]

Today, the art of fiddling remains in a state of change—as it has been since viols first crossed the Mississippi. Trends include out-migration of musicians in search of employment and a dwindling in the numbers of square dances. Some young fiddlers are even focusing on fiddle contests and the performances that will garner competition success, rather than on traditional tunes and styles of playing. Nevertheless, the fiddling tradition remains strong in Arkansas. It is kept vital by local folk music societies, a handful of luthiers, and the state's annual Old-Time Fiddling Championship, a competition and reunion of vernacular violinists held each autumn at the Ozark Folk Center in Mountain View.

If the fiddle maintained its following into the twentieth century, the tradition of clogging and square, country, and set dancing seemed threatened. The number of dancers declined, partly because of opposition from some religious authorities and also in connection with what might be called proto-urbanism. As "city" music, particularly jazz in its many forms, and accompanying styles and attitudes spread from urban areas, do-si-dos and promenades must have seemed old-fashioned, somewhat "early American." As America, even its

6   Biographical information on George Shrader is derived from Arkansas History Commission cataloguing description metadata for the Shrader fiddle in their collection: http://ahc.digital-ar.org/cdm/singleitem/collection/p16790coll17/id/223/rec/17 (accessed July 17, 2015).
7   Nancy McDonough, *Garden Sass: A Catalogue of Arkansas Folkways* (New York: Coward, McCann and Geohegan, 1975), 232-233; "Violet Hensley the Whittlin' Fiddler of Yellville" (Official Website). http://violethensley.com/ (accessed July 17, 2015).
8   Beisswenger, *Ozarks Fiddle Music*, 12; William K. McNeil, *Ozark Country* (Jackson: University Press of Mississippi, 1995), 98–99; see also Howard W. Marshall, *Play Me Something Quick and Devilish: Old-Time Fiddlers in Missouri* (Columbia: University of Missouri Press, 2013).

non-urban zones, entered the Jazz Age, the traditions of called dancing and the accompanying social activity seemed doomed to extinction. Fortuitously, or perhaps ironically, and certainly improbably, the father of one of the most potent forces of modernization would also throw a life-line to the declining square dance.

Henry Ford, one of the godfathers of modern American auto culture, grew up on a farm outside of Detroit, Michigan. When he was ten, he learned to scrape out a few fiddle tunes and joined a local dancing club, which featured called dances accompanied by fiddle and hammered-dulcimer music. Dances featured at this and other local clubs included both square and round dances, as well as novelty dances such as the ripple, the gavotte, the sea side polka, and various waltzes. Ford evidently enjoyed himself in these early dancing days. In 1910, already a coming producer of automobiles, he sponsored a reunion of his old dancing club featuring "old time dancing... consisting of square dances, Virginian Reels and old fashioned polkas."

Multi-record set of dance music commissioned by Henry Ford as part of his campaign to revitalize old-fashioned dancing, ca. 1940s.

Over the next few years, Ford became more and more of a public figure, particularly with the success of his Model T, so he was regarded as an authority not just on efficient industrial practice but also on larger cultural matters. And what mattered to him more and more, particularly in the aftermath of the Great War, was what he saw as the cultural threats of the modern world. His main bugbears were Wall Street bankers, war profiteers, and what he considered to be the International Jewish Conspiracy; the influence of this cabal, Ford hinted, extended even to popular music. In 1921, articles alluded to "Jewish jazz" becoming the new national music and popular music being controlled by the "Jewish song trust."[9]

At the same time, Ford began hosting old-fashioned dances in a corner of one of his Dearborn factory buildings, featuring music from fiddles and even a *cimbalom*, a Hungarian variant on the hammered dulcimer. Ford sought out old-time musicians for these soirees and hired dancing teacher Benjamin Lovett in 1924 to study, record, and teach old-time dances, including square dances, to his guests. The next year, Ford established a dance and etiquette class for Dearborn children, overseen by Lovett. Lovett, in addition to teaching, compiled a dance manual along lines suggested by Ford. Because dance calls varied across the country, it was, Ford thought, desirable that they be standardized and formalized in order to revive and preserve them. The book

---

9   Paul M. Gifford, "Henry Ford's Dance Revival and Fiddle Contests: Myth and Reality," *Journal of the Society for American Music* 4, no. 3 (2010): 312–313. Gifford acknowledges Ford's anti-Semitism but suggests plausibly that his promotion of old-time music and dance had more to do with his personal dismay at the effects of the Great War than his prejudices; in his own words, "I'm trying in a small way to help America take a step, even if it is a small one, toward the saner, sweeter idea of life that prevailed in prewar days." (Gifford, 313)

"Good Morning": After a Sleep of Twenty-Five Years, Old-Fashioned Dancing Is Being Revived by Mr. and Mrs. Henry Ford appeared in 1926. It contained instructions and calls for square dances, contra dances, and round dances of various kinds, plus etiquette guidelines. An introduction expressing what were considered to be Henry Ford's views on dancing made his aim explicit:

> Denunciation of the dance by the protectors of public morals has usually been occasioned by the importation of dances which are foreign to the expressional needs of our people....The balance is now shifting toward that style of dancing which best fits with the American temperament. There is a revival of that type of dancing which has survived longest amongst the northern peoples. The time has swung in favor of such dances as are described in this book.[10]

The dances, classes, and book made clear Ford's interest in reviving old-fashioned square dancing and the genteel fun it afforded. His advocacy inspired others. Fiddling competitions appeared across the nation during the winter of 1925–26, and some continued into the period of the Great Depression.[11] Square dancing, too, enjoyed a modest popularity that continued into the 1930s and even beyond.[12]

Along with Henry Ford and Benjamin Lovett, a third name stands high on the list of those culpable for the continuation of square dancing: Lloyd "Pappy" Shaw. Shaw was superintendent of the Cheyenne Mountain (Colorado Springs, Colorado) high school in the 1930s. Shaw was a fan of traditional dancing and encouraged his students to dance, too, by offering summer classes to dancers, callers, and national folk dance leaders. His approach melded the traditional dance styles with modern "western attire." Shaw organized a student square-dancing demonstration team that performed in New York, Boston, Los Angeles, and New Orleans, serving as missionaries for this new take on an old dance tradition, which would become known as modern square dancing.[13]

During World War II, square dancing was hurled farther, broadcast through the medium of USO canteen dances. After the war, GIs brought memories of these dances home with them. One scholar of the square dance has noted that at the end of the war, "square dancing experienced a rise in popularity among the urban population....As the modernized post-war society developed, square dancing was transformed into a recreational

10   *"Good Morning": After a Sleep of Twenty-Five Years, Old-Fashioned Dancing Is Being Revived by Mr. and Mrs. Henry Ford* (Dearborn, MI: Dearborn Publishing Co., 1926), 8. Online at http://babel.hathitrust.org/cgi/pt?id=uc1.$b281688;view=1up;seq=9 (accessed July 17, 2015).
11   One such contest was held in Joplin, Missouri, in 1926. Eleven years earlier, in 1915, a large fiddlers' convention had been held in Hot Springs, Arkansas. The state of Arkansas in this instance anticipated even Henry Ford.
12   In 1934, a sort of Ozark folk culture boom took place, with local folk festivals featuring traditional music and dance organized in three Missouri towns and Eureka Springs, Arkansas. In the 1940s, both Blanchard Springs and Eureka Springs would host folk festivals.
13   Herb Egender interview, 2004, Square Dance History Project, http://squaredancehistory.org/items/show/203 (accessed July 17, 2015). Egender was a member of Shaw's 1938 Cheyenne Mountain Dancers, the legendary square dance demonstration team. See also: "Dr. Lloyd 'Pappy' Shaw," http://www.callerlab.org (accessed July 17, 2015). This biographical sketch is hosted by "Callerlab," an organization set up to train and standardize calling for square dancers the world over.

activity on a par with sports and other hobbies."[14] With this growth emerged professional callers, dress codes,[15] magazines, and, inevitably, organizations.

The National Square Dance convention organized in 1951, but two years earlier, Arkansas modern square dance enthusiasts Otis Higgins and Richard Dick formed the Arkansas State Square Dance Federation (ASSDF) to promote modern square dancing in the state by sponsoring and organizing events and publishing a newsletter, as well as providing insurance for dancers.[16]

Through the post–World War II decades, the ASSDF oversaw a blossoming of interest in square dancing, clogging, and "round dancing" across the state. At one point in the 1980s, the subscription list for its quarterly newsletter, *The Modern Square*, exceeded 1,000, and the Little Rock area was home to about twenty local square dance clubs.

In 1975, Representative Ted Risenhoover of Oklahoma introduced a House Joint Resolution to make the square dance the national dance of the United States. This measure failed, as did a succession of similar efforts over the next dozen years or so.[17] In 1988, proponents of the idea shifted their tactics to the state level, hoping to build a *de facto* designation one state at a time, much as the apostles of the Prohibition movement did in the early twentieth century. The movement began with a head start: Oregon, Washington, Alabama, and Tennessee had already moved to so honor the square dance. In 1988, Oklahoma joined the movement, with California adopting the square dance as the state's folk dance (the West Coast Swing was accorded "state dance" honors). Idaho joined the fold in 1989, with Illinois and Massachusetts heeding the call in 1990.

And finally, in 1991, it was Arkansas's turn to face the music. A concurrent resolution authored by Senator Jack Gibson of District 35 proposed designating the square dance as the official American folk dance of Arkansas. It won quick approval and was signed into law by Governor Bill Clinton on February 7, 1991, as Act 93.

Act 93 resembled measures introduced across the nation by promoters of organized modern square dancing. The bill posited a long history of called, or "cued," dancing in North America and Arkansas and cited the association of square dancing with family recreation. It defined square dancing as incorporating virtually all called or cued dances—including clogging, contra, and line dancing—and asserted that official designation would "enhance the cultural stature of Arkansas both nationally and internationally."

---

14   Margot Gunzenhauser, *The Square Dancing and Contra Dance Handbook* (Jefferson, NC: McFarland & Co., 1996), 4. Gunzenhauser, an American folklorist and traditional dance caller who lives in Denmark, has acknowledged the paucity of scholarship on the origins of traditional and modern called dances: "Unfortunately, much of what one reads in square dance books about the development of folk dancing in the United States is speculative at best and pure nonsense at worst." (Gunzenhauser, *Square Dancing*, 1).

15   Square dancing dress codes were and remain formal but friendly. A pamphlet issued by the United Square Dancers of America traces the history of square dancing and dancing attire in folksy fashion; sets out general principles of proper attire for square dancing, contra dancing, clogging, and country-western dancing; and ends on a watchful note: "Evolution and change are inevitable, constant processes and square dancing is no exception....When we want to show people what we represent, we wear the square dance costume that distinguishes us from those not in our activity....The reason our square dance activity has outlived so many other styles is the close adherence to rules of the dress code and behavior on a national scale." Education Committee of the United Square Dancers of America, "Evolution of Square Dance Attire," 1997, http://www.usda.org/booklet/B01803.pdf (accessed July 17, 2015).

16   Arkansas State Square Dance Federation. http://www.assdf.com/ (accessed July 7, 2015).

17   As, for that matter, did the congressional career of Representative Risenhoover, whose quest for a third term was squelched at the primary level after a newspaper article revealed details of his housekeeping in Washington, including his sleeping on a heart-shaped waterbed. Carolyn Hannemann, "Theodore Marshall Risenhoover," http://www.okhistory.org/publications/enc/entry.php?entry=RI011 (accessed July 17, 2015).

To date, thirty-two states have designated an official dance; of these, twenty-four states have made official the square dance's prominence.[18] Square-dance enthusiasts have not abandoned their national aspirations: U.S. House Resolution 645 of 2003, whose co-sponsors included Arkansans Marion Berry and John Boozman, proposed to designate it the national folk dance. The measure died in committee, but it will probably rise again, although a 2009 *Wall Street Journal* article noted that the United Square Dancers of America, which bills itself as "the only national dancers' association organized by dancers for dancers and operated by dancers," put its national-designation campaign on hold until it could find a sponsor for such a bill.[19]

The flame of modern square dancing still burns in Arkansas, although the number of local clubs has declined to fewer than twenty and subscriptions to *The Modern Square* have dropped to about 200. Nevertheless, in 2014, Little Rock and North Little Rock hosted the 63rd annual National Square Dance Convention; 3,823 registrants from every state and ten foreign countries came to Little Rock, dressed sharp and western, and passed a good time in good company. In addition to recorded music and live callers, the convention featured three evening contra dances featuring the Arkansas Country Dance Band, Springhill, and the Old 78s, ensuring that the long association between live fiddling and the square dance—however generously construed—would be honored.[20]

The Ozark Folk Center in Mountain View is the home of the only park in America devoted to the preservation of Southern mountain folkways and music.

18   *Netstate Guide to State Symbols*, http://www.netstate.com/states/tables/state_dances.htm (accessed July 17, 2015).

19   Mary Pilon, "Strictly Come Square Dancing: Historian Digs Into Dance's History," *Wall Street Journal*, December 16, 2009, http://blogs.wsj.com/speakeasy/2009/12/16/strictly-come-square-dancing-historian-digs-into-dances-history/ (accessed July 17, 2015); United Square Dancers of America, http://www.usda.org/folkdn.htm (accessed July 17, 2015). The organization claims on its website that thirty-one states so far have adopted the square dance as the state folk dance; this figure conflicts with other tabulations but may reflect the optimism necessary for driving the national-designation effort.

20   National Square Dance Convention, http://www.63nsdc.com/Program/report/rpt_cnt_regbystate_pub.asp (accessed July 17, 2015).

For further reading:

Arkansas State Square Dance Federation. http://www.assdf.com/ (accessed July 17, 2015).

Beisswenger, Drew, and Gordon McCann. *Ozarks Fiddle Music*. Pacific, MO: Mel Bay Publications, 2008.

Cochran, Robert. "Arts, Culture, and Entertainment." *Encyclopedia of Arkansas History & Culture*. http://www. encyclopediaofarkansas.net/encyclopedia/entry-detail.aspx?entryID=386 (accessed July 17, 2015).

Goerzen, Chris. "George Cecil McLeod, Mississippi's Fiddling Senator and the Modern History of American Fiddling." *American Music* 22 (Fall 2004): 339–379.

Gunzenhauser, Margot. *The Square Dancing and Contra Dance Handbook*. Jefferson, NC: McFarland & Co., 1996.

Mangin, Julie. "The State Folk Dance Conspiracy: Fabricating a National Folk Dance." *Old-Time Herald* 4 (Spring 1987): 9–12.

Marshall, Howard W. *Play Me Something Quick and Devilish: Old-time Fiddlers in Missouri*. Columbia: University of Missouri Press, 2013.

McDonough, Nancy. *Garden Sass: A Catalogue of Arkansas Folkways*. New York: Coward, McCann and Geohegan, 1975.

Randolph, Vance, and Frances Emberson. "The Collection of Folk Music in the Ozarks." *Journal of American Folklore* 60 (April 1947): 115–125.

United Square Dancers of America. http://www.usda.org/folkdn.htm (accessed July 17, 2015).

Ware, David. "Official State Dance a.k.a.: Square Dance." *Encyclopedia of Arkansas History & Culture*. http://www. encyclopediaofarkansas.net/encyclopedia/entry-detail.aspx?entryID=3147 (accessed July 17, 2015).

———. "Official State Musical Instrument a.k.a.: Fiddle." *Encyclopedia of Arkansas History & Culture*. http://www. encyclopediaofarkansas.net/encyclopedia/entry-detail.aspx?entryID=3142 (accessed July 17, 2015).

Worster, Ann Phillips. "Violet Brumley Hensley." *Encyclopedia of Arkansas History & Culture*. http://www. encyclopediaofarkansas.net/encyclopedia/entry-detail.aspx?entryID=4698 (accessed July 17, 2015).

York, Joe. *Violet Hensley: 74 Fiddles*. Arkansas Living Treasure Film Series. http://www.historicarkansas.org/alt-film-project/violet-hensley (accessed July 17, 2015).

"And they traveled on forever"

Albert Bigelow Paine's **The Arkansaw Bear** *(1898) chronicled the fanciful adventures of a fiddling black bear named Horatio and a plucky young human runaway named Bosephus. Much of the book's charm lies in the illustrations by Frank Ver Beck.*

CHAPTER 11: STATE SONGS

Of Thee We (Try) to Sing

When discussing state songs (at least in polite company) one walks a knife-edge over a bed of nails. It smarts to maintain one's balance, but falling to one side or the other will hurt just as much, if not worse. The difficulty lies in the utter vulnerability of so many of these odes and anthems. It is far too easy to crack wise about far too many state songs, particularly those of states other than one's own.

This vulnerability may be inevitable. Patriotic songs, like their prose cousins, aim high. They try to express feelings and aspirations above the everyday, beyond the practical or immediate. They speak of greater things, but their authors are human, and, as such, are subject to limitations of vocabulary, of experience, of proportion. Their compositions can fall prey to overstatement or didacticism or things that play well at home but do not travel well beyond state borders. Too many seem spun from noble-sounding and high-minded stuff that rings hollow (though hopeful) in politicians' speeches over the years and decades. For instance:

> *All hail to grand old Bay State, the home of the bean and the cod!*
> *Where Pilgrims found a landing and gave their thanks to God.*
> *A land of opportunity in the good old U.S.A.*
> *Where men live long and prosper, and people come to stay.*
> — "All Hail to Massachusetts," by Arthur J. Marsh (adopted 1966)[1]

---

1   "State Songs," Secretary of the Commonwealth of Massachusetts. http://www.sec.state.ma.us/cis/cissng/sngidx.htm (accessed August 16, 2015).

Still others opt for the booster voice—cataloguing a state's natural treasures and opportunities for work or play. Others will slip in historical references or even well-meant instructional matter; Maryland's state anthem, written in 1861, has a topical quality that lends a little of the intense *frisson* that characterizes *La Marseillaise*:

The despot's heel is on thy shore,
Maryland!
His torch is at thy temple door,
Maryland!
Avenge the patriotic gore
That flecked the streets of Baltimore,[2]
And be the battle queen of yore,
Maryland! My Maryland!

— "Maryland, My Maryland," by James Ryder Randall, written 1861, adopted 1939[3]

Alaska's state song, adopted some years before statehood, explains the iconography of that state's flag:

Eight stars of gold on a field of blue—
Alaska's flag. May it mean to you
The blue of the sea, the evening sky,
The mountain lakes, and the flow'rs nearby;
The gold of the early sourdough's dreams,
The precious gold of the hills and streams;
The brilliant stars in the northern sky,
The "Bear"—the "Dipper"—and, shining high,
The great North Star with its steady light,
Over land and sea a beacon bright.
Alaska's flag—to Alaskans dear,
The simple flag of a last frontier.

— "Alaska's Flag," words by Marie Drake, music by Elinor Dusenbury, adopted 1955[4]

A state song need not be a musical masterwork in order to be memorable—although "singability" is a desirable quality. The best state songs combine adequate musical qualities with an attempt on the part of the composer or composers to either entertain listeners, inspire them, or sing a love song to the state; sometimes, very rarely, a state song will manage two out of three—hitting all three targets is hard, though not impossible.

---

2   A cheery reference to the casualties of the Pratt Street Riot of April 19, 1861, in which raw Federal troops being conveyed across Baltimore were confronted by an armed secessionist mob waving some sort of "rebel" flag. The troops were attacked, then returned fire: eight civilians and three soldiers were killed.

3   Maryland State Archives, *Maryland Manual On-Line*, "Maryland at a Glance: State Song." http://msa.maryland.gov/msa/mdmanual/01glance/html/symbols/lyricsco.html (accessed August 16, 2015).

4   "Alaska Kids' Corner." State of Alaska. http://alaska.gov/kids/learn/statesong.htm (accessed August 16, 2015).

Currently, forty-eight of the fifty states have designated one or more songs as official state songs.[5] The most venerable of these adoptions dates to 1911,[6] with a slight upsurge of such activities occurring in the 1930s and again in the 1960s, before enthusiasm for such designations took off in the 1970s. During that decade, twelve state songs were adopted; in the 1980s, nineteen; in the 1990s, seventeen. Since 2000, twenty-four have been added to the national state-song songbook. For many states, once is not enough; Arkansas has so designated no fewer than four compositions. (Only three states—Massachusetts, New Hampshire, and Tennessee—have adopted more.) The styles of Arkansas's state songs include devotional anthem, sprightly folk melody, and 1980s vintage country-pop. The earliest was adopted contemporaneously with the flowering of progressivism in Arkansas and marked a popular appreciation of the state's natural beauty and agricultural bounties, turning away from the "hillbilly" Arkansas of early twentieth-century popular imagination. Subsequent state song adoptions largely followed in this vein, although one attempted to straddle musical and philosophical fences, with at best mixed results.

What goes into a state song?

Like state seals, they contain hopes and aspirations, but also sentiments—or occasions for them. They may be composed for the purpose or suborned from other contexts. Ideally, a state song should be worthy of being part of popular culture but not necessarily come from it—it is supposed to represent something higher.

Such was not the case with the song earliest and longest associated with Arkansas. Arkansas's first unofficial song was likely the fiddle tune known popularly as "The Arkansas Traveler."[7] Its origins are a little obscure; it certainly was born elsewhere. Several sources attribute the melody to Jose Tasso of Cincinnati, Ohio, a Mexican-born concert violinist and composer who has been described as "the premier dance and concert fiddler up and down the Ohio River [of the 1840s]."[8] Was Tasso the composer of "Arkansas Traveler"? Whether or not he was, he certainly helped popularize it: sheet music for the song was published by Tasso's usual publisher in

---

5   This includes categoric variations such as state anthem, state rock song, state lullaby, state cowboy song, state land rush song (no prize for guessing which state claims this category), state gospel song, state polka, state song (traditional), state song (popular), state ode, state waltz, state ballad, state cantata, U.S. Bicentennial song, U.S. Bicentennial march song, U.S. Bicentennial school song, U.S. Bicentennial rap song, state children's song, state bilingual song, state march, state environmental song, official bluegrass song, official country and western song, official patriotic song, official historical song, official state flower song, state hymn, and others. Notably and perhaps to their credit, neither New York nor New Jersey have to this point ventured to designate official songs. "Official State Songs." http://www.netstate.com/states/tables/state_songs_year.htm (accessed August 16, 2015); see also Michael J. Bristow, *State Songs of America* (Westport, CT: Greenwood Press, 2000).

6   Some twentieth-century adoptions were of songs with origins in the previous century, such as "Maryland, My Maryland." Or, for that matter, "The Arkansas Traveler." Better late than never.

7   Sometimes rendered as "Arkansas Traveller." The doubled "l" was commonly used in the first half of the nineteenth century; it faded from common use after the Civil War but is still considered acceptable, if archaic.

8   Charles K. Wolfe, *Kentucky Country: Folk and Country Music of Kentucky* (Lexington: University Press of Kentucky, 2015), 16.

1847. By this time, the tune was already strongly associated with a tale often credited to Kentucky-born "Colonel" Sandy Faulkner, an early Arkansas fiddler, tall-tale teller, generally unsuccessful office-seeker, and similarly unsuccessful farmer. Faulkner was fond of telling a tale "on himself," in which he recounted a conversation he had supposedly enjoyed with a rural squatter, punctuated by the squatter playing the opening bars of the well-known fiddle tune "Arkansas Traveler." Faulkner's tale became a popular comic monologue and proved to "have legs" beyond the state's borders, doing much to establish a popular image of Arkansas as a place populated by rural eccentrics. The heart of the story, in which Faulkner (in his guise as the traveler) establishes common ground with the squatter by showing that he can play "the turn of the tune" (the second half of the music) and thus is offered all the hospitality that the squatter can muster, is easily and frequently misinterpreted as a patronizing joke at the expense of rural Arkansawyers. Thanks to comedians who told and retold the tale, elaborating and sometimes coarsening the story, for years both before and after Sandy Faulkner's death in 1874,[9] both the song and the story became etched into the American popular consciousness. They were also both loathed by Arkansas's gentrifiers who, in the last years of the nineteenth century, sought to disassociate themselves from high jinks and high-speed fiddling alike.[10]

◇ ◇ ◇

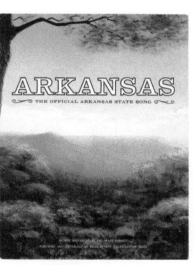

The first officially recognized state song owed nothing to the folk fiddling tradition or comic rural stereotypes. In 1916, Eva Ware Barnett, a classically trained composer and sometime professor of music at Ouachita Baptist College (now Ouachita Baptist University) in Arkadelphia, published "Arkansas," an anthem that substituted a graceful and genteel characterization of the state for the older "hillbilly" image. By one account, Barnett was inspired by a call from the United Daughters of the Confederacy for a state song, since the group's Jonesboro chapter was disconcerted by the discovery that the state had no song to call its own.[11] Barnett, who although a trained musician was a first-time composer, rose to the occasion. Her anthem name-checked flowers and crops, and contained words of nostalgia, with the narrator looking back to a carefully tailored and idealized past:

"Arkansas, The Official Arkansas State Song" pamphlet, Eva Ware Barnett, 1963.

---

9   One such was the celebrated Mose Case, an albino African American guitarist and comic performer. Case was hailed by many as the premier American guitarist of his day; his arrangement of "The Arkansas Traveler," published as sheet music in Buffalo, New York, made him famous, and his performance of the same tune was widely praised. Case died in New York City in 1885. Another who built on the foundations of Faulkner's tale and the tune was actor and impresario Frank Chanfrau, whose touring production of *Kit, the Arkansas Traveller* (penned by T. B. DeWalden and Edward Spencer, neither of whom are known to have had any ties to the Arkansas) was a theatrical favorite around the nation from 1871 until 1899. In *Arkansas/Arkansaw: How Bear Hunters, Hillbillies, and Good Ol' Boys Defined a State* (Fayetteville: University of Arkansas Press, 2009) historian Brooks Blevins discusses both this play and other incarnations of the Arkansas Traveler character and story.

10   William B. Worthen, "Arkansas Traveler," *Encyclopedia of Arkansas History & Culture.* http://www.encyclopediaofarkansas.net/encyclopedia/entry-detail.aspx?entryID=505 (accessed August 16, 2015). Worthen, longtime director of the Historic Arkansas Museum, ably summarizes the history of both painting and song and explains the early twentieth-century reaction to Arkansas's rough and rural image. See also Mary Hudgins, "Arkansas Traveler—A Multi-Parented Wayfarer," *Arkansas Historical Quarterly* 30, no. 3 (Summer 1971): 145–160.

11   "Arkansas Was First Effort of Mrs. Eva Barnett," *Jonesboro Weekly Sun*, January 15, 1917, 8.

I am thinking tonight of the Southland,

Of the home of my childhood days,

This was almost certainly calculated and deliberate. The early years of the century saw conscious attempts on the part of the state's leaders to dispel old stereotypes, or at least the wrong kinds. Barnett's lyrics evoked visions of a bucolic, be-flowered, and fertile state that always provided a warm welcome and safe shelter for "her children." The lyrics are draped in terms gracious but no less stereotypical for all of that, a sort of farrago of golden chestnuts:

Where the roses are in bloom

And the sweet magnolia too,

Where the jasmine is white

And the fields are violet blue...

The song's second verse switched from floral references to agricultural ones, suggesting the natural fecundity of Arkansas's croplands:

There the rice fields are full,

And the cotton, corn and hay,

There the fruits of the field

Bloom in the winter months and May.

Barnett's composition was so well received that the legislature designated it the official state song in 1917. State senator John Carter introduced a concurrent resolution noting that Arkansas had never before adopted an official song and asserted that Barnett's "Arkansas" was recognized by most schools in the state as the state song. Having established, or at least claimed, that "Arkansas" was the *de facto* state song, he urged that it be made so *de jure* as well. The measure was approved on January 12, after a rousing quartet performance in which the wife of State Senator A. W. Garrett of Okolona took the soprano part.[12] Barnett retained the copyright for the song, the music for which, published by Little Rock's Central Music Co., apparently sold steadily through the next two decades.

In 1939, the office of Secretary of State C. G. "Crip" Hall prepared a pamphlet of information about the state, including the words and the music to "Arkansas." According to later testimony by Secretary of State's Office employees, Barnett offered no objection to this free publication. The pamphlet, bearing Hall's name, was issued in 1940, an election year; 60,000 copies were distributed. In June 1940, however, Barnett filed a claim against the state for $3,000 in damages, asserting that the free distribution (characterized as having been done for political purposes) had injured sales of her sheet music, on which she collected about five cents per copy. The case was argued on June 24, 1941, in U.S. District Court. On June 25, Barnett's lawyers opted for a "no suit" action, effectively withdrawing the charge while retaining the option of reopening the case within a year. The reason remains murky, but reportage of the day suggested that inexperience with copyright law, coupled with the possibility that Barnett had granted informal permission for the song to be published in the pamphlet, made her

---

12   *Arkansas Gazette*, January 13, 1917, 3.

case a weak one.[13]

The next episode in the case began on June 20, 1943; newspapers reported that Governor Homer Adkins had appointed a committee to choose a new state song. A few days later, Barnett withdrew "Arkansas" from consideration as the next official state song. The committee's response to this withdrawal is undocumented, but apparently word got out concerning this vacancy, as a mid-September newspaper article indicated that several songs had been submitted to the panel for consideration.[14]

And then, there was...silence. Over the next four years, little progress was made. The 1947 General Assembly authorized formation of a new state song commission, in light of the existing one's failure to inspire, discover, produce, or commission a worthy successor to "Arkansas." The new body, chaired by the head of the University of Arkansas Department of Music, received many suggestions, some complete with words and music, but ultimately reached back into the previous century for Arkansas's new theme song. On November 10, 1948, the commission adopted "The Arkansas Traveler" as the title and melody of the official state song, inviting the public to send in lyrics for consideration.[15]

In the next year, the commission issued lyrics to the old fiddle tune with no indication of their parentage.[16] Two verses offered a nostalgic recapitulation of the traditional tale of the Arkansas Traveler, denatured of any lingering traces of frontier-era authenticity:

On a lonely road quite long ago,
A trav'ler trod with fiddle and a bow;[17]
While rambling thru the country rich and grand,
He quickly sensed the magic and the beauty of the land[18]

The refrain departed from the gentrified recap to offer sentiments worthy of any progressive booster:

For the wonder state we'll sing a song,
And lift our voices loud and long.
For the wonder state we'll shout hurrah!
And praise the opportunities we find in Arkansas.

---

13 *Arkansas Gazette*, June 26, 1941, 11. Before the case came to a hearing, Secretary of State Hall was contacted by two other claimants to the title of state song. One, Miss Mary Allen of Little Rock, claimed that her 1915 composition, "Take Me to Arkansas, the Best State of All" was copyrighted before Barnett's "Arkansas" and should have been designated the official state song since it contained such patriotic phrases as "the Ozarks," "the healing waters of Hot Springs," and "the apple blossoms and cotton fields so white." The other claimant, A. N. Harris of Pine Bluff, asserted that his "Down Where the Arkansas Flows" had been written several years earlier but not copyrighted until 1940; it was written, he said, for inmates of the Boys' Industrial School "after several years of vagrancy or petty crimes" (he did not specify if the misbehavior had been the boys' or his own). *Arkansas Gazette*, June 15, 1941, 10.

14 *Arkansas Gazette*, June 27, 1943; September 22, 1943, 6.

15 "Traveler Now Official Melody for State Song," *Arkansas Gazette*, November 11, 1948, 7.

16 Raising suspicions that their author was kin to either Penelope Ashe or Alan Smithee.

17 Although, in the story, it is clear that the traveler is on horseback; the popular lithograph (based on a painting by Arkansas artist Edward P. Washbourne) shows the horse to be a white charger with elegant lines, equivalent to tooling around today in a high-end sports car.

18 To infer this from Faulkner's monologue requires a leap of imagination notable even for those used to contemplating the "magical realism" of household economics. In Faulkner's tale, the traveler stops at the squatter's cabin looking for a dry place to rest, some food, forage for his horse, and whiskey, since it has been a cold, wet day in the saddle.

THE ARKANSAS TRAVELLER
SCENE IN THE BACK WOODS OF ARKANSAS.

TRAVELLER... TO SQUATTER... CAN YOU GIVE ME SOME REFRESHMENTS AND A NIGHTS LODGING? — SQUATTER. NO SIR — HAVEN'T GOT ANY ROOM, NOTHIN TO EAT (FIDDLES AWAY) — TRAVELLER... WHERE DOES THIS ROAD GO TO? — SQUATTER... IT DONT GO ANYWHERE... IT STAYS HERE... (STILL FIDDLING) — TRAVELLER... WHY DONT YOU PLAY THE REST OF THAT TUNE? SQUATTER — DONT KNOW IT —

Edward P. Washbourne's original 1858 painting of the Arkansas Traveller was quickly turned into a large-format lithograph by Leopold Grozelier of Boston. After the Civil War, a smaller, cruder version of the print was issued by Currier & Ives of New York, famous for mass-produced colored lithographs. The same firm issued a second print, "The Turn of the Tune," possibly working from sketches left unfinished by Washbourne at the time of his death in 1860.

THE TURN OF THE TUNE
TRAVELLER PLAYING THE "ARKANSAS TRAVELLER"

SQUATTER... WHY STRANGER I'VE BEEN TRYING FOR YEARS TO GIT THE TURN OF THAT TUNE... COME RIGHT IN... JOHNNY TAKE THE HORSE AND FEED HIM... WIFE GIT UP THE BEST CORN CAKES YOU CAN MAKE... SALLY MAKE UP THE BEST BED... HE CAN PLAY THE TURN OF THAT TUNE... COME RIGHT IN AND PLAY IT ALL THROUGH STRANGER... YOU KIN LODGE WITH US A MONTH FREE OF CHARGE...

120

As far as can be told, the legislature never acted to ratify the commission's choice, but this updated version of the "Traveler" served nonetheless as the state's *de facto* official song from 1949 to 1963. Despite its traditional roots, it did not prove popular, perhaps because of the awkward scansion of its verses. Barnett's "Arkansas" remained popular, particularly with school choirs, and eventually the composer's unhappiness with the state moderated.[19] The legislature acknowledged the unpopularity of the replacement state song in its 1963 session, when it approved an unusually frank resolution introduced by Roscoe Brown of Craighead County. House Concurrent Resolution 19 asserted that the words to "The Arkansas Traveler" did little to develop pride in or respect for the state and that, moreover, doubt existed as to whether it ever had been officially adopted as the state song. Claiming that Barnett's anthem best described Arkansas's "attractions, traditions and loyalties," the resolution proclaimed "Arkansas" the official song...provided that Barnett would assign its copyright to the secretary of state. Which she did.

Governor Orval Faubus signed the resolution on March 4, 1963, restoring "Arkansas" to its former status. On November 5, 1963, Secretary of State Kelly Bryant hosted a reception for Barnett at the State Capitol, at which the songwriter autographed copies of the sheet music, which would be distributed free to the public upon request.[20]

No serious challenge to the status of "Arkansas" was mounted until 1971, when the state Senate voted to designate "Arkansas Waltz" by Bill Urfer of Heber Springs and Cletus Jones of Benton as the official state waltz. The song extolled Arkansas's scenery, its agriculture, and even the athletic prowess of its flagship college teams:

> *Your teams win almost every game*
> *Those Hogs and Indians are hard to tame*[21]
> *When you hear the call they've got the ball*
> *That's Arkansas.*

The House did not follow suit in endorsing the song. In 2005, Cletus Jones told musicologist Stephen Koch, "I was in there the whole session; it came up on three resolutions." Objections over a verse stating that a person has to leave the state to get a job bogged down consideration: "They wasted time on that when they needed to be a-doing something worthwhile," recalled Jones.[22] Ultimately the Senate approved a solo resolution on March 10, 1971, which served as an expression of sentiment but carried with it no official designation.[23]

In 1985, another challenge to Barnett's anthem was mounted. In February, Representative Robert "Sody" Arnold of Arkadelphia introduced House Bill 824, which proposed to replace Barnett's song with another composition, also titled "Arkansas," written by Billie Francis Taylor and Keith Hays. Arnold claimed that few Arkansans knew the words to Barnett's "obscure but official" anthem; he noted that the only time he

19   Another obstacle to reconciliation had been removed by the 1961 death of the long-serving Secretary of State C. G. Hall, Barnett's old *bête noir*.
20   *Arkansas Gazette*, November 3, 1963, 19A.
21   The second reference is to Arkansas State University's athletic teams, known from 1931 to spring 2008 as the Indians, subsequently as the Red Wolves. Before 1931, they were "Aggies" or "Farmers" (1911–1925), "Gorillas" (1925–1930), and "Warriors" (1930–1931).
22   Stephen Koch and Max Brantley, "Jones' Arkansas Waltz," *Arkansas Times*, May 12, 2005. http://www.arktimes.com/arkansas/jones-arkansas-waltz/Content?oid=866293 (accessed August 16, 2015).
23   State of Arkansas, General Assembly, Senate Resolution 24, file copy, Arkansas Secretary of State's Office.

remembered hearing it was during an impromptu performance in the House chamber by the late Representative William Thompson of Marked Tree. Ultimately, though, chivalry prevailed—Arnold took steps to end the consideration of his bill after learning that Barnett's daughter, Martha Fors of Little Rock, had cried upon learning that her mother's song might be scrapped.[24]

And there the matter sat and might have stayed for decades to come, but for the approach of Arkansas's sesquicentennial in 1986. The 150th "birthday party" for the state occasioned renewed interest in the state's history and heritage; in the sessions immediately before and after the sesquicentennial year, the legislature adopted several state symbols and also called for a competition to compose what would be designated the state's official sesquicentennial song. Nearly 500 submissions competed for the honor, some from established musicians and some from unknowns. From the scores of compositions, two attracted the most notice: "Oh, Arkansas," written by Little Rock musician Terry Rose and veteran Chicago-based songwriter Gary Klaff, and "Arkansas (You Run Deep in Me)" by veteran Nashville composer and Mallet Town native Wayland Holyfield.[25]

Wayland Holyfield

"Oh, Arkansas," as recorded by Rose, was a patriotic secular hymn to the state. Rose's lyrics repeated an introductory indicative phrase, "It's the spirit of—," followed each time by an element of the state's landscape or population. Each verse contained six such invocations, followed by the chorus invoking friendship, the Razorbacks, and the explicit identification of the state as a member of a larger polity:

> *Oh Arkansas, oh Arkansas, Arkansas U.S.A.*
> *It's the spirit of friendship, it's the spirit of hope.*
> *It's the Razorbacks every game they play.*
> *Oh Arkansas, oh Arkansas, Arkansas U.S.A.*

Much of the power of the song can be traced to Rose's heartfelt delivery. His country-tinged baritone swelled with authentic affection for his home state while the melody, composed by the creator of such storied commercial tunes as Budweiser's "This Bud's for You," "Ace Is the Place with the Helpful Hardware Man," and "How About a Nice Hawaiian Punch," strode confidently forward, ending in a stanza of repeated "Oh Arkansas, Arkansas U.S.A."[26]

---

24 Barnett had died, full of years and honors, in 1978; the Cotton Plant native is buried in Little Rock's Rosemount Cemetery.

25 The previously announced winner of the contest seems to have attracted little notice. The overlooked creation was "Arkansas Land," composed by Ann Ballard of Light in Greene County. Ballard was already an established, prolific songwriter with more than 200 country and gospel titles to her credit (*Arkansas Gazette*, June 19, 1986, A19, C1).

26 Margaret Carroll, "A Dozen Dynamic Duos," *Chicago Tribune*, May 15, 1985.

"Arkansas (You Run Deep in Me)" was created as a corporate gift to the state. Arkansas Power and Light Company (AP&L) commissioned veteran songwriter Holyfield to both compose and perform the song. He later termed the assignment "the toughest challenge I think I've ever had," adding that he did not want it to be a travelogue or an anthem. To record it, he assembled a group of musicians with Arkansas roots in RCA Victor's Nashville studios, the birthplace of the smooth "countrypolitan" Nashville sound. The recording's production values were high and the meter catchy, but the lyrics set the song apart from its peers: it was nothing less than a love song. The narrator sets the tone by recalling Arkansas, a place he has left but remembers fondly. The verses play with familiar Southern images and elements—magnolias, Delta levees hosting moonlit dances, whippoorwills—plus some less familiar, at least in popular song: frogs, mallards, the Ozarks. These are presented as fond memories, recalled wistfully and with warmth, but the final, affirmative verse invokes nothing less than the physical heart and namesake of the state:

And there's a river rambling through the fields and valleys,
Smooth and steady as she makes her way south,
A lot like the people whose name she carries.
She goes strong and she goes proud.

AP&L presented the song to the state in a ceremony on the capitol steps on January 24, 1986, before a small crowd that included the composer, state officials, State Sesquicentennial Committee Chair Tom Dillard, and the president of AP&L.

The recording was widely played during the sesquicentennial year; AP&L underwrote both recording costs and production of cassette copies of the song for distribution to Arkansas broadcasters, plus a thousand copies to be sold on behalf of the committee to raise funds. "Oh, Arkansas" was widely performed live throughout the year by Rose, a regionally popular performer. It was also performed and championed by Little Rock television meteorologist and pianist Ned Perme.

The popularity of the two songs encouraged Representative Bill Stephens of Conway to introduce a resolution designating both as official state songs while reserving for Barnett's "Arkansas" the honorific of official state anthem. A story in a local paper jested that Stephens's House Concurrent Resolution 1003 "plucks two songs from last year's Sesquicentennial hit parade."[27] The same article noted that "it's not as though Arkansas doesn't already have a state song" and described the scene in the House chamber as Stephens played Rose's recording of the song on a small cassette player. A few House members, including Representative David Matthews of Lowell, sang along.

An additional measure, House Concurrent Resolution 1007, designated the displaced "Arkansas Traveler" as the state's official historic song. The resolution's sponsor, Bob Fairchild of Fayetteville, declined to sing the song, claiming tone deafness; the *Arkansas Gazette* reported that Representative Pat Flanagin of Forrest City voted against the measure, claiming that the state "was loaded up with songs."[28]

Since 1987, no serious effort has been made to either add to or winnow the state's state song quadruvium.

---

27   Bob Wells, "A Toe-Tapping Tune for the Tuneful State," *Arkansas Gazette*, January 24, 1987, 1A.
28   *Arkansas Gazette*, February 3, 1987, 8.

Holyfield's "Arkansas (You Run Deep in Me)" is the best-known, or perhaps the most often heard, of the four; his original recording remains a familiar background to public service announcements, documentaries, and school assemblies. The Arkansas Secretary of State's Office offers lyrics for all four official state songs on its website, as well as in packets of materials distributed annually to grade school classes across the state. The office receives fifty to 100 requests per year for copies of the printed music to one or all of the songs, usually from school teachers, choir directors, or civic groups. Commercial recordings of the state songs are not readily available, but the wide distribution of cassette copies of the Rose and Holyfield compositions ensures that they can be found on the resale market. In 2006, Meme Hagers, a teacher at Fayetteville's Vandergrift Elementary School, devised *Down in the Arkansas*, a musical play incorporating the official state songs as well as others with an Arkansas connection. A recording of this play was underwritten by the Arkansas Arts Council and distributed to schools across the state, providing teachers with simple instrumental accompaniments to the state songs, encouraging students to sing along. The new recordings of all four state songs offered teachers and others an opportunity to revisit previously held notions and assumptions about the compositions. Supported by a lyrical banjo accompaniment, "Arkansas" became less an anthem than a gentle and genial lullaby. "Arkansas Traveler" was offered both in vocal and simple instrumental performances as well as in its original fiddle form, played with clarity and verve by Holly Smardo, sometime concertmaster of the North Arkansas Symphony Orchestra. The vocal arrangement demonstrated that, at the very least, the lyrics-by-committee were not entirely un-singable: the children's chorus sang at a relaxed enough a pace that even the song's crowded refrain could be understood. Smardo's recordings of both the main "Arkansas Traveler" melody and the "turn of the tune" made it easy for listeners to fill in the "soundtrack" to the original Arkansas Traveler tale.

Down in the Arkansas rendered a possibly greater service to the twinned state songs adopted in 1987. Since their release, both songs—"Arkansas (You Run Deep in Me)" particularly—had become familiar to Arkansas audiences in their original recorded forms. It is hard to break the aural paradigm of a well-recorded song, but Hagers's student singers allowed listeners to enjoy the compositions on their own: no glossy Nashville production values, no intricate accompaniments, no reverb...just songs sung carefully and with feeling. It is safe to say that *Down in the Arkansas* did not lessen Arkansans' attachment to the original arrangements, but it forced the songs to stand on their own—revealing that they were indeed songs worth repeating and cherishing. Rose and Holyfield were confirmed as worthy additions to a select company which included an albino comedian, a Mexican-born Ohio fiddler, a serially disappointed office-seeker, a former music teacher intent on eradicating the Arkansas hillbilly from the popular imagination, and the modest members of not one but two commissions who tried their best to pull off a near-impossible feat: creating a new state song worth singing.

For further reading:

Blevins, Brooks. *Arkansas/Arkansaw: How Bear Hunters, Hillbillies, and Good Ol' Boys Defined a State.* Fayetteville: University of Arkansas Press, 2009.

Bristow, Michael J. *State Songs of America.* Westport, CT: Greenwood Press, 2000.

Hladczuk, John, and Sharon Schneider Hladczuk. *State Songs: Anthems and Their Origins.* Lanham, MD: Scarecrow Press, 2000.

Hudgins, Mary. "Arkansas Traveler—A Multi-Parented Wayfarer." *Arkansas Historical Quarterly* 30, no. 3 (Summer 1971): 145–160.

Ware, David. "Official State Songs." *Encyclopedia of Arkansas History & Culture.* http://www. encyclopediaofarkansas.net/encyclopedia/entry-detail.aspx?search=1&entryID=3153 (accessed August 16, 2015).

Welky, Ali. "Wayland Holyfield." *Encyclopedia of Arkansas History & Culture.* http://www.encyclopediaofarkansas. net/encyclopedia/entry-detail.aspx?search=1&entryID=4381 (accessed August 16, 2015).

Worthen, William B. "Arkansas Traveler." *Encyclopedia of Arkansas History & Culture.* http://www. encyclopediaofarkansas.net/encyclopedia/entry-detail.aspx?search=1&entryID=505 (accessed August 16, 2015).

CHAPTER 12: STATE FRUIT AND VEGETABLE

The South Arkansas Vine-Ripe Pink Tomato—Or, Now Let Us Praise Famous Nightshades

It happens when you hit the road, heading north by northwest out of Arkansas. You go through the high plains of Kansas or Oklahoma, which turn into the high plains of Nebraska or Colorado before "roughening" a little as you approach the front range of the Rockies. You start to see isolated (increasing in frequency as you head northwest) examples of a modest slogan: "Famous Potatoes." It's not on billboards or bumper stickers or graffiti-tagged overpasses. Instead, the pride and joy of the sovereign state of Idaho, one of the famous omnibus states admitted to the Union in the closing decade of the nineteenth century, is writ large across vehicle plates for all the world to see. This doubtless provokes many chuckles, but in a way, it is also comforting and even impressive—a state secure in itself, its sense of self, can afford to celebrate its most homely asset, the ubiquitous tuber. Idaho has towering mountains, crystalline lakes, jaw-droppingly beautiful forests, volcanic expanses, and much more, but the license plate shows that the state chooses to be remembered for something modest. But there is something fine and good in that modesty.

Arkansas does not go quite so far in staking its identity on a product of the soil, but one of its state symbols certainly should rank with the tuber of Idaho. In 1987, the Arkansas General Assembly conferred official state symbol status on the "South Arkansas Vine-Ripe Pink Tomato," a staple of Arkansas gardens and for many years an economic mainstay of the southeastern part of the state. Act 255, introduced as House Bill 1480, asserted the aesthetic and culinary excellence of the Arkansas-grown tomato and determined that, because it was technically a fruit but generally consumed as a vegetable, it should serve as both fruit and vegetable in the state's collection of official symbols.[1]

The story of the designated famous tomato is tied up in botanical mysteries, colonial legacies, transatlantic exchanges, and the changing profile of Arkansas agriculture in the late nineteenth and early twentieth centuries, as well as market forces beyond the state's borders interacting with something else—perhaps we can call it "pride in product." And, of course, there's a festival involved. And an eminent journalist. So, what's not to like?

To begin with, it's worth looking at the roots, so to speak, of the tomato. It is of the family *solanaceae*—the nightshades—which is an interesting plant group, as it yields both foods and poisons. In Europe, the family members include the henbane and belladonna—known to have powerful poisonous or psychoactive effects on humans.[2] Only one Old World member of the family was reckoned edible: the aubergine (or eggplant), which was relatively rare in European gardens. This may be hard to believe, given the way it takes over a garden, but rare it was, and there you have it.

In the New World, the *solanaceae* tended to be edible. They include tobacco (not strictly edible, but...), potatoes, tomatillos, and even peppers. What unites these? What makes a *solanaceae* a *solanaceae*?

The name Solanaceae derives from the genus *Solanum*, known to those who eschew the Latin taxonomic tangle as nightshades. The etymology of this Latin word is, alas, unclear. The name may come from a perceived resemblance of certain solanaceous flowers to the sun and its rays. One species of *Solanum* is known as the "sunberry"—which, come to think of it, would be a pretty good nickname for a grape tomato.[3] Another hypothesis is that the name enjoys a degree of etymological consanguinity with the Latin verb *solari*, meaning "to soothe," presumably referring to the pharmacological properties of some of the psychoactive species of the family, which in times past doubtless afforded solace to some, and certainly something a bit more final to others.

For whatever the reason, European visitors to the New World quickly picked up on the similarity in

1   The tomato is, botanically speaking, a berry: it forms from the flower of its plant and contains and protects its seeds, just like blueberries and blackberries do. This characteristic is what distinguishes vegetables from fruits. The former are usually leaves, stalks, stems, buds, or roots and do not contain the seeds necessary for reproduction. In 1893, the panel of eminent ethnobotanists known collectively as the U.S. Supreme Court ruled in *Nix v. Hedden* that the tomato was in fact not a fruit, but rather a vegetable; it based this ruling on the ways in which tomatoes were prepared and served. The Court essentially decided that a tomato is a vegetable because people think it is, regardless of its scientific classification. And the same goes for zucchini. Justia: U.S. Supreme Court. https://supreme.justia.com/cases/federal/us/149/304/case.html (accessed July 6, 2015.)
2   Henbane, or "stinking nightshade," was known in medieval Europe for its anesthetic qualities, as well as for producing visual hallucinations and a sensation of flight. Belladonna or "deadly nightshade" contains potent alkaloids in both its foliage and fruit which, tradition holds, were used by the wives of both Caesars Augustus and Claudius to commit murder.
3   A good nickname, perhaps, but alas, it is not to be. The sunberry is a purplish berry, bred by famed American horticulturist Luther Burbank. It resembles the garden huckleberry (*Solanum scabrum*), another nightshade grown in Africa as a leaf crop and sometimes used as a dye. This is not to be confused with the black or thin-leaved huckleberry (*Vaccinium membranaceum*), the official state fruit of Idaho. All clear?

appearance between some dangerous foliage at home and plants they encountered here. Thus, they concluded, tomatoes might be poisonous, like their European cousins, the nightshades. In fact, the green tomato stems and leaves do contain an alkaloid which can be lethal to humans in large enough amounts; unripe green tomatoes, however, carry only trace amounts of the poison and ripe red tomatoes are free of it.

But this is discussing the cart somewhat in advance of the horse. How did we get to those ripe red tomatoes? Or, for that matter, the pink ones?

The species *Solanum lycopersicon*, of which today's tomatoes are subspecies, originated in a smallish strip of land on the Pacific coast of South America, land now belonging to Peru, Ecuador, and Chile. This region includes high altitudes and low altitudes, wet areas and dry areas, so a number of varieties of *solanaceae*—one might dub them prototomatoes—emerged from this natural nursery. Most of these resembled or foreshadowed only faintly the tomatoes of today, or even a century ago.

No one can say for sure when these plants were first cultivated; ethnobotanists surmise that the plants slowly naturalized their way northward as a weed which, at some point, pre-contact peoples noticed and sampled, discovering them to be edible. This must be conjectural, but it describes a likely chain of events. What is known at one "end" is the area of origin; at the other end is 1519, the arrival of Spanish conquest forces in central Mexico, the heart of the Aztec empire. Montezuma was there, Cortes was there...and so were tomatoes or, as the vegans of Tenochtitlan called them, *tomatl*. They still did not look much like modern supermarket tomatoes: they were small, irregular, "pleated," with varying numbers of cavities. Some were purple, some were pink, some yellow, others orangey-red—but all colors were consumed with enthusiasm by the Mexican people. They went home with the conquistadores, to be sprung on an Old World waiting for new fruit.

It appears that seeds and fruit came home to Spain in the early sixteenth century as the conquerors of Mexico returned to give accounts of their doings and discoveries. By the mid-1500s, the word *tomate* appears in Spain—derived from the Aztec *tomatl*. Within a few more years, these exotic arrivals and their seeds spread as far as Italy and the Low Countries. Conventional wisdom has suggested that these were assumed to be poisonous, hence were relegated to the role of ornamental exotics, but someone, surely, was not averse to taking a bite or two out of the exotic imports. In 1592, a Spanish priest and gardener mentioned that there were two or three kinds of tomatoes that bore segmented fruit that turned red; he noted that they were said to be "good

> Take a half dozen tomatoes that are ripe, put them to roast in the embers, and when they are scorched, remove the skin diligently and mince them finely with a knife. Add onions, also minced finely, to discretion; hot chili peppers, also minced finely; and thyme in a small amount. After mixing everything together, adjust it with a little salt, oil and vinegar. It is a very tasty sauce, both for boiled dishes and for anything else.
>
> Antonio Latini, *Lo Scalco alla Moderna* (1692), Translated by Rudolf Grewe, "The Arrival of the Tomato in Spain and Italy: Early Recipes." *Journal of Gastronomy* 3, no. 2 (Summer 1987).

for sauces." A contemporary of his, English botanist John Gerard, recorded that he had received seeds of these "apples" from both Italy and Spain, where, he wrote, "they do eat [tomatoes] with oil, vinegar, and pepper mixed together as sauce for their meat, even as we in these cold countries do mustard."[4]

And, just as they had migrated from the New World to the Old, tomatoes found their way into the gardens of the North American colonies. Contrary to the old saw of early Americans shunning the tomato out of a belief that it was poisonous, its cultivation in the warmer parts of the English colonies was well-established by the time of the American Revolution. By the late seventeenth century, it is known that tomatoes were grown in the Caribbean and the Carolinas; tomatoes were part of the diet of residents of New Orleans in the eighteenth century and by the second decade of the nineteenth century, were cultivated throughout the Mississippi and Ohio valleys. The source of the seeds is unknown, but various possibilities suggest themselves. In the Southeast, perhaps they were brought from Spanish America, or from England or France, where tomatoes were not uncommon. Or, French refugees from the slave revolt in Haiti may be credited with bringing both seeds and the custom of cooking with tomatoes to America's coastal cities.

While tomatoes were grown and consumed early in the southern colonies/states, they were slower to gain acceptance farther north. From New York northward, it was not until the third decade of the nineteenth century that tomatoes finally lost the last odium of being possibly poisonous or otherwise dangerous. After 1830, tomato seeds became available pretty much anywhere in the Republic.

Tomato packing in Monticello, ca. late 1930s.

The tomato represented a triumph of variegation. By the 1880s, nearly 200 varieties were known and a decade later, nearly 400 variety names were listed by the U.S. Department of Agriculture, a fitting close to what had become the century of the tomato. Older ribbed varieties shared garden space with the larger, rounded and smooth types developed by American breeders. Juicy slicing tomatoes in a wide variety of colors were available, as were smaller ones such as cherry, grape, and even currant tomatoes; for cooking down, plum, pear, or "paste" tomatoes offered lower moisture than the slicers and more "meat," making them ideal for sauces and other cooking. In the decades following the Civil War, consistent commercial tomato

---

4   Lawrence Davis-Hollander, *The Tomato Festival Cookbook* (North Adams, MA: Story Publishing, 2004), 245.

> ## East India Tomato Sauce
> Skin and remove the seeds from three dozen fine, ripe tomatoes, work the pulp through a fine sieve, boil the watery particles away until you have reduced it about one half; add three ounces powdered green ginger, fifteen cloves garlic, bruised, two wineglassfuls of tarragon vinegar, two ounces salt, one-quarter ounce of mild red pepper (cayenne); let the whole boil once, put it into wide-mouthed bottles, cork and seal. This recipe is an excellent one, but to please the American palate use half the quantity of garlic.
>
> Thomas Jefferson Murrey, *Murrey's Salads and Sauces* (New York: Charles Dillingham, 1884)

seeds appeared. Many of the early commercial varieties were developed by Alexander Livingston, who developed the Paragon in 1870 and the Acme in 1875; these would in time both become "heirloom" tomatoes and be the basis of many other successful hybrid tomatoes, grown across the nation.[5]

Arkansas grew up with the tomato, attaining statehood as the tomato finally came into its own as an American cash and household crop. Tomatoes generally remained domestic garden crops until the 1880s, when the first canning plants appeared, offering a way to preserve the bounty of harvest which would otherwise spoil while awaiting shipment to market.

Tomatoes appeared early in Arkansas; locals apparently did not share the old fear of death by love apple. One prominent Arkansan who championed the tomato was lawyer and journalist Albert Pike, who encouraged its cultivation in order to provide his state with a little dietary diversity. The Arkansas tomato remained mainly a home-garden-and-local-market proposition until the advent of canning, which allowed surpluses to be hygienically preserved in tinned iron cans, thus making them both durable and transportable.[6] The state's first commercial canning plant was opened in Yocum in Carroll County in the 1880s; in years to come, processing operations and tomato sheds popped up in both the Ozarks and the southeastern part of the state, which became Arkansas's two great tomato-producing zones. After tomato blight afflicted the Ozark tomato fields in the 1940s, those farmers turned to other crops, leaving the tomato market to the southeastern zone which centered on Bradley County and in particular the town of Warren. Beginning in the 1920s, farmers grew tomatoes there.

And lo, they were pink.

Pink tomatoes (that is, ones whose pinkish skin is translucent and whose ripe interior looks pink instead of red when the fruit matures to the breaker stage) form a small part of the mass tomato market today but were once a significant portion of the tomato supply. Pinks tend to taste slightly more acidic than red varieties, balanced with a pleasing initial sweetness. Early successes among commercial pink tomato seeds included three from the godfather of commercial tomato seed, Ohioan Alexander Livingston: Livingston's Beauty, Livingston's

---

5   Information on Alexander Livingston can be best gleaned from the horse's mouth: His 1893 autobiography, suggestively titled *Livingston and the Tomato*, remains available in print from the Ohio State University Press.

6   Canning was an early-nineteenth-century innovation which matured by mid-century. One of the leaders in the field was the firm of Campbell & Anderson of Camden, New Jersey, founded in 1869; Campbell's canned tomatoes and tomato soup became justly renowned wherever historic archeologists analyzing trash middens are found.

Magnus, and Livingston's Main Crop Pink. Other successful pink varieties, hallowed names in the halls of heirloom tomato enthusiasts, included the pink Brandywine, the General Grant, the Gulf State Market, and the Mortgage Lifter, first propagated in 1922.

Just why the Bradley County farmers came to adopt the pink tomato is unclear, but Leah Forrest Sexton, the reigning historian of the Arkansas tomato industry, notes that pink tomatoes were first sold commercially in Bradley County in 1923, a year characterized by depressed profits on cotton. Several farm families were guided by County Agent C. S. Johnson to experiment with various kinds of garden produce to supplement their cotton earnings. They found that they could start tomato plants from seeds in a hot bed[7] and transfer them to covered cold frames prior to planting them in the fields. The technique worked well, and the pink tomatoes found ready buyers, leading more Bradley County farmers to experiment over the next two decades with pink tomatoes. By the 1940s, the district's name had been made on the strength of its dependably fine pinks.[8]

If this were a fairytale, it would be enough to write, "and they all lived happily ever after" at this point, then amble into my garden to see if one of my Arkansas Traveler pinks has ripened enough to harvest. But there is more to tell about tomatoes—about their marketing, about shifting times and tastes and, happily, about some good things lasting.

One part of the Bradley pink story involves the steps the Bradley County farmers took to market their produce. Until 1949, individual growers sold and distributed their own tomatoes. This was inefficient, to put it mildly. For those with faraway customers, bound by contracts, this could involve a drive of hours or even days

---

7   A technique involving a framed and covered raised bed founded on a thick layer of animal manure, which supplies both heat through decomposition and nutrients to the growing plantlets. In regions where manure was in short supply, gardeners built enclosed "hot houses" heated by fires and flues. Remains of some of these have been found in the Ozark National Forest. Presumably, manure was plentiful enough in southeastern Arkansas so that the simpler self-heating hot beds prevailed.

8   Leah Forrest Sexton, "Tomato Industry," *Encyclopedia of Arkansas History & Culture.* http://www.encyclopediaofarkansas.net/encyclopedia/entry-detail.aspx?entryID=5526 (accessed July 6, 2015).

☐ 3x4 24 ct   ☐ 4x4 32 ct

ARKANSAS

Arkansas
GROWN

TOMATOES

☐ 5x6 60 ct

bearing fragile produce (the pinks of that time were thin-skinned and prone to cracking, so they were best sold individually wrapped in tissue). The year 1949 saw the first of three Bradley County tomato auctions established. The first was for the Hermitage neighborhood, followed by auction markets for Warren and Monticello. Farmers would bring in their truckloads of tomatoes to a main shed, and something like a live tobacco auction would ensue, followed by the farmers taking their produce to the individual bidders' sheds. The bidders would pay cash on the crate head and be responsible for arranging further transport for the tomatoes. The system worked well but gradually gave ground to the current broker system, in which gratification is deferred (and so is payment). The last Bradley County tomato auction was held in 2001.

By 2001, much had changed in terms of both crops and markets. Bradley County's famed pink tomatoes were not the same ones grown in the 1920s. The first pink tomato grown commercially in Bradley County was almost certainly the Gulf State Market tomato, often simply referred to as the Gulf State.[9] The breed grew in Bradley County for close to thirty years, well into the 1950s, but proved susceptible to Fusarium wilt, a disease that can damage and kill plants. To fill the gap left by the Gulf State, the U.S. Department of Agriculture (USDA) developed a wilt- and crack-resistant pink, the Pink Shipper, which entered the market in 1957. This might have remained the dominant pink of Bradley County, but, in 1961, Dr. Joe McFerran and Jack Goode from the University of Arkansas Cooperative Extension Service (UACES) experimented with different varieties of pinks, including the old Gulf State. McFerran crossed the Gulf State with a wilt-resistant USDA-numbered strain: the result was the Bradley Pink. Eventually, however, even this "neo heirloom" proved vulnerable to a variant of the wilt, which led to the development in 1968 of the crack- and wilt-resistant Arkansas Traveler pink tomato, still a favorite of growers and gardeners.

For many years, Arkansas remained one of the nation's top producers of marketed tomatoes. In the late 1960s, as many as 900 farmers in and around Bradley County grew and made at least part of their livelihood from the famous pink tomatoes, ripened on the vine and packed in tissue. But change was in the air. Californian and, later, Mexican growers whittled away at the Arkansas market portion. These growers produced large red tomatoes—often picked while immature and then bathed in ethylene gas and salt water to ripen them. By the 1990s, there were only 200 Bradley County growers and dwindling; today, only a handful of farms near Warren produce commercial quantities of tomatoes. Most of these are "pinks by courtesy"—since the 1980s, Bradley County growers

Children at the Bradley County Pink Tomato Festival in Warren.

have also produced reds, which are thicker-skinned, slower to mature (therefore less particular as to moment of harvest), and generally more robust than the older pink varieties—thus, more profitable, at least most years. The Bradley County practice is to harvest these in their pink stage—that is, at breaker, when they are turning

---

9   This strain was first identified in 1917 by a Mississippi grower; it was refined and propagated by the Livingston Seed Company.

from green to red—rather than picking them green and forcing their ripening. This is a riskier way of raising market tomatoes, with more wastage than green-harvesting, but the difference, say tomato connoisseurs, is in the flavor. And the flavor is all.

Today, Arkansas does not show high among the sixteen states whose tomato production is ranked by the USDA's National Agricultural Statistics Service. In 2011, Arkansas stood tenth in the nation for fresh market yield and production; two years later, its ranking was two places lower.[10] The tomato is, nevertheless, the state's largest vegetable crop, despite erratic production figures: in 2008, about 3,000,000 pounds of fresh market tomatoes were produced, but in 2014, the figure dropped to near 1,500,000.[11]

Regardless of production figures, though, affection for the pink tomato—either pink by type or by time of picking—remains strong. This affection is in part kept vital by the Bradley County Pink Tomato Festival, which made its debut on a hot June day in 1956. It was a one-day event, an opportunity to throw a party honoring both the characteristic crop of the county and the workers who made it a success. Events and entertainers were added each year; the festival has become a nearly week-long affair, complete with a street dance; tomato eating, cutting, and packing competitions; arts and crafts; and a mainstay since 1956: the All-Tomato Luncheon.

If the festival is one hardy perennial, another is the yearly column by *Arkansas Democrat-Gazette* editor Paul Greenberg which sings a love song to ripe tomatoes—locally grown, picked when they are ready, and never forced to a state of edibility.

> To recapture the thrill, take one Bradley County Pink. Note the vivid color, the simple heft, the way it was made for the human hand....Then slice evenly, noting the fine texture. Be careful of the juice. No, don't taste yet. Barely sprinkle with just a little coarse salt, then make a tomato sandwich using two slices of brown bread and...just the lightest little hint of unsalted butter, nothing more. Now. And you know what time itself tastes like.

—Paul Greenberg, "The Fruit of Time," *Arkansas Democrat-Gazette*, June 20, 2001, G3.

The tomato's renown is, of course, also perpetuated by its designation as the state's official fruit and vegetable. In 1987, State Representative John Lipton of District 90, whose constituency included Bradley County, introduced the measure which would become Act 255, conferring official status. The measure asserted the aesthetic and culinary excellence of the Arkansas-grown tomato, both fruit and vegetable, but described a type rather than specifying a species because there existed no registered breed styled "South Arkansas Vine Ripe Pink Tomato." Thus, this symbol of Arkansas has a certain mystery to it. The designation raises hopes that any red or pink tomato may grow up to become an example of the state symbol, so long as it is harvested at just the right moment.

---

10   U.S. Department of Agriculture, National Agricultural Statistics Service, Vegetables 2013 Summary (March 2014). http://www.nass.usda.gov/Publications/Todays_Reports/reports/vgan0314.pdf (accessed July 6, 2015).

11   U.S. Department of Agriculture, National Agricultural Statistics Service, Delta Region Vegetables 2014 Summary. http://nass.usda.gov/Statistics_by_State/Mississippi/Publications/Crop_Releases/Fruit_Nut_Vegetable/2015/msvegetablejan15.pdf (accessed July 6, 2015).

For further reading:

Bir, Sarah. "From Poison to Passion: The Secret History of the Tomato." *Modern Farmer*, September 2, 2014. http://modernfarmer.com/2014/09/poison-pleasure-secret-history-tomato/ (accessed July 6, 2015).

Bradley County Pink Tomato Festival. http://www.bradleypinktomato.com/ (accessed July 6, 2015).

Davis-Hollander, Laurence. *The Tomato Festival Cookbook*. North Adams, MA: Storey Publishing, 2004.

Gentilcore, David. "Taste and the Tomato in Italy: A Transatlantic History." *Food and History* 7, no. 1 (Spring 2009).

Greenberg, Paul. "The Fruit of Time." *Arkansas Democrat-Gazette*, June 20, 2001.

Grewe, Rudolf. "The Arrival of the Tomato in Spain and Italy: Early Recipes." *Journal of Gastronomy* 3, no. 2 (Summer 1987).

Livingston, Alexander W. *Livingston and the Tomato* (reprint edition). Ohio State University Press, 1998.

Murrey, Thomas Jefferson. *Murrey's Salads and Sauces*. New York: Charles Dillingham, 1884. http://vtechworks.lib.vt.edu/handle/10919/10339 (accessed July 6, 2015).

Sexton, Leah Forrest. *The History of the Bradley County Pink Tomato Industry*. MA thesis, Henderson State University, 2014.

———. "Tomato Industry" *Encyclopedia of Arkansas History & Culture*. http://www.encyclopediaofarkansas.net/encyclopedia/entry-detail.aspx?entryID=5526 (accessed July 6, 2015)

Ware, David. "Official State Fruit and Vegetable, a.k.a.: South Arkansas Vine Ripe Pink Tomato." *Encyclopedia of Arkansas History & Culture*. http://www.encyclopediaofarkansas.net/encyclopedia/entry-detail.aspx?search=1&entryID=3156 (accessed July 6, 2015).

Williams, Lamor. "Pink, Red, Beautiful, Flavorful: A Look at Tomato Farming in Arkansas." http://www.arfb.com/mobile/headlines/2014/pink_red_beautiful_flavorful_a_look_at_tomato_farming_in_arkansas/ (accessed July 6, 2015).

CHAPTER 13: STATE MAMMAL

Or, Visions of Deer Camp Dance in My Head

In considering the white-tailed deer, Arkansas's official state mammal, it is worth musing for a moment about why it is a symbol of Arkansas—or, rather, what does it say about us? On one level, it is emblematic of the state's game population, a stand-in for all the Wild Things. On another, it is the visible reminder of a great success—the intentional restoration and careful perpetuation of the state's cervid population, through the actions of hunters, conservationists, and the Arkansas Game and Fish Commission. This is a happy-ending story, and a glorious one, too.

But this last version is incomplete. It's not wrong, mind you, but focusing on the happy ending makes more sense if we remember Little Nell lashed down on the train tracks with the 8:15 to Moosejaw headed her way. What almost happened to the deer should remind us to not take what we may grandly refer to as the "bounty of nature" for granted. We almost didn't have the white-tailed deer here, at least in quantities to call abundant, or even healthy.

Today, deer are the attainable Holy Grail for Arkansas hunting season. Wild turkeys will give one a merry chase, but deer season retains the cachet. Going into deer camp is a fall ritual enjoyed by thousands, and oh, it is a time: time to live out Nessmuk's axiom that "We do not go to the green woods and crystal waters to rough it, we go to smooth it. We get it rough enough at home."[1] Nessmuk was in some ways a spiritual ancestor of the hunter of today. His frustrations were not the same as ours, but chances are good that he would recognize the look in the eyes of men and women who get enough of the rough at home, in the office, on the commute to and fro, in the parking lot at the mall, in the [your pet everyday hell here]. Nessmuk had the idea that going into the wilds was restorative, and those colleagues who disappear at the beginning of each of the deer seasons come back in some ways restored. It is possible that they've never heard of Nessmuk, but they live his prescription. Cots and air mattresses are the rule now, instead of the browse beds of yore—and gas stoves in place of the campfire, not to mention better bug dope, clothes that will keep you dry, and GPS technology to take away the sinking feeling that you've strayed too far past the edge of the maps in your pocket. But the frisson of the tradition is still there, as are

Virginia Deer.

the iron Dutch ovens, the feel of hunting boots needing to be softened up before cross-country stalk, and the smells of bug repellent, gun oil, smudge fires, and camp cooking. And going out into the woods to seek the deer makes this possible.

So, where to start?

Maybe with the land. I like to think that to the early European entrants into "Arkansaw," this place must have seemed like an ocean of trees. Hardwoods, softwoods, tall ones and scrubs—Arkansas had it all. Something like ninety percent of the surface area of what is today's state was a wild vastness of timber—both deciduous and evergreen.

If the woods were the ocean, then the wild things that ran through the trees were the fish. The bison were the whales. The wolves, coyotes, and alligators were the sharks, and so forth. What were the snakes, or the squirrels, or the many birds? I can't say; I will leave this for someone else to work out. But, I will go so far as to suggest that the deer were the dolphins. Swift, graceful, canny—like their gray sea-brethren, the deer added grace notes to the woodlands.

◊ ◊ ◊

When we say "deer," we speak of the local flavor of the large family of mid-sized mammals native to the United States, Canada, Mexico, Central America, and South America as far south as Peru and Bolivia. In the

---

1   "Nessmuk" (George Washington Sears), *Woodcraft and Camping* (New York: Forest and Stream, 1884), p. 13. Sears, who adopted the pen name of "Nessmuk" to honor a member of the Narragansett nation who befriended him when he was a boy, was an early advocate of lightweight camping and the restorative powers of the outdoors. After early years rambling and holding a wide assortment of manual jobs, Sears became a Pennsylvania shoemaker; in addition to this "day job," he was a frequent contributor to *Forest and Stream* magazine (today published as *Field and Stream*).

Americas, the white-tail (or white-tailed deer) is the most widely distributed wild ungulate.

In North America, the species is most thickly distributed east of the Rocky Mountains; elsewhere, the black-tail, or mule, deer has long predominated. On the other hand, a combination of agricultural land clearing and climate change has expanded some of the white-tail's range. One finds white-tailed deer in aspen parklands and along river bottoms in the central and northern Great Plains, and in similar settings among the foothills of the northern Rocky Mountain regions from South Dakota and Wyoming to southeastern British Columbia, as well as just about everywhere east of the line, including west Little Rock residents' home gardens. Clearly, this animal is adaptable.

During the nineteenth and early twentieth centuries, naturalists identified what they thought were as many as thirty or even forty subspecies of white-tailed deer, based on variations of size, and markings and other physical characteristics. The deer of "historic Arkansas" were probably either *Odocoileus virginianus virginianus* (the most common and widely distributed subspecies) or *Odocoileus virginianus macrourus*, usually known as the Kansas white-tail. The present-day picture has been complicated by instances of trapping and transplanting for

English photographer Eadweard Muybridge (1830–1904) is known for his pioneering work on animal locomotion in 1877 and 1878, which used multiple cameras to capture motion in stop-motion photographs.

purposes of repopulation. The white-tail of today's Arkansas is generally the *Odocoileus virginianus*—literally, the hollow-toothed Virginia deer.

The Arkansas white-tail is a large, even-toed mammal with large ears and, as one might expect from the name, a long, bushy tail that is white underneath. Males are larger than females, and they exhibit forward-pointed antlers with unforked tines. Height at the shoulder ranges between 26 and 42 inches, and weight usually falls between 88 and 300 pounds—although this may seem an undermeasurement to anyone who has carried a white-tail carcass out from the back country.

In terms of nourishment and habitat, the white-tailed deer is notably adaptable. It lives on forest edges, in open woodlands, and in brush or areas growing back after being logged. Any place with ample browse will suit the white-tail: they feed on leaves, twigs, and shoots of multiple tree species, as well as on grass and broad-leaf plants, fruits, berries, mushrooms, and, in autumn, acorns.[2] The deer are ruminants; that is, they have four digestive chambers through which food passes before reaching the intestines. The details of what happens in which chamber may be elided over at this point (see references for more information on deer digestion). Suffice it to say that the deer's digestive tract is designed to eke the most nutrition out of any quantity of food.

The breeding season for Arkansas deer begins in late September and continues over winter through February. Traditionally, the season started about three weeks earlier in the north of the state than in the south, but long-term climate shifts may play hob with this; come back in a decade and check, please. The outcome of the "rut," the period of intense reproductive activity, is the appearance of fawns, beginning in late March and continuing into late spring. Life expectancy for these young is variable. With a little luck—in the form of good browse, plenty of water, and hunters who cannot shoot straight—deer live as long as seven or eight years in the wild, with a very few living to the ripe old age of fourteen or fifteen.

We may never know the full extent of the deer population of pre–European contact Arkansas, but we do know that deer formed an important part of the domestic economies of the Native American nations and villages that predated European development. In a cave at Petit Jean State Park are drawings of animals that look a lot like deer[3]; archeologists have unearthed tools made of antlers. When Spanish explorer Hernando de Soto crossed the river into proto-Arkansas, he met native residents wearing clothes of deer skin. Henri Joutel, the chronicler of the last expedition of French explorer René-Robert Cavelier, Sieur de La Salle, makes mention of abundant deer.

With French, and then Spanish, colonization beginning in the late seventeenth century and continuing by fits and starts in the eighteenth, deer assumed a new role: currency. Where once deer, like bison and other animals, had been direct subsistence elements, now they also provided media of exchange, as native populations and new European transplants developed trading relationships. The Mississippi Valley's natives played a vital role in the colonial economy, supplying meat, hides, tallow, and agricultural produce in exchange for desired

---

2   A scholarly paper on deer grazing suggests, perhaps inadvertently, that deer's favorite graze usually consists of whatever grain, fruit, or vegetables a farmer has growing at any given time.

3   To be fair, as long as they don't look like fish or bison or mammoths, prehistoric animal drawings tend to all look like deer.

trade goods. These locally produced commodities both fed the colonists and provided goods (hides and tallow, in particular) that the colonists or their proprietors could sell elsewhere in North America or in Europe. Goods were not sold for money, but instead were bartered: a flintlock musket might be worth sixteen deerskins or five buffalo hides; four more deer hides might purchase powder and shot for a season's hunting. This trading system created a mutual dependence between Europeans and Native Americans. It also encouraged the hunting of wild game beyond the immediate needs of one's family or community.

Explorers and other visitors of the early national period similarly found deer to be abundant. As Lieutenant James B. Wilkinson descended the Arkansas River from near present-day Muskogee, Oklahoma, in 1806, he saw (and recorded his impressions of) thousands of bison, elk, and deer.[4] The Hunter-Dunbar expedition up the Ouachita River in 1804–1805 yielded similar observations. Euro-American settlers' land clearing and over hunting crowded bison populations westward. Arkansas's populations of the eastern elk, which lived in the pine and hardwood forests, disappeared by around 1840.

The white-tails, however, were either numerous enough or adaptable enough (or both) to tarry longer. They provided a valuable part of rural Arkansans' subsistence, and deer hides and tallow remained commodities that could be sold or exchanged.[5] Some doubtless were killed for sport, but the low human population density of Arkansas probably helped keep the hooved population healthy.

This dynamic shifted, though, toward the end of the nineteenth century, as land use became more intensive and expansive: expansion of agriculture, livestock grazing, and timber cutting disturbed and destroyed habitat. A more dramatic challenge came in the form of an influx of over hunting, particularly in the lowlands of the northwestern part of the state. In post–Civil War years, both market hunters and sportsmen began to make significant inroads into the wild populations of the area. This was facilitated by the construction of railroads through the region: hunters, for fun or profit, could take the St. Louis, Iron Mountain and Southern Railway south into the game-rich "sunken lands," fishing and hunting game birds and deer, secure in the knowledge that they were unrestricted by any effective federal or state laws. In this way, hunting shifted, as it had during

---

4   Lieutenant Wilkinson was a subordinate of Major Zebulon Pike, who sent him <u>down</u> the Arkansas, while Pike proceeded <u>up</u>. Wilkinson's father was General James Wilkinson, a self-promoting Revolutionary War veteran who, in spite of having proven himself unable to fulfill the duties of clothier-general to the army, was encouraged and supported by no less a personage than George Washington. Beginning in 1787, Wilkinson *pere* worked as a spy and agent provocateur for the Spanish crown, plotting to create Spanish dependencies out of western U.S. territories. He appears to have conspired with Aaron Burr, then arrested the former vice president, thereby saving his own bacon. Ironically and perhaps providentially, while in 1806 the younger Wilkinson was sent down the Arkansas River, his commander, Pike, headed west, only to fall into the hands of Spanish authorities. Had he stayed with Pike, Wilkinson might have had one of those embarrassing "our people employ your father" moments. The younger Wilkinson attained the rank of captain in the U.S. Army and was killed while serving under his father, who was commanding U.S. troops at the Battle of Dauphin Island in Mobile Bay in 1813. His father survived investigations and courts-martial, his treasonous complicity with Spain widely suspected but never proven until long after his death in 1820. The younger Wilkinson, an able explorer of the Arkansas valley, is largely forgotten today, while his father is memorialized by streets in Frankfort, Kentucky, and in New Orleans; a county name in Georgia; and the opprobrium of such historians as Robert Leckie, who characterized Wilkinson as "a general who never won a battle or lost a court-martial." Theodore Roosevelt, with his customary charity, said of Wilkinson *pere*: "In all our history, there is no more despicable character."

5   German sportsman and traveler Friedrich Gerstäcker described the economics of a community along the St. Francis River made up of hunters and squatters, who "often brought in the produce of the forest, such as bear's fat, honey, smoked deer-hams, skins and bear-hides, which they exchanged for powder and shot, whiskey and the other luxuries of forest life." Gerstaecker, *Wild Sports in the Far West* (1847), quoted in Keith Sutton ed., *Arkansas Wildlife: A History* (Fayetteville: University of Arkansas Press, 1998), 26.

colonial times, from direct subsistence to a form of subsidy—for some, at least, who lived in the game lands. Food for tables competed and even lost ground to hunting that brought in money. Restaurants north of Arkansas often featured wild game from the sunken lands, particularly from the Big Lake area; iced venison, ducks, fish, and even frogs were loaded onto the trains and sent north to market.

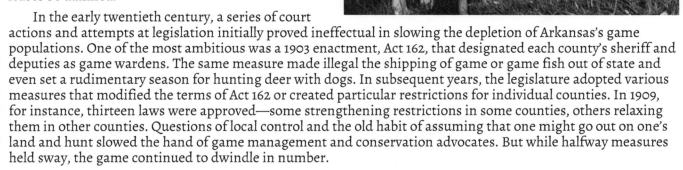

Locals profited, but the enthusiastic over hunting by out-of-staters caused friction as well, as the pattern of locals' subsistence hunting was long established and the interlopers competed with them for game. St. Louis hunters turned to leasing land from timber companies, hoping to reserve choice tracts for their exclusive hunting use, but locals ignored the posting notices and vandalized hunting camps built for the "dudes" from outside. For the locals, the wet forest lands constituted a commons from which they would not be excluded, leases be damned.

In the early twentieth century, a series of court actions and attempts at legislation initially proved ineffectual in slowing the depletion of Arkansas's game populations. One of the most ambitious was a 1903 enactment, Act 162, that designated each county's sheriff and deputies as game wardens. The same measure made illegal the shipping of game or game fish out of state and even set a rudimentary season for hunting deer with dogs. In subsequent years, the legislature adopted various measures that modified the terms of Act 162 or created particular restrictions for individual counties. In 1909, for instance, thirteen laws were approved—some strengthening restrictions in some counties, others relaxing them in other counties. Questions of local control and the old habit of assuming that one might go out on one's land and hunt slowed the hand of game management and conservation advocates. But while halfway measures held sway, the game continued to dwindle in number.

It may have been concern over dropping game populations, or widespread irritation over measures meant to either protect the game or liberate would-be hunters from the restrictions of such protection, but something shifted in 1915. In that year, the General Assembly acted to create the Arkansas Game and Fish Commission (AGFC). Keith Sutton of the AGFC notes that "this was not an easy decision...even though the shortage of game and fish obviously was growing more acute every year.[6] Act 124, which created the commission, was the brainchild of Junius M. Futrell, a senator (and future governor) from Paragould. The act set seasons and limits for certain species, including deer. It also imposed a license fee of one dollar for deer and made it illegal to

---

6   Sutton, *Arkansas Wildlife*, 54.

hunt without a license. Other fees and protections were imposed and, to make it all work, the act stipulated the creation of a system of wardens and deputies, who would be supported by the license fees and any penalties. In addition, the work of the wardens would be overseen by an unpaid five-person commission with a broad remit.[7]

To suggest that this act marked the beginning of deer recovery in Arkansas would constitute pulling a very long bow. To begin with, no reliable count had been made of wildlife populations in the state. Anecdotal evidence, such as dropping reports of harvested game, made the pattern clear enough, however. In its first annual report, the commission was qualitatively precise, if numerically indefinite: Arkansas had "a few bear, fewer beavers, some otter, prairie hens, wild turkeys and white-tailed deer." The report opined that the remaining numbers could be the basis of population recovery but not if the annual harvest continued to greatly exceed the number of animals born.

The absence of deer, after decades of their seemingly unlimited abundance, made their recovery a high priority for the commission. Initially, efforts focused on setting reasonable bag limits and enforcing them. In 1917, the Arkansas legislature closed the doe season and instituted a limited buck season to try to coax the resident population above the estimated 2,000. When this proved unproductive, the commission started trapping and purchasing animals for brood stock. In 1926 and 1927, deer were imported from four states, including a batch of thirteen fawns from North Carolina, courtesy of the National Forest Service.

The floods of 1927 set the recovery program back, and hard: Arkansas's deer population dropped to an estimated 500 head by 1930. Over the next few years, however, herds in refuges showed signs of significant increase. A public-relations campaign to discourage killing does gained some ground, although a parallel effort to ban using dogs in deer hunting met strong opposition and little success for many years.

This frustration did not, however, detract from the overall picture of advance in the effort to restore deer populations. What turned the tide was the combination of managed seasons, refuges, "stocking" with animals from outside the state, and, beginning in 1945, a program of transplanting excess deer from overpopulated districts to ones with small populations and more carrying capacity.[8] One good index of this is the number of legal deer harvested per year: in 1938, a total of 203 such kills were recorded. In 1942, the number topped 1,000. By 1952, it stood at 6090 and, in 1992, the number reached comfortably over 110,000.

Thus, it made sense when, in March of 1993, the Seventy-Ninth General Assembly approved House Bill 2110, which designated the white-tailed deer as the official mammal of the state of Arkansas. The bill, introduced by Representative Arthur F. Carter of the Second District (Carroll County, plus parts of Newton and Madison Counties), was signed into law by Governor Jim Guy Tucker as Act 892 on April 5, 1993. Arkansas is not alone in

---

7   The commissioners were charged with (among other duties) setting policy, promoting fish stocking and game preserves (the latter to be accomplished with no expenditures of public funds), supervising, law enforcement, and appointing wardens. Setting seasons and bag limits, however, was to be the work of the state legislature.

8   Another factor was the adoption, in 1944, of Amendment 35 to the state constitution. This finally placed management and regulation of all wildlife resources under the authority of the Arkansas Game and Fish Commission, giving it greater autonomy to take steps as necessary to keep populations stable and healthy (see Sutton, *Arkansas Wildlife*, Chapter 11, for discussion of the impact of Amendment 35).

paying tribute to the white-tailed deer: ten other states have selected *Odocoileus virginianus* as an official symbol.[9] Several of them have something in common with this state—they almost lost the white-tail. Details of recovery vary from state to state, but it is notable and a good thing that they—WE!—are cognizant of what might have been, and how close we came to losing the white-tail.

Today, the status of the white-tailed deer in Arkansas is fairly secure. The population topped 500,000 in the mid-1980s and, today, the AGFC maintains it at around 1,000,000. As the herd has grown, the commission has promoted population stabilization as a goal for deer management. Hunters are by and large happy, and the tradition of heading off to deer camp remains alive, allowing those who "rough it" in their offices, shops, and workrooms to follow Nessmuk's restorative prescription.

For further reading:

Arkansas Game and Fish Commission. *Annual Report* (Little Rock, 1915).

———. Deer Harvest Reports. https://www.ark.org/agfc/gamecheck/reports.php (accessed June 28, 2015).

Deckman, Dale. *Distribution and Subspecies of the North American White-tailed Deer.* Sturgeon Bay, WI: White-tails Unlimited, 2003.

Kissell, Robert E., Jr., and Philip A. Tappe. "Response of an Arkansas White-tailed Deer Population to Harvest." *Journal of the Arkansas Academy of Science* 59 (2005): 199–202.

Sealander, John, and Gary Heidt. *Arkansas Mammals: Their Natural History, Classification and Distribution.* Fayetteville: University of Arkansas Press, 1990.

Sutton, Keith, ed. *Arkansas Wildlife: A History.* Fayetteville: University of Arkansas Press, 1998.

Ware, David. "Official State Mammal." *Encyclopedia of Arkansas History & Culture.* http://www.encyclopediaofarkansas.net/encyclopedia/entry-detail.aspx?entryID=3154 (accessed June 28, 2015)

Whitaker, John. *Audubon Field Guide to North American Mammals.* New York: Knopf, 1996.

---

9   Wisconsin was the first, in 1957, followed by Pennsylvania (1959), South Carolina (1972), Mississippi (1974, as the state's designated land mammal, the bottlenose dolphin, grabbed the marine mammalian honors), Nebraska (1981), Illinois (1982), New Hampshire (1983), Ohio (1988), Oklahoma (1990), and Michigan (1997).

CHAPTER 14: STATE NICKNAME AND CREED

Some Good Words, Cognomens, and Credos

Words matter. They are subtle things and powerful, even though flat (in printed form) and fleeting when spoken. Most official state symbols are not words: they are instead for the most part physical, tangible things, although they may be fleeting in their own right, such as butterflies or short-blooming flowers, which remind us to enjoy such things as they pass by. Such symbols may suggest or embody ideas, but they are not ideas in and of themselves. Words, on the other hand, are the things humans use to express the essence of ideas. They are concretions of concepts, mental electricity set down in code. Most states have designated at least one word or phrase within their lists of state symbols; Arkansas enjoys two (or three, if one counts the state motto inscribed upon the state seal—but that has been dealt with elsewhere in this volume so you, gentle reader, are spared a second disquisition on THAT topic): an official state nickname and a state creed. The former is widely known, the foundation of our state's touristic promotion efforts, while the latter is relatively obscure, as is often the case with well-meaning attempts at putting big ideas into mere words.

To begin with, it is worth considering the nature of nicknames, and the difference between ones chosen <u>for</u> you and ones chosen <u>by</u> you.

Nicknames applied to a person, thing, or place by others are often honest, if insensitive, indications of how something is seen or understood by others; they can carry with them a slight element of mockery or at least amusement at the expense of whatever is being nicknamed. The latter, on the other hand, can represent attempts to pre-empt such characterizations, often as expressions of aspirations or pride. This can be successful, but those who would coin their own nicknames should be cautious: Like state songs or mottos, such names or phrases can take on a slightly risible quality when regarded by outsiders.

Many geographical places are known by titles, or alternative names, which can have positive implications. Paris, for example, is the "City of Light," New York is the "Empire State," the other New York (Manhattan, at least) is "The Big Apple," and New Jersey is the "Garden State." On the other hand, some alternative names or titles are more truthful than flattering, though they are borne with pride by their subjects: "Windy City" (Chicago); "Auld Reekie" (Edinburgh, Scotland); "Ice Box of the Nation" (Big Piney, Wyoming). Still others are aspirational or allude to history: "The Old Dominion State" (Virginia); "The Old Line State" (Maryland); "The Beaver State" (Oregon). It has been suggested that it is not *strictly* correct to call such titles "nicknames," even though the term itself means "other name"; usage pecksniffs will gripe that such appellations are often used to boost the status of such places, contrary to the usual role of a well-chosen nickname or "cognomen."

◊ ◊ ◊

Many places or communities, particularly in the United States, adopt such alternate names because it is believed that they can help establish a place's identity, helpful both for attracting outsiders to visit, settle, or even invest, and also for giving citizens an identity around which to unite.

Such alternate assignations are thus believed to have a purpose, both economic and civic: a good enough moniker,[1] beloved by those it represents and recognized by others, can be a powerful thing, although those who try too vigorously to promote a new community ideology or myth using such an agent are probably doomed to failure. Nevertheless, such nicknames are believed to have economic value, although this is inevitably hard to measure. Perhaps it is safest to assert that a well-chosen sobriquet[2] makes it easier to promote and publicize a town or state, by establishing a sort of characterizational shorthand signature for it.

Since its earliest days, Arkansas has been popularly known by a succession of nicknames. The earliest were unofficial and tinged lightly (or sometimes not) with humor, reflecting popular perceptions of a largely rural state. Later adoptions, spaced at intervals throughout the twentieth century, arose from desires to distance Arkansas from the rough-and-ready image formed during its earliest decades. These new "known-bys" abandoned folk culture or historical references in favor of earnest promotional intent, as Arkansas's boosters sought to remake the state's image in a way they hoped would attract the positive attention of outsiders.

Arkansas's earliest recorded nicknames made reference to characteristic features of the region. In the first half of the nineteenth century, Arkansas was noted for its population of Louisiana black bears (*Ursus americanus luteolus*), one of sixteen black bear species found in the United States. Though not as huge or reputedly fierce

---

1   Generally defined as "name" or "nickname." Sorry.
2   Also generally defined as "nickname." On the bright side, the correct pronunciation is in the French manner, "so-bree-kay," rather than the English "so-bri-ket," thus establishing a sort of spiritual affinity with the state whose name is likewise pronounced à la manière Française.

as their grizzly and Kodiak cousins to the west and north, these bears were nevertheless the kings of the Arkansas wild. Adults are about 50 to 75 inches long from nose to rump, measure 35 to 48 inches at the shoulder when on all fours and can reach over 6 feet tall when standing erect. Male black bears are known to exceed 600 pounds, though in Arkansas, adult males today range from 130 to 300 pounds and adult females from 90 to 150 pounds. Bears have good eyesight and an excellent sense of smell; that prominent nose is not there just to make them look cute. A black bear stands on its hind legs with its nose in the air to scent the wind, searching for culinary opportunities; they can detect carrion (which they will scavenge, since they are not quite the gentle vegans that campers might wish for) or a freshly filled garbage can (which they will open, examine, dump, examine, dine from, and discard) at considerable distances. They are excellent swimmers, can outrun any Olympic athlete, and are particularly adept at climbing trees, which more than one surprised camper or hunter has discovered to their deep chagrin.[3]

These qualities and others made bears superb foragers but not necessarily the most accommodating neighbors for the human populations of early Arkansas. Bears were hunted by Native Arkansans for their meat, hides, teeth, and claws; in colonial days they were pursued by what we would call commercial hunters. Visitors to Arkansas Territory saw bears or evidence of them in settlers' cabins, where bear meat was on the table and bear robes covered floors; bear oil and bear grease also provided cash or exchange for backwoods families. Bears were hunted without restriction, in large part because the supply seemed almost inexhaustible. This abundance inspired the sobriquet of "The Bear State," which remained in common use past the beginning of the next century.

Change, however, was in store for Brother Bear. A combination of lost habitat and overhunting led to a declining population; in some parts of the state, bears were relatively scarce as early as the 1840s. Following the Civil War, increasingly urbane (use this term with some caution) Arkansawyers became intolerant of bear-related property damage and the periodic bear attacks on livestock or even humans. Market hunters and locals seeking to fill their Dutch ovens thus hunted the bear with less sportsmanship and reverence than vehemence and efficiency. By 1927, the bears that had once dominated Arkansas's canebrakes and swamp woods were

3   Rebecca McPeake, Don White Jr., and Rick Eastridge, "Encountering Bears in Arkansas," University of Arkansas Division of Agriculture Cooperative Extension Service, http://www.agfc.com/species/documents/nuisance_bears.pdf (accessed August 14, 2015); "Black Bear," Arkansas Game and Fish Commission, http://www.agfc.com/species/pages/SpeciesWildlifeDetails2.aspx?Title=Black%20Bear (accessed August 14, 2015).

almost gone: fewer than fifty remained in the wetlands along the lower White and Cache Rivers. The Arkansas Game and Fish Commission called a halt to the bear slaughter that year, and what had once been the Bear State had become something else.[4]

While "the Bear State" became the best-known Arkansas cognomen of the nineteenth century, a couple of others were common enough in those times to warrant mentioning. One, "the Toothpick State," referenced the early custom of men commonly carrying large sheath or belt knives, usually for purposes of self-defense.

What is an "Arkansas toothpick"? The question still vexes edged-weapon scholars and enthusiasts; the "toothpick" is sometimes termed a large dagger or a bowie knife (in its many variants), something carried in a belt scabbard, or tucked into the trouser-waist or even lodged in the upper of a tall boot, ready to be slipped out and brandished in the event of imminent mayhem or gentlemanly discourse on the streets of Arkansas Post (or, for that matter, on the floor of the Arkansas House of Representatives). The knowledgeable William Worthen of the Historic Arkansas Museum suggests that in the years before the Civil War, "Arkansas knife" and "Arkansas toothpick" were terms used interchangeably with "bowie knife." "Bowie knife" was itself a term applied with some latitude. It was inspired by a knife made by Washington (Hempstead County) blacksmith James Black for either gambler and duelist James Bowie (latterly celebrated for his bravery in the War for Texas Independence) or his brother Rezin. This knife was descried by Rezin Bowie as simply "a hunting knife"; knives later made by Black as copies of that famed instrument featured "coffin" handles, silver-wire wraps or ornaments on the handle scales, a cross-guard of nickel-silver or brass, and a clip point.[5] Such "toothpicks" served as common inexpensive sidearms, suitable for dining, butchering, and dueling or other interpersonal violence. They soon became fixed in the national imagination, connected to the state from which one famous example had sprung.[6] The messy dispatching by knife of one Arkansas state representative

At the end of the Civil War, Confederate President Jefferson Davis was unfairly accused of fleeing Union troops dressed as a woman; in this caricature he at least carries a Southern tradition in his petticoats.

---

4   See C. Fred Williams, "The Bear State Image: Arkansas in the Nineteenth Century," *Arkansas Historical Quarterly* 99, no. 2 (Summer 1980), generally, for insight into the genesis of Arkansas's rustic, game-y, and violent reputation. By century's end, the bear had also become a thing of anthropomorphic nostalgia, as depicted in Albert Bigelow Paine's *Arkansaw Bear: A Tale of Fanciful Adventure* (New York: R. H. Russell, 1898).

5   William Worthen, "Arkansas and the Toothpick State Image," *Arkansas Historical Quarterly* 53 (Summer 1994): 161–190. In present times, the term "Arkansas toothpick" is usually reserved for double-edged daggers, slender but stout enough in section to withstand hard use, ranging in size from a small boot-knife to something a little shy of a Roman *gladius*. Regardless of size, the "toothpick" is a knife designed primarily for fighting. For detailed information on such blades, see Harold L. Peterson, *American Knives: The First History and Collectors' Guide* (New York: Charles Scribner's Sons, 1958) and Norm Flayderman, *The Bowie Knife: Unsheathing an American Legend* (Woonsocket, RI: Andrew Mowbray, 2004).

6   The author has seen examples of both American and Sheffield-made knives identified as "Arkansas [or "Arkansaw"] toothpicks," testifying to the state's reputation.

by another in 1837[7] cemented the new state's renown as a violent place and helped inspire a new and not particularly pleasant cognomen for Arkansas: "the Toothpick State."[8]

One last early nickname for Arkansas deserves mention: "Rackensack." The derivation of the word "Rackensack" has been analyzed with no single sure source ever identified, but by the end of the 1840s, it was established as a burlesque synonym for rural Arkansas, particularly the hills of the western part of the state. One idea is that "rackensack" derives from an Osage word denoting the Ozark Plateau. Another theory is that the name arose during the Mexican-American War, from a description of Arkansas troops as able to "rack and sack a town faster than anyone." How this description could have gained wide currency so quickly is another matter altogether, but support for the name being current during the war comes from a painting by Samuel E. Chamberlain, illustrating his memoirs of the Mexican War published in 1956 as *My Confession*. The picture is a side view of a pair of field guns, cascabel knobs seeming to touch and their trails crossed; on the left, a flag bears the motto "Extend the Area of Freedom." To the right is a similar flag which informs the viewer that "Rackensack is in the Field."[9] The true origin of the word may ultimately be as hard to pin down as that of Toad Suck in Faulkner County, but it matters little at this remove; it was used by residents as a humorous reference to both themselves and their area. Moreover, the name could cross state lines. In the 1870s, a Missouri-born former Confederate soldier named Edward Cave arrived in the Tucson, Arizona, area. He became a prospector working the Cave Creek district north of today's Scottsdale. He was something of a local character and went by the nickname of "Old Rackensack"; he located some valuable deposits including the district's first gold mine and also wrote letters to the editors of the Phoenix newspapers on diverse topics.[10] Regardless of the word's origin, it became an insider's nickname—used by Arkansawyers themselves—alluding to an older and less-settled past time. The word and its spirit live on in the Rackensack Folklore Society, organized in the 1960s to preserve and pass along the traditional music and culture of the people of Arkansas, particularly those of the Ozarks.

These early Arkansas aliases survived the end of the century but, by 1900 or so, they were viewed with impatience by modernizing citizens who sought to dispel the state's long-established "hillbilly" reputation. One of the most energetic apostles of this new, modern Arkansas was educator and politician Charles Hillman Brough. During two terms as governor (1917–1921), he earned a reputation as a reformer in the Southern Progressive mold. After leaving office, he worked energetically with the Arkansas Advancement Association

---

7   On December 4, 1837, House Speaker John Wilson stabbed Representative Joseph Anthony to death at the climax of a brawl on the floor of the House of Representatives, in front of the rest of the legislators. Wilson pled self-defense and was acquitted, but he did not escape punishment: He was expelled from the legislature after censure for his conduct. John Ferguson, *The Old State House—Some Questions and Answers* (Little Rock: Arkansas Commemorative Commission, 1968), 8–9.

8   Latter-day attempts to refine or gentrify the meaning of this early cognomen have been unconvincing at best; in 2004, the author was informed by an Arkansas native and member of the Daughters of the American Revolution that the phrase referred to the huge stands of tall, straight-as-a-toothpick pine trees that covered much of the state in its early days. A variation on this gloss offers the assertion that "toothpick" refers to the instruments of oral hygiene made from the abundant hardwood trees of Arkansas. Sigh.

9   Samuel E. Chamberlain, *My Confession: Recollections of a Rogue*, with introduction and postscript by Roger Butterfield (New York: Harper and Brothers, 1956), 128.

10   Kraig Nelson, "A Short History of Cave Creek," Desert Foothills Land Trust, http://dflt.org/testdflt/newsletters/31-current/111-history-of-cave-creek (accessed August 14, 2015).

(AAA), a group of businessmen who worked to dispel old stereotypes in hopes of attracting in-migration and investment in the state. One of Brough's particular goals during his time with the AAA was the adoption of an official nickname or promotional slogan for the state. Brough's choice was "the Wonder State," referencing the state's dramatic scenery and vast resources. In 1923, the Arkansas legislature responded: Senate Concurrent Resolution 2, approved on January 26, proclaimed that "hereafter

Arkansas shall be known and styled 'the Wonder State.'" In support of this brave attempt at self-nicknaming, the resolution asserted that the state "excelled all others" in its natural resources and that its agricultural prowess was recognized internationally; the resolution hailed the publicity work of the AAA which, it claimed, had "so indelibly stamped upon the mind of the world that Arkansas is The Wonder State…'" and went so far as to dismiss the old, unofficial "Bear State" sobriquet as "a misnamer [sic]."[11]

Brough continued to work for the next several years on behalf of the AAA, mainly giving speeches extolling the state's beauty, resources, business resources, and high general standard of morality. He worked hard to counter the "hillbilly" image of the state and developed the thesis of Arkansas's self-sufficiency, based on its diversity of resources.[12]

Brough placed great importance on the adoption of a new and improved alias for Arkansas, but although "Wonder State" enjoyed official sponsorship, it did little to change perceptions of Arkansas as an underdeveloped forest and agricultural colony full of rural eccentrics, undereducated people, violence, and

11   Acts of Arkansas 1923, pp. 802–803; see also E. J. Friedlander, "'The Miasmatic Jungles': Reaction to H. L. Mencken's 1921 Attack on Arkansas," Arkansas Historical Quarterly 38, no. 1 (Spring 1979): 63–71.

12   C. Fred Williams, "Arkansas's Image," Encyclopedia of Arkansas History & Culture. http://www.encyclopediaofarkansas.net/encyclopedia/entry-detail.aspx?entryID=1 (accessed August 14, 2015); Foy Lisenby, "Charles Hillman Brough," in Timothy P. Donovan and Willard B. Gatewood Jr., eds. The Governors of Arkansas: Essays in Political Biography (Fayetteville: University of Arkansas Press, 1981), 149–50. Brough is remembered for asserting that "if a fence was built around Arkansas," the state would be self-sufficient; the potential in this statement for inspiring facetious state nicknames and slogans is nearly as vast as the resources of which he was so proud.

swamps. The popularity in the 1930s of entertainers Bob Burns and "Lum and Abner" (Chester Lauck and Norris Goff), who traded in broad, Arkansas-referenced humor, likewise did little to dispel this image; meanwhile, the state's business and manufacturing sectors attracted little outside investment.[13]

In 1953, Arkansas's legislators moved to place "Wonder State" on the figurative mantel, alongside "Bear State" and "Toothpick State." House Concurrent Resolution 26, introduced by Representatives "Dooley" Womack of Ouachita County and J. T. Slack of Clark County, began by stating the obvious: "Wonder State" had been the official nickname or popular name of the state since 1923.[14] The resolution acknowledged that like the state's earlier, unofficial names, "Wonder State" had been justified by the conditions of its times, but that times had changed and it no longer commanded popular appeal. There had been a "definite and wholehearted trend," however, toward the phrase "Land of Opportunity" ever since it had first appeared on license plates back in 1941. Now, in light of the bright prospects for the state's economy, it was time to proclaim "Land of Opportunity" the official nickname of the state. The measure was approved in the House on March 4, in the Senate on March 12, and signed into law on March 27, 1953.[15]

This legislative *coup de sobriquet* did not appear from out of a clear, blue Arkansas sky; it was part of a long-running campaign of "rebranding," one that carried on the work begun by Brough.

It is just possible that Brough had been right, that what Arkansas needed in order to thrive was a really good new alias. "Wonder State" had not worked out, possibly because it sounded like something tied to or inviting what is today known, with a slight tone of dismissal, as "magical thinking." It was too earnest, too general, too—well, just not quite the right phrase. And there matters stood until the 1940s, when a group of businessmen began redoubled efforts to promote economic development and, consequently, encourage Arkansas's best and brightest to either stay in the state or return home.

Key to this effort was Hamilton Moses, president of Arkansas Power and Light (AP&L). When he became president of AP&L in 1941, the company had already begun promoting the "Arkansas Plan," a program to increase public demand for electricity and to solicit outside investments in Arkansas companies.

In 1941, probably at Moses's suggestion, a new slogan appeared on Arkansas vehicle license plates: "Land of Opportunity." Moses, a politically skillful corporate leader, was also as dedicated to Arkansas development as Brough had been; under his direction, AP&L assumed a key role in promoting Arkansas as a destination for business. Moses worked with a group of business leaders, known as the Committee of 100, whose promotional literature bore the same nickname as the state's license plates. In 1943, Moses organized a group of the state's business leaders that became the foundation of the Arkansas Economic Council, which revived the old AP&L "Arkansas Plan" but gave it a new focus. Instead of seeking outside money to fund locally hatched enterprises, the new plan concentrated on persuading national corporations to locate facilities in Arkansas. The council's work bore fruit as postwar Arkansas's industrial employment rose significantly. It therefore made sense in 1953

---

13   This perceived lack of outside investment may have had something to do with the long-running economic doldrums of the Great Depression. War production requirements plus the revitalization of the lumber industry in the late 1930s would lead to economic growth during the 1940s, probably independent of any effects, positive or negative, of state nicknames.

14   This marked the first official mention of it being styled a nickname—take that, usage pecksniffs!

15   *Acts of Arkansas*, 1953, p. 1511.

for the state's solons to embrace the motto that had graced license plates for more than a decade already; even the words of the then-current state song, "Arkansas Traveler," seemed to endorse the evolution, managing to invoke the Brough-era nickname in one line, then use the O word in the next:

For the Wonder State we'll shout Hurrah!

And praise the opportunities we find in Arkansas.

During the 1980s, Arkansas's outreach to tourists became more aggressive than before, reflecting a maturing understanding of tourism as a growth industry. So, the Arkansas parks system began promoting Arkansas as "the Natural State," and the nickname proved popular, largely eclipsing the older "Land of Opportunity" in public esteem and currency. In March 1995, Representative Dennis Young of Miller County introduced House Bill 2051 to amend the Arkansas Code, designating "The Natural State" as Arkansas's official nickname (no mention was made of the existing one). Citing the state's "unsurpassed scenery, clear lakes, free-flowing streams, magnificent rivers, meandering bayous, delta bottomlands, forested mountains and abundant fish and wildlife," the bill proposed to make official a change that had already largely been effected.

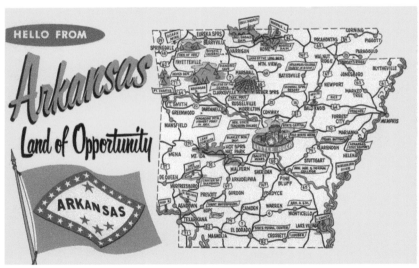

The move was not, however, universally supported. "Land of Opportunity" retained its partisans, who would surface on March 24, when the measure came up for a roll call vote in the Arkansas House. Before the vote was recorded, special permission was granted for members to wear red hats bearing the new nickname.[16] All seemed smooth sailing at first: the roll call vote yielded 63 votes for the bill and 23 against, with 51 needed to pass—a comfortable margin. Following the vote, however, Representative Frank Willems of the Twenty-Sixth District (Logan and parts of Franklin and Johnson Counties), one of the 23 opponents, requested a Sounding of the Ballot; his request was supported by four other members. In this procedure, a clerk of the House, working from the tally of the electronically recorded roll call, asked each of the affirmative voters to confirm that he or she had in fact voted in favor of the bill. Those not responding, for whatever reason,[17] would see their prior votes disallowed or "challenged." Eleven "ayes" were successfully challenged, which reduced 2051's margin of those in favor to a single vote: the final recorded tally was 52 in favor, 23 opposed, 23 absent, and two choosing to vote "present." The matter passed to the State

16   House Journals 1995, Vol. 4, pp. 3107, 3905; David Ware, "State Nicknames, a.k.a. Official State Nickname," *Encyclopedia of Arkansas History & Culture.* http://www.encyclopediaofarkansas.net/encyclopedia/entry-detail.aspx?entryID=3150 (accessed August 14, 2015).

17   Such as, in this instance, having temporarily left the chamber for a break.

Senate, which ratified the House's approval and sent it on to Governor Jim Guy Tucker on April 12. On April 19, the legislature was informed that Tucker had approved the bill without signing it into law.[18]

Arkansas has not only a nickname, or several of them, but also a creed. For those who, in the words of Francis Bacon, "delight in giddiness or count it a bondage to fix a belief," "creed" may count as an honorary four-letter word because there is something non-negotiable about the very notion of a creed. The word comes to us from the Latin *credo*, translated as "I believe." In Old English it is was rendered as *creda*—a statement of Christian belief. Although usually connected with religious belief, "creed" has a wider meaning: it designates the principles which an individual or an associated body holds so strongly that they become the springs and guides of conduct.

Who or what can boast of having a creed? Most religious faiths, certainly Western ones do, although some sects emphasize scripture over such summaries of core beliefs. Professions do—perhaps the best known is the Hippocratic Oath, which is still taken, in modified form, by physicians, but other "credentialed" professions do, too, including stenotypists and court reporters, military members of all ranks, and lawyers.[19] Many of these, particularly for attorneys, were and are as much codes of practice as statements of beliefs. Creeds tend to be terse documents, perhaps because the ideas they contain need little artistic elaboration.

Polities may also adopt or pay service to creeds. Some of the best come from organic documents of a nation; a case in point is the Declaration of Independence. Others seem to spring from a desire to clear up some unfinished business, or to remind citizens/members of what things bind them together. Several sovereign states have adopted creeds: North Dakota (1926), Georgia (1939), Alabama (1953), and Arkansas (1972).

The germ of the Arkansas Creed was contained in House Concurrent Resolution 2 of 1969, introduced

18   House Journals 1995, Vol. 4, pp. 3905, 3918; Vol. 5, pp. 5150, 5167. The author thanks House Parliamentarian Buddy Johnson for his lucid explanation of and comments on the "Sounding of the Ballot" parliamentary maneuver.

19   The court reporters' creed is a relatively recent document, first promulgated in 1982. It is a vigorous assertion of the existence of the profession throughout history as well as statement of pride in profession: "My Profession protects the truthful witness, and I am a nemesis of the perjurer. I am a party to the administration of justice under the law and the court I serve. I discharge my duties with devotion and honor. Perhaps I haven't made history, but I have preserved it through the ages. In the past I was called scribe. Today I am the court reporter that sits in the courts of our country. I am the stenographer that sits in the United States Congress. I am the Verbatim Court Reporter!" http://www.courtreportersmuseum.info/creed.htm (accessed August 14, 2015).

by State Representative Roscoe Brown of Jonesboro. Brown said that it "promoted the ideals of liberty and democracy among a proud people." Brown alluded to the American form of government being challenged by enemies of democracy and pointed out that 1969 marked the sesquicentennial of the formation of Arkansas Territory and its government; these considerations made it proper that a creed be written for and adopted by the state. The resolution spelled out the steps by which the creed would be created. First, a commission of dignitaries would sponsor a state-wide contest. The winning composition would be designated as the "Arkansas Creed" and the author would receive a testimonial plaque. The resolution was approved on February 28 and sent on to Governor Winthrop Rockefeller, who signed it on March 4. On March 3, 1970, state historian Dr. John Ferguson was officially appointed head of the Creed Commission.

The committee first met on June 10 of that year. It included Ferguson, Maurice Dunn of Hot Springs, Dr. Claude Babin of Monticello, Education Commissioner Arch Ford, and Representative Brown. In December, the committee issued rules for a creed-writing contest. They solicited entries of 250 words, editable to eighty words or less. The deadline for submissions was initially February 1 but was later reset to May 1, 1971, due to a paucity of entries.

From a field of ninety-one entries, thirteen semifinalists were selected. Committee members, in addition to some interested outsiders, were asked to choose the best and rank the rest. One outside evaluator, *Arkansas Gazette* archivist Margaret Ross, did not consider any of the submissions suitable for designation. After several meetings, the top three contestants were chosen: Charlotte Colston of Monette High School, Evelyn Archer of El Dorado High School and...State Representative Brown. The committee decided that none of these would be declared the clear winner, so Ferguson took up the task of composing a creed that incorporated elements of the three finalists' submissions.[20] Ferguson's text was adopted, with minor amendments, by the committee on April 26, 1972, and submitted to Governor Dale Bumpers for his approval. Bumpers promulgated the new Arkansas Creed on August 1, 1972:

> "I believe in Arkansas as a land of opportunity and promise. I believe in the rich heritage of Arkansas and I honor the men and women who created this heritage. I believe in the youth of Arkansas who will build our future. I am proud of my state. I will uphold its constitution, obey its laws, and work for the good of all its citizens."

The Arkansas Creed is not often recited but remains official, although it was not inserted into the state code, like other designated state symbols were.[21] Perhaps the best last word on the subject of the creed was delivered by Representative Brown on the occasion of its official debut: "No creed is better than the practice of it."[22]

---

20   Dr. John Ferguson, interview with the author, September 25, 2001; additional material from *Arkansas Creed Selection Committee, 1969–1972*, Small Manuscripts Collection, Arkansas History Commission, Little Rock, Arkansas.

21   Despite the provisions of HCR 2, no testimonial plaque was awarded to Ferguson for his work in creating the final text of the creed. HCR 2 had also stipulated that a copy of such a plaque would be deposited with the Arkansas secretary of state, but diligent searching has not revealed one or any documentation of its delivery.

22   "At Last Arkansas Gets Creed," *Arkansas Democrat*, August 1, 1977, 5.

For further reading:

Arkansas Creed Selection Committee 1969–1972. Small Manuscripts Collection, Arkansas History Commission, Little Rock, Arkansas.

Blevins, Brooks. *Arkansas/Arkansaw: How Bear Hunters, Hillbillies, and Good Ol' Boys Defined a State.* Fayetteville: University of Arkansas Press, 2009.

———. *Hill Folks: A History of Arkansas Ozarkers and Their Image.* Chapel Hill: University of North Carolina Press, 2002.

Dew, Lee A. "On a Slow Train through Arkansaw: The Negative Image of Arkansas in the Early Twentieth Century." *Arkansas Historical Quarterly* 39, no. 2 (Summer 1980): 125–35.

Lisenby, Foy. *Charles Hillman Brough: A Biography.* Fayetteville: University of Arkansas Press, 1996.

Paine, Albert Bigelow. *The Arkansaw Bear: A Tale of Fanciful Adventure.* New York: R. H. Russell, 1898.

Shea, William L. "A Semi-Savage State: The Image of Arkansas in the Civil War." *Arkansas Historical Quarterly* 48, no. 4 (Winter 1989): 309–28.

Williams, C. Fred. "Arkansas's Image." *Encyclopedia of Arkansas History & Culture.* http://www.encyclopediaofarkansas.net/encyclopedia/entry-detail.aspx?entryID=1 (accessed August 14, 2015).

———. "The Bear State Image: Arkansas in the Nineteenth Century." *Arkansas Historical Quarterly* 39 (Summer 1980): 99–111.

CHAPTER 15: STATE GRAIN AND STATE SOIL SERIES

Made for Each Other

A variety of terms are used when one is speaking of the soil of the Delta lands of the Mississippi valley—terms that are more or less unintelligible to someone who has not grown up near the river, depending on the land for his or her sustenance. Delta blogger John McKee has observed that many such terms, such as "sand-blow," "rice land," or "gumbo," describe the balance of clay and sand in a patch of soil.[1] Where sand and silt have accumulated in a waterway, the stream will in time choke itself out and look for somewhere else to run. It will leave behind soil that is fertile, absorptive, and permeable, as it is well-drained. It will hold water long enough but not keep it around too long. This sort of land is particularly sought by cotton farmers.

Sandy land is the traditional dream of Delta farmers—but not all Delta land is so gifted. From a river comes not just sand and silt, but also clay, which is a cohesive soil, meaning that its particles will stick together. Those particles remain in suspension until deposited in a low point. Look for places where water stands on the surface a long time and you will find clay there, not letting water find its natural level easily. These are called "bottoms" and they are sometimes covered in "buckshot," little round globs of clay that has dried

1   John McKee, "Delta Dirt: Sand, Clay, and a River's Love," *Delta Bohemian*, December 23, 2010, http://www.deltabohemian.com/delta-dirt-sand-clay-rivers-love/ (accessed July 19, 2015).

and cracked. When this bottom soil is dry, it is buckshot; when properly wetted, it is termed gumbo and becomes the land where highway tires fear to go. The bottoms are found, oddly enough, some distance away from the river. The bottoms hold water too long and well to suit most cotton, but there is another crop which takes to them neatly indeed: rice, the official grain of Arkansas.

The story of rice in Arkansas is the story of adaptation, a sea change in staple crops. It involves an old system in failure or at least steep decline, an ancient crop, and a Midwestern transplant who became the apostle of that crop. Rice, a staple of human consumption for thousands of years, entered North America when it was first planted in South Carolina in the early 1690s. While rice was cultivated in small amounts in Arkansas as early as 1840, it did not become a major crop in the state until the early years of the twentieth century, after which it rose to prominence as a signature staple, made possible by a clayey soil series underlying the bottoms of eastern Arkansas. This soil or, rather, series of soil layers, has been recognized by the Arkansas State Legislature as an official state symbol, just like the grain whose cultivation it makes possible and profitable.

◇ ◇ ◇

From its earliest times, Arkansas was an agricultural zone. In territorial days, farmers made up some 90 percent of the population. During territorial and early statehood days, the uplands were farmed by small, largely self-sufficient landholders (either owning or squatting in anticipation of getting land cheaply through pre-emption). The late and sorely missed Arkansas historian C. Fred Williams noted that even if the new Arkansans claimed 100 acres or more, they generally farmed less; a hill country farm might have no more than thirty acres planted. These acres would contain some salable staples, such as corn or cotton, plus cereals, potatoes, vegetables, and perhaps tobacco. The rest of the land would be left as woodlands, sources of timber as well as range for a few head of livestock. Most of what was raised served for

Carlisle Rice Mill Company, Carlisle (Lonoke County), ca. 1910.

subsistence. Any cotton grown would be sold, usually as the farm family's main source of cash or credit for the year.[2]

The decade of the 1840s saw an evolution, as planters (or their agents) ventured into Arkansas in search of fertile new soil for cotton production. They found what they were looking for in the alluvial plains of the Arkansas Delta country: expanses of rich and flat sandy land, which was both well-watered and well-drained. In short, it was cotton land. In the past, would-be farmers had hewn to the hillsides, well away from the inconvenient truths of snakes, other riverine pests, and seasonal inundation. Now, the great fertility of the

2   C. Fred Williams, "Agriculture," *Encyclopedia of Arkansas History & Culture.* http://www.encyclopediaofarkansas.net/encyclopedia/entry-detail. aspx?search=1&entryID=385 (accessed July 19, 2015).

Train load of rice, ca. 1912.

alluvial soils, worked by chattel slave labor, drew antebellum agribusiness to the wet flatlands of the eastern reaches of Arkansas. Arkansas Delta cotton sold for top money at the Memphis markets. Arkansas's population grew (particularly its enslaved sector) and, by the eve of the War Between the States, cotton reigned as the king of Arkansas's staples.

The Civil War ended much of the Old Order of Arkansas cotton culture, largely because it did away with the "tied" (or chained) labor force upon which that culture had depended. What emerged in the postwar years was a new system, one in which antebellum landowners or their successors partnered with tenants or share croppers, allowing (again, quoting Williams) underclass farm hands and landowners alike to meet mutual needs. Some new, small freehold farms were established under the terms of the Southern Homestead Act of 1866, but these were few in number, and their owners, like tenant farmers and sharecroppers, were forced by tight credit and market realities to grow what had been grown before the war: cotton, the readily salable commodity of Arkansas fields.

But cotton was a shaky foundation for agricultural recovery. After cotton farmers enjoyed a brief postwar period of high prices for cotton, prices slumped, due to market gluts from both domestic and overseas production. Through the end of the century cotton prices averaged 11 cents per pound. "New South" advocates preached the gospel of diversification beginning in the late 1870s. In pockets of the state, new crops took hold, such as fruit or truck produce (including, after 1920, Arkansas's celebrated tomatoes). Most farmers, however, found it hard to successfully diversify. By the start of the twentieth century, Arkansas Delta farmers needed a supplemental staple crop and needed it badly. It would come—from south of the border—but planted and promoted by a hardy Midwestern transplant.

◇ ◇ ◇

Oryza sativa—Asian rice—was domesticated from the wild grass *Oryza rufipogon* roughly 10,000–14,000 years ago, in the middle Yangtze and upper Huai river valleys of China. The two main subspecies of rice—*indica* (prevalent in tropical regions) and *japonica* (prevalent in the subtropical and temperate regions of East Asia)— are now believed to have derived from this common domestication. Another cultivated species, *Oryza glaberrima*, was domesticated much later in West Africa.

Rice and farming implements dating back at least 8,000 years have been found in China. Cultivation spread down the rivers over the following 2,000 years, reaching south Asia by approximately 2500 B.C.E. From there, it spread to the west. The crop may well have been introduced to Greece and the neighboring areas of the Mediterranean by returning members of Alexander the Great's expedition to India around 344–324 B.C. From Greece, rice spread gradually throughout southern Europe and to a few locations in northern Africa.

The Moors brought Asiatic rice to the Iberian Peninsula in the tenth century. Muslims also brought rice to Sicily, from where it made its leap to the mainland: by 1475, its cultivation was promoted by Ludovico Sforza, Duke of Milan. After the fifteenth century, rice spread throughout Italy and then France, later propagating to all the continents during the age of European exploration.

Rice was introduced to Latin America and the Caribbean by European colonizers. Spanish conquerors brought Asian rice with them to Mexico in the 1520s; the Portuguese and their African slaves introduced it at about the same time to colonial Brazil. Recent scholarship suggests that enslaved Africans played an active role in the establishment of rice in the New World and that rice, either African or Asian rice prepared in traditional African ways, was an important crop from an early period. Rice dishes characteristic of West Africa remained a staple among their enslaved descendants in the Americas.

Rice came to North America before 1700, likely imported with enslaved Africans obtained from the west coast of Africa. One version of the rice "origin story" spins a fanciful picture of a brigantine forced to take shelter in Charleston (through which 40 percent of all American slave imports passed, which makes it likely that the ship in question was in fact a slaver) in 1685 with its master, Captain John Thurber, giving a local worthy a bag of seed rice; from this, the story goes, sprang Carolina (and by inference American) rice culture.[3] The story may have a grain of truth to it. What is clear is that in the early eighteenth century, rice proved the first successful crop for South Carolina. The colony had been founded in 1670, but its settlers struggled for its first thirty years. By about 1700, however, they discovered that Asian rice grew well in the inland swamps of the Low Country. This product brought consistently high prices in England, and the colony prospered and expanded. Later, because of the extraordinary success in South Carolina, the rice plantation system was extended farther south into coastal Georgia, where it also prospered.[4]

> ## To make a cheap rice pudding
>
> Get a quarter pound of rice and a half pound of raisins stoned, and tie them in a cloth. Give the rice a great deal of room to swell. Boil it two hours; when it is enough, turn it into your dish, and pour melted butter and sugar over it, with a little nutmeg.
>
> Hannah Glasse, *The Art of Cooquery Made Plaine and Easy* (1788)

By the middle of the nineteenth century, rice growing had spread, in a limited way, to other southern states, including North Carolina, Florida, Mississippi, Alabama, and Louisiana; some was apparently grown in Arkansas as well. After mid-century, cultivation increased in southwestern Louisiana and Texas, so much that by the 1890s, the product of these two states led the nation. Arkansas agriculturalists, however, were slow to commit to rice as a main staple crop.

◊ ◊ ◊

At the heart of any good epic tale should be a central visionary character, around whose perception or charisma or strategic skills swirl the winds of change and progress. For the Israelites, Moses; for the American

---

3   Historians of South Carolina differ over the details of the introduction to the colony of Madagascar gold seed rice, which apocryphally came via Captain Thurber's brigantine in 1685. Supporters of the Thurber story have claimed that the gold rice was the first to be introduced to South Carolina, only to be gradually displaced by white rice. Indications are strong that, in fact, Carolinians grew white rice in the seventeenth century, with gold rice being introduced after the American Revolution. Either way, colonists successfully grew small amounts of the grain in the Charlestown colony by 1690. James H. Tuten, *Lowcountry Time and Tide: The Fall of the South Carolina Rice Kingdom* (Columbia: University of South Carolina Press, 2010), 10–12.

4   Another economic activity that prospered in connection with rice culture was the importation of enslaved Africans from the rice-growing regions of West Africa. South Carolina rice planters were willing to pay extra for slaves from what they knew as the Rice Coast or the Windward Coast who brought with them knowledge of rice culture, which their masters utterly lacked. See Joseph Opala, *The Gullah: Rice, Slavery, and the Sierra Leone-American Connection*, Yale University Gilder Lehrman Center for the Study of Slavery, Resistance, and Abolition, http://www.yale.edu/glc/gullah/cont.htm (accessed July 19, 2015). See also: Daniel C. Littlefield. *Rice and Slaves: Ethnicity and the Slave Trade in Colonial South Carolina* (Baton Rouge: Louisiana State University Press, 1981) and Tuten, *Lowcountry Time and Tide.*

colonists turned revolutionaries, Washington; for the peanut, George Washington Carver; for Arkansas rice, there is…William H. Fuller of Carlisle in Lonoke County, who is frequently credited with creating the interest in rice production through an experimental farm in 1902. Following his example, the story goes, rice production caught on in various counties on the Grand Prairie, as well as the Mississippi River Delta region and the Arkansas River Valley.

William Fuller relocated from Nebraska to Lonoke County in 1895, part of a modest migration of northern farmers who were attracted to the Grand Prairie by cheap land and railroad access to markets.[5] In the following year, Fuller and neighbor Hewit Puryear left Lonoke with a team and wagon on a month-long, thousand-mile hunting trip to the coastal marshes of Louisiana. Along the way, near Crowley, Louisiana, Fuller and Puryear stopped to visit an irrigated rice farm; the operation so intrigued Fuller that the two men spent additional time visiting a Crowley rice plant, gathering information on rice culture. When Fuller and Puryear returned to Lonoke County, they carried with them rice seed and the conviction that the clayey soil of the Grand Prairie would be "a good rice country if we had the water."[6]

And water they had, plenty of it; the challenge would be to get it out of the ground and onto the field. Fuller initially planted three acres of rice, flood-watered by a pair of four-inch wells. The rice grew well until his pumps broke down. The plants withered, but he had proven the concept, at least to his satisfaction. Now, the devil was in the details. In 1898, Fuller returned to Louisiana and spent four years learning the rice business, returning to Lonoke County in 1903. The next year, he sowed seventy acres of rice, which yielded an average of 75 bushels of rice per acre. The proof was in the paddies; in 1905, 1,000 groundwater-irrigated acres were planted, and, in 1906, nearly 6,000 were committed to rice. In that year, farmers could command $1.89 per hundredweight of rice—nearly $1.00 per bushel—and average yields that year topped 38 bushels per acre. With profits galore in prospect, farmers planted, and businesses such as rice mills and pump service shops sprang up to support them. The rice boom was on, made possible by ample groundwater for flood irrigation and a local soil well-suited to the needs of rice farming: that "buckshot" ground.

Underlying about 200,000 acres of eastern and southeastern Arkansas, including much of the Grand Prairie, is what is known as the Stuttgart soil series. It was named in 1964 for Stuttgart in Arkansas County and is made up of several soils, layered in a predictable order, although the thickness varies. Stuttgart series soils typically exhibit three layers: the upper two layers are of different silt loams, and the subsoils are rich in red and gray silty clays. The high percentage of clay in the subsoil gives it a slow permeability—that is, water tends to stay on or just below the ground surface, percolating slowly back into the aquifer. This makes the Stuttgart series ideal for rice culture since rice is a crop that, in the words of one farmer, "likes it hot and likes it wet."

The Stuttgart series is described by soil scientists as a member of a soil family of fine, smectitic, thermic albaquultic hapludalfs. The series is a member of the order *alfisol*; these are highly fertile, leached forest soils,

5   Author John Gould Fletcher raises the possibility that Fuller came to Arkansas earlier; he asserts that Fuller, born in Ohio in 1843, came to the state as a young man "to engage in what, no doubt, was sufficiently unproductive farming." John Gould Fletcher, *Arkansas*, reprint edition (Fayetteville: University of Arkansas Press, 1989), excerpted in: *University of Arkansas Rice Extension News* vol. 1, no. 2 (Winter 2009): 8.
6   William H. Fuller, "Early Rice Farming in Grand Prairie," *Arkansas Historical Quarterly* 14 (Spring 1955): 72.

whose subsoils are clayey. **Hapludalfs** are soils of humid climates. The **albaquultic** subgroup means that the series exhibits an abrupt textural change from layer to layer, has a moderately high water table during part of the year, and has a base saturation of less than 60 percent at 50 inches below the top of the subsoil. **Thermic** refers to an average annual soil temperature of 15 to 22 degrees Celsius (59° to 72° Fahrenheit). **Smectitic** indicates that the subsoil clay is dominated by minerals that expand when wet and contract when dry. **Fine** means the soil contains a high percentage of fine silt and clay particles. The official series description notes that the solum thickness—that is, the surface and subsoil layers

which have undergone the same soil-forming processes and conditions, and are the levels in which topsoil formation occurs—range from 60 to more than 80 inches.[7]

◊ ◊ ◊

Rice is usually planted beginning at the end of March, continuing through early June. Most of the planting is done in (relatively) dry fields by seed-drill, supplemented by "broadcast" seeding.

After planting comes irrigation, in the form of flooding: the edges of fields are usually leveed or raised in order to better retain water. Flood irrigation begins in late May or early June, after the rice seedlings have sprouted and produced four or five leaves. Harvest follows, beginning in August and continuing into October.

From its beginnings on a handful of Lonoke County acres, Arkansas's rice industry has spread statewide. In 2014, approximately 1,480,000 acres were harvested in rice statewide, spread across forty counties. The greatest concentration of rice production remains in the eastern part of the state, from the Grand Prairie north toward the bootheel of Missouri. Other areas with significant rice production include the Arkansas, Ouachita, and Red River valleys. Yields in 2014 averaged 7,560 pounds of rice per acre, for a total of 11,195,700,000 pounds or (if large numbers give you a headache) 5,590,400 short tons of rice. Prices for all rice that year (that is, medium- and long-grain rice combined) ranged from 14 to 14.6 cents per pound; as for the total value, you do the math. The result was that for 2014, Arkansas remained the nation's largest producer of rice, growing a little less than half of the nation's total.[8]

7   "Stuttgart" the Arkansas State Soil, U.S. Department of Agriculture, Natural Resources Conservation Service Bulletin. http://www.nrcs.usda.gov/wps/portal/nrcs/detail/ar/programs/?cid=nrcs142p2_035042 (accessed July 19, 2015). An alternate description has been advanced by researchers who characterize the soil as being fine, montmorillonitic (exhibiting significant presence of a type of clay), thermic typic natrudalfs (indicating the presence of exchangeable sodium).

8   USDA Economic Research Service, Rice yearbook 2015, http://www.ers.usda.gov/data-products/rice-yearbook-2015.aspx (accessed July 19, 2015) Table 1: "U.S. rice production, supply, use, and season-average farm price, total rice and by class"; USDA/NASS Crop Production Summary 2014, issued January 2015 http://www.usda.gov/nass/PUBS/TODAYRPT/cropan15.pdf (accessed July 19, 2015), "Rice Area Planted and Harvested, Yield, and Production by Class—States and United States: 2012–2014."

Most of the rice grown in Arkansas is of the long-grain variety, while other states (such as California) produce more short-grain and medium-grain rice. About 90 percent of the rice consumed in the United States is grown in the United States, and the United States is also the fourth-leading exporter of rice (exporting rice especially to Mexico, Canada, Haiti, and Japan). While more than half of the rice produced is served whole, rice also is an ingredient in processed food, pet food, and...beer. The brewing company Anheuser-Busch is reputed to be the largest single purchaser of U.S. rice, buying as much as eight percent of the annual crop; it owns rice mills in Arkansas and California.

◊ ◊ ◊

If there is a heart of Arkansas's rice empire, it is Stuttgart, the seat of Arkansas County. Founded in the 1870s as a German immigrant colony, it grew slowly in its first years despite railroad access and determined efforts to diversify through industrialization (to ease the area's dependence on stock raising and haying).

Stuttgart's fortunes changed with the arrival of rice as a staple crop. A trial plot was planted in 1902; it proved so successful that by 1907, enough rice was planted in the area to justify erection of a rice mill, completed in October of that year. In the years following World War I, rice prices tumbled and soared by turns, leading to uncertainty among Arkansas's rice producers as to how best to weather the storms of the market. In January 1921, a group of Arkansas rice farmers met in Stuttgart to discuss how they might attempt to stabilize the situation, as well as their prospects. Later that year, they formed a cooperative, the Arkansas Rice Growers' Cooperative Association, and moved to lease rice mills so that they could market their own rice as a finished product. Despite early setbacks, this first co-op persevered and inspired the creation of several rice-drying cooperatives scattered across Arkansas's expanding rice production area. In 1948, the Rice Growers' Cooperative first marketed its products under the trade name of "Riceland"; after a merger with a parallel croppers' cooperative, the organization adopted the name Riceland Foods in 1970. Stuttgart remains its headquarters. The city proudly claims the title of "Rice and Duck Capital of the World."

Rice and *duck*?

The Stuttgart soil series may be the perfect underpinning for rice, but it supports other crops as well. In Arkansas, these are usually listed as corn, soybeans, and other small grains, but crop and soil studies generally miss sight of two additional significant attributes of Stuttgart: waterfowl and those who hunt them. Millions of waterfowl fly south each winter to the Mississippi Delta and other regions of Arkansas. They are drawn by what one might call the eastern Arkansas trifecta: location, wetlands, and forage.

Decades of game observation have revealed that migrating waterfowl (and other birds) in the United States follow four broad routes: the Atlantic Flyway on the East Coast, the Pacific Flyway on the West Coast, the Central Flyway along the Rocky Mountains and their eastern slope (including the western edge of Arkansas), and the Mississippi Flyway, which brings birds to eastern Arkansas. The Mississippi Flyway describes a tall cone, the wide northern end of which begins in the prairies of central Canada and the northernmost tier of states. The flyway narrows as it crosses Missouri, so that it covers mainly the eastern half of Arkansas before narrowing further as birds head south for the Gulf of Mexico. Ducks and geese begin showing up in Arkansas as early as late summer and their numbers increase as the weather cools. By December, millions of these travelers populate

PLOWING IS DONE BY TRACTORS IN THE RICE BELT, NEAR STUTTGART, ARK.

waterways and wetlands across the state.

A second element of eastern Arkansas's "duck magnetism" consists of its abundant wetlands; the soil series that keeps water close to the surface ensures ample wetlands for ducks to rest in during their migrations. The work that decades of farmers have done to level these fields and to keep water on them has made them nigh well irresistible to waterfowl flocks looking for an agreeable place to rest from the hard work of migrating. The third element is forage, and in this, the rice paddies of eastern Arkansas excel: most ducks, including the mallard, feed from grains and seeds, as well as acorns and aquatic insects, which abound in Arkansas wetlands. The rise of rice cultivation in eastern Arkansas in the early decades of the twentieth century, and consequent large duck populations, made the region profoundly attractive to both fowl and fowlers. The overhunting, both by residents and by out-of-state sport and market hunters, that led to the so-called "Big Lake Wars" was not a result of the rice boom but had a profound effect in the form of the creation of the state's Game and Fish Commission, which would ultimately take responsibility for managing and preserving waterfowl populations.

Today, Arkansas plays host to over two dozen species of geese and ducks. These include dabbling ducks such as teal, wood ducks, and mallards; diving (or sea) ducks including the canvasback, the bufflehead, and the goldeneye; and the black-bellied whistling duck, mergansers, and Canada geese. Populations vary by season and with climate shifts—a dry year will encourage waterfowl to try their luck elsewhere—but annual wildfowl population surveys help index the rise and fall of the population. The 2015 Midwinter Survey of the Mississippi Alluvial Valley of eastern Arkansas produced an estimate of 1,227,194 ducks, including over 925,000 mallards.[9]

To harvest such a crop requires hunters. Many hunters. Hunters from Arkansas, hunters from elsewhere. Hunters with money and hunters with little. Hunters with Remington 870s and treasured Winchester Model 12s, camouflaged synthetic-stocked wonders, well-worn Auto-5s, or maybe, once in a great while, something like an A.H. Fox Super Fox side-by-side with Burt Becker barrels.

And they come to the Grand Prairie; they come to Stuttgart.

A 2011 survey revealed that approximately 572,000 Arkansans participated in some sort of hunting, racking up an impressive 10,006,000 person/days of hunting; non-residents spent an additional 961,000 hunting days in Arkansas fields. Residents and non-

◇ ◇ ◇

"A duck call in the hands of the unskilled is one of conservation's greatest assets."

—Nash Buckingham, *De Shootinest Gent'man*, 1941.

◇ ◇ ◇

9   Arkansas Game and Fish Commission, *Aerial Waterfowl Survey Report*, January 5–9, 2015. http://www.agfc.com/resources/Publications/AerialWaterfowlSurveyJan2015.pdf (accessed July 19, 2015).

residents alike devoted significant pocket change to the pursuit of pursuit: a sum of over a billion dollars was spent by Arkansas hunters on food and lodging, transportation, hunting equipment, and related expenses. This survey did not break down expenditures by region or hunting season, but the Grand Prairie sees its share of the harvest: about seventy duck clubs and resorts are to be found within an hour's drive of Stuttgart, and during hunting season, their patrons bring, by a 2005 estimate, a million dollars per day to Stuttgart.[10]

A state soil is a soil that has special significance to a particular state. According to the National Resources Conservation Service (which, back in simpler times, was known as the Soil Conservation Service), each state in the Union (including those which once were Confederated) has selected a state soil, twenty of which have been legislatively established. These "Official State Soils" share the same level of distinction as official state flowers and birds.

The first state to designate a distinctive dirt was Nebraska, which memorialized the Holdrege series in 1979. The next state to take the plunge was Vermont, which honored the Tunbridge soil series in 1985. Other states followed in desultory fashion over the next decade, suggesting no particular rush on the part of Arkansas's sister states to designate the earthy foundations of their respective fortunes. The year 1997, however, saw a seeming outburst of soil consciousness: no less than four states designated official soils that year: Alabama, California, West Virginia, and Arkansas.[11]

Act 890 of the Arkansas General Assembly of 1997 designated the Stuttgart soil series the official state soil. The bill was introduced by Representative Wanda Northcutt of District 81, which encompassed parts of five counties (Arkansas, Desha, Jefferson, Lonoke, and Prairie) noted for their agricultural production founded, literally, on the presence of the Stuttgart soils. Northcutt's measure noted that other states "having significant concerns for soil, have by legislative enactment chosen a locally unique soil series as their official state soil" and asserted that Arkansas, too, cared about its soil. It continued with language extolling the soil's contributions to the state's agriculture, forests, and pasturelands, as well as its wildlife habitats, beautiful landscapes, homes, and communities. The catalogue of justifications ended with an anticlimactic but frank "WHEREAS, the State of Arkansas has yet to designate a state soil...." The measure was approved on March 27, 2007. Perhaps predictably, it lacked an emergency clause.

In choosing a state grain, Arkansas is part of a much smaller, more exclusive club. To date, only four states have designated an official state grain: Minnesota (wild rice, 1977); Wisconsin (corn, 1989); California (rice, 2013); and Arkansas.[12] Rice was designated the official grain of the state by Act 513 of the Eighty-Sixth Arkansas General

10   Glen R. Sparks, "Ducks and Rice Are Staples in Stuttgart, Arkansas," *The Regional Economist*, October 2005, https://www.stlouisfed.org/publications/regional-economist/october-2005/ducks-and-rice-are-staples-in-stuttgart-ark (accessed July 19, 2015).

11   California's choice of state soil series, the San Joaquin, is also known as a good one in which to grow rice, as well as other irrigated crops such as wheat, figs, almonds, and grapes, as well as for pasturage. Like the Stuttgart series, San Joaquin soils formed in old alluvium, although in uneven topography rather than the riverine flatlands of the Stuttgart. A hardpan layer a few feet beneath the surface restricts roots and water percolation. San Joaquin soils are classified in USDA soil taxonomy as **fine, mixed, active, thermic abruptic durixeralfs**.

12   Or, perhaps, the number might be 4.5; half credit goes to Illinois, which in 2003 designated popcorn, which certainly qualifies as a grain, as its official state snack. Sigh.

Assembly. Introduced by Representative Bruce Maloch of Magnolia in Columbia County, the act was approved on March 27, 2007. The measure was as plain and unornamented as its subject; no justifications were offered for the designation, and a peculiar disclaimer assured that no state agency's publication would be required to be revised in order to list or display the state grain. It would be permissible, however, to include the information in future publications or revisions of existing ones.

For further reading:

Arkansas Game and Fish Commission. *Aerial Waterfowl Survey Report, January 5-9, 2015.* http://www.agfc.com/resources/Publications/AerialWaterfowlSurveyJan2015.pdf (accessed August 10, 2015).

Fuller, W. H. "Early Rice Farming on Grand Prairie." *Arkansas Historical Quarterly* 14 (Spring 1955): 72–74.

Gates, John. "Groundwater Irrigation and the Development of the Grand Prairie Rice Industry." *Arkansas Historical Quarterly* 64 (Winter 2005): 394–413.

Littlefield, Daniel C. *Rice and Slaves: Ethnicity and the Slave Trade in Colonial South Carolina.* Baton Rouge: Louisiana State University Press, 1981.

Opala, Joseph. *The Gullah: Rice, Slavery and the Sierra Leone-American Connection,* Yale University Gilder Lehrman Center for the Study of Slavery, Resistance, and Abolition. http://www.yale.edu/glc/gullah/cont.htm (accessed August 10, 2015).

Sparks, Glen R. "Rice and Ducks Are Staples in Stuttgart, Arkansas." *The Regional Economist* (October 2005). https://www.stlouisfed.org/publications/regional-economist/october-2005/ducks-and-rice-are-staples-in-stuttgart-ark (accessed August 10, 2015).

Teske, Steven. "Rice Industry." *Encyclopedia of Arkansas History & Culture.* http://www.encyclopediaofarkansas.net/encyclopedia/entry-detail.aspx?search=1&entryID=380 (accessed August 10, 2015).

Tuten, James H. *Lowcountry Time and Tide: The Fall of the South Carolina Rice Kingdom.* Columbia: University of South Carolina Press, 2010.

Ware, David. "Official State Grain, a.k.a Rice." *Encyclopedia of Arkansas History & Culture.* http://www.encyclopediaofarkansas.net/encyclopedia/entry-detail.aspx?search=1&entryID=5250 (accessed August 10, 2015).

Williams, C. Fred. "Agriculture." *Encyclopedia of Arkansas History & Culture.* http://www.encyclopediaofarkansas.net/encyclopedia/entry-detail.aspx?search=1&entryID=385 (accessed August 10, 2015).

CHAPTER 16: STATE HISTORIC COOKING VESSEL

Or, If the Pot Calls the Kettle Black, What Does the Kettle Call the Pot?

A Dutch oven is not, strictly speaking, an oven. Nor is it demonstrably Dutch in origin. Its design is immediately recognizable in its generalities—flat bottom, tight lid, stout bail-style handle—but has many variations, some large, others obscure. It is iron, except when it is steel, or aluminum, or even ceramic. It is deep, usually, but can also be shallow. With its tight lid in place and covered in campfire coals or charcoal briquettes, it can serve as an oven, as its name suggests. Using this vessel, you can stew, braise, boil, bake, fry, or roast. Available in good hardware and sporting goods establishments, it is almost never the lightest vessel for a particular cooking task or technique, but it is competent in most uses. For preparing savory baked goods and succulent main courses outside the confines of a kitchen, it is unexcelled. Success requires practice, yet the vessel is forgiving: If a disaster occurs, simply scrape out the evidence, re-season the metal, and try again.

The Dutch oven is one of the characteristic cooking vessel of early America and pioneer Arkansas, the general form of which has endured for more than two centuries. In recognition of this, it is one of Arkansas's officially designated state symbols: official historic cooking vessel. John G. Ragsdale Jr. of El Dorado, whose scholarship has added much to popular appreciation of the Dutch oven, praises "the magnificent service the vessels have provided through the past centuries and continue to provide for us today."[1]

The Dutch oven was designated in 2001 as the state's "historic cooking vessel" to indicate and celebrate the good work of the cooking implement in Arkansas's history. Dutch ovens were brought into the state by Euro-American explorers and settlers and were in wide use by the early 1800s. By the time of statehood, anecdotal evidence suggests that most Arkansas households probably had Dutch ovens in use in their hearths or cooking fires; their use continued long afterward. Today, campers, hunters, Cub and Boy Scouts, and even backyard chefs who enjoy the challenge of plumbing the secrets of this storied antique carry on the tradition of Dutch oven cookery.

The Dutch oven in its usual form is neither a pot nor a kettle; it is instead an inspired hybrid. A pot is traditionally understood as a cooking vessel that tapers inward toward the top; a kettle will taper toward its base. Pots of earlier days were more often bulbous than straight-sided, while kettles tended toward straight walls. Either might have a lid fitted on it, pots perhaps a little more often. Pots tended to have rounded bottoms, while kettles were stamped flat. Both were commonly suspended over fires, hence they were made with "ears" from which they were suspended.

A classic Dutch oven combines elements of pot and kettle. It is a high-sided cast-metal vessel, usually with three integral legs which provide both support and space for coals to heat the oven from the bottom. The typical Dutch oven has a flat bottom and a tight-fitting lid to contain the heat and moisture inside. The top is heavy enough to restrain a little pressure but loose enough to allow dangerous pressure to escape. This is no pressure-cooker, a time bomb ready to explode by the campfire.

The lid has a central bail or knob handle, allowing it to be removed during cooking to observe or stir the cooking food. The oven body has ears cast integral with it located at or near the rim. These may be vertical or horizontal in orientation; their purpose is to allow it to be lifted by a bail or hooks. The sides of the oven usually have vertical walls with a smaller diameter at the bottom than the top. The lid is either near flat or in the shape of a very shallow dome, with a raised rim in place to help to hold coals. Some deep pots with straight, tapered sides; a fitted top; and a handle protruding from one side in addition to bail ears have been styled "Dutch ovens," but Dutch oven fundamentalists sometimes quibble: The oven should be portable, and the handles just get in the way.[2]

◇ ◇ ◇

The question of the origin of the term "Dutch oven" is a little murky.

The traditional story, recounted by Ragsdale and others, connects the name to early Hollander prowess in

1   John G. Ragsdale, *Dutch Ovens Chronicled: Their Use in the United States* (Fayetteville: University of Arkansas Press, 1981), xi.
2   John Ragsdale and others refer to these as "hearth ovens," since the handle can be useful for moving the pot in and out of the fireplace's heat. Doing this with a full pot requires a strong grip and very efficient insulation; the handle will, after a while cooking, be as warm as the oven itself and will hold that heat for some time.

casting iron, which both led to cast-iron pots being imported into England from the Low Countries in the late 1600s and inspired what some might call a bit of English ingenuity.[3] In this version, in 1704, English foundry owner Abraham Darby travels to Holland to inspect the casting of brass vessels in dry-sand molds. Returning to England, the story goes, he improves on the Dutch method, developing a technique for sand-casting iron vessels, for which he receives a patent in 1708. From this point, the story goes, he goes into production of iron pots at Coalbrookdale, which were then exported to the ends of the earth, or wherever the British could sell them. Ragsdale, echoing previous students of the implement, suggests that the sobriquet "Dutch oven" owes its character to Darby having adapted the Dutch system in order to get his own patent.

Well, maybe.

Abraham Darby was indeed a vital figure in the rise of metalworking in England's industrial evolution. The son of a Staffordshire Quaker farmer, he first set up making malt mills for breweries, but in about 1703 or '04, he went into partnership with other Quakers of Bristol to form a brass "battery," where he and his associates employed "Dutchmen" to make brass pots and pans using a trip hammer. Darby also experimented with other techniques for producing hollowware, developing a method for casting pots in "greensand" molds, previously used only for smaller castings.[4] This enabled pots to be mass produced and to be thinner than those made by the traditional process of casting in loam molds.

What gave Darby the idea? In the early eighteenth century, Dutch craftsmen were using cast iron to make hollowware (pots and pans). Iron was cheaper than brass or other cuprous alloys, had a higher melting point, and was more impact-resistant, although tending to be brittle and prone to rusting. Darby went to the Netherlands in 1704 to study Dutch foundrymen's methods. He set up a small works in Bristol, the Cheese Lane Foundry, which initially cast brass pots. Soon, however, Darby and apprentice Quaker John Thomas began to experiment with new (and cheaper) ways of making hollowware out of iron. In 1707, they patented their innovative sand-casting method. Now they could produce cast-iron pots at a good price, undercutting their Dutch counterparts.

All of this is well and good but does not really explain the name. Abraham Darby did not use it to describe his vessels and, in fact, he went on quickly to larger things. In 1709, he moved to Coalbrookdale in Shropshire, on the Welsh border, where all the raw materials he needed for making iron were close at hand. He took over a derelict furnace there and rebuilt it. He started to experiment again, this time using coking coal instead of charcoal to smelt the iron. Coking coal was plentiful, had fewer impurities, and produced a better quality of metal, so it was a vast improvement. This change of fuel was a major breakthrough, and the consequent mass production of quality iron helped accelerate the Industrial Revolution.[5]

Other writers suggest that the earliest Dutch ovens were cast in Pennsylvania or Massachusetts, where iron ore and coal for heat in the processing of the cast iron were available. The purported creator's name is not known

---

3   Others might call it industrial espionage or intellectual piracy.
4   "Greensand" is, in fact, damp sand, "green" like "green" wood. It is used to make expendable molds and, in addition to silica sand, includes small amounts of clay and sometimes coal.
5   M. W. Finn, "Abraham Darby and the Coke-Smelting Process." *Economica* 26, no. 101 (February 1959): 54–59; "Abraham Darby I," Quakers in the World, http://quakersintheworld.org/quakers-in-action/271 (accessed August 10, 2015). See also T. S. Ashton, *Iron and Steel in the Industrial Revolution* (Manchester, UK: Manchester University Press, 1924) and H. Hamilton, *The English Copper and Brass Industries to 1800* (London: Longmans, Green & Co., 1926).

but is sometimes alluded to as a cook who, in the early 1700s, commissioned a local foundry to make a distinctive vessel of his own design, which proved so successful that high demand caused a rush of more ovens to be cast. This origin story plays well to the American tradition of celebrating individual innovators, but there is no known name to associate with the development of the inspired hybrid design—nor does this version of the vessel's creation explain the name, except to the extent that if Pennsylvania is selected as the place of origin, there is a "Dutch" connection in the form of the Pennsylvania Dutch (Deutsch, as in German) culture which is, of course, neither Dutch nor metallurgically inclined.

Or, is the name a sly dig at a makeshift?

Let us leave the oven by the side of the etymological road for the time being and look at "Dutch." The word shows up in English in the fourteenth century and was used at first to refer to Germans in general; by the seventeenth century, the sense had narrowed to mean "of the Netherlands," which coincided with these same Hollanders becoming a united, independent state and incidentally the subject of English commercial and military attention and rivalry.[6]

With that rivalry arose a dismissive or pejorative association: the word "Dutch," when used as an adjective, was long a dismissive descriptor used by English speakers for things they regarded as inferior, irregular, or contrary to normal (i.e., English) practice.[7] Examples of this dismissive spin include Dutch treat (no treat at all; everybody pays their own way), Dutch uncle (the kind who dispenses not-always-useful advice instead of treats), Dutch widow (prostitute), Dutch bargain (in which, of two parties to a transaction, one gets much the better end of the deal than the other), Dutchman (in the building trades, a piece or wedge inserted to hide the fault in a badly made joint or to plug a hole or cover a gap; in theater, a narrow strip of cloth to conceal the joining spot between two scenery flats), and, of course, Dutch courage (the sort contained in a gin bottle).[8]

Cook lifting lid full of coals from Dutch oven used for baking bread, ca. 1939.

The *Oxford English Dictionary* notes that the term "Dutch oven" appears around 1769. The OED lists it among the words describing things from Holland, but perhaps it is here used in the slighting sense. By this time, the dismissive or pejorative adjectival use of "Dutch" was well-

---

6   In Holland itself, *duitsch* was used to describe people from what is today's Germany; in the English colonies of North America, "Dutch" referred to immigrants from the Rheinland (Rhineland) or Germanic-speaking Switzerland. This makes sense, *ja?*

7   Curiously, the English have never attempted to attach this adjective to the custom of driving on the right-hand side of the road, contrary to the best British practice. The author, in his salad days, heard several English acquaintances refer to this as "Continental," perhaps expressing mystification or envy rather than patronization.

8   The Dutch themselves figured out what their rivals from "Perfidious Albion" were up to. For decades, they went along with it, grumbling all the way to the bank. But in 1934, Dutch officials were ordered by their government to stop using the term "Dutch." Instead, they were to rewrite their sentences so as to employ the official "Netherlands" or a derivative thereof. See Hugh Rawson, *Wicked Words* (New York: Crown Publishers, 1989).

established, so it is reasonable to at least suspect that the name reflects someone cocking a snook at the idea of the iron-pot-as-oven. Association of Holland with the manufacture of cheap iron pots likely reinforced the suitability of this familiar name. Whatever the reason, the term for the vessel was known and used by the mid-eighteenth century. And it crossed the seas: Ragsdale has established that, in 1775, a notice in the *Pennsylvania Gazette* listed Dutch ovens for sale made by the Batsto Iron Works of Batsto, New Jersey, founded in 1766 along the banks of the Batsto River.[9]

◇ ◇ ◇

To understand the appeal of the Dutch oven, it is worth looking at the state of the cooking art in the eighteenth and early nineteenth centuries, particularly the ways in which baked goods were made. It was not until well into the nineteenth century that iron cooking ranges with integral ovens were common, even in established towns. Instead, household cooking was done in a fireplace or hearth, usually floored with flagstones and featuring some arrangement for suspending a pot over the fire.[10] Often, kitchen hearths included a "bake oven," a small cave of brick or stone built into the side of the hearth, with a small door which opened into a larger, domed space and flue. Using this oven was not uncomplicated. First, the responsible cook would build a large fire inside the bake oven, stoking it and allowing it to burn for several hours. The fire heated the stone and brick of the oven. Once it had burned down, the coals and ashes were scraped out, the interior quickly swabbed to remove still-smoldering ash, and then foods to be baked were placed inside, often directly on the hot stone floor. The heat radiating from the brick and stone would then cook the contents of the oven over the course of several hours.

The oven was a wonderful thing—but not every household had one, particularly in the developing homesteads and communities of America's westward expansion. Moreover, using the oven required a commitment of time and attention. An efficient cook would usually prepare many loaves of bread, pies, and dishes such as baked beans all at once in this way, to make best use of the work that had gone into preparing the

9   Ragsdale, *Dutch Ovens Chronicled*, 62; See also Barbara Solem, *Batsto Village: Jewel of the Pines* (Medford, NJ: Plexus Publishing, 2014), 12-13 for full text of the June 7, 1775, advertisement as well as a good concise history of the iron works. The contents of the advertisement, which touted "A Great variety of iron pots, kettles, Dutch ovens, and oval fish kettles, wither with or without covers, skillets of different sizes, being much lighter, neater and superior in quality to any imported from Great Britain..." plus other large kettles, sugar mill-gudgeons, grating bars of different lengths, grist-mill rounds, weights of all sizes, Fuller plates, stoves of different sizes, sash weight, and forge hammers. This all constituted a stout nose-thumbing directed toward Britain and the restrictions of the Iron Act of 1750, a Parliamentary measure that restricted the manufacture of finished iron products while encouraging the production of pig iron for export to Britain.

10   Native American women baked bread by wrapping a cornmeal dough in leaves, then cooking it either on a hot stone or in the ashes of a fire. This technique was the same as used in cultures around the world over millennia. In England, baking on the hearth is associated with King Alfred of Wessex (849–899). The tradition continued into the modern era; it was common for pioneer households to consume "ash cakes" baked on the swept stone floor of a heated hearth.

oven for use. Also, in warm weather, the oven was a very hot neighbor. Baking was an all-day process, and even after the coals had been raked out of the oven, the stone or bricks would radiate heat not just into the oven but also into the surrounding room for many hours. In winter, this was doubtless welcome, but warmer months encouraged ways to get around the use of the built-in oven. The iron pot known as the Dutch oven offered an attractive alternative. It could rest in the hearth or even outdoors and, with a little care, could produce modest quantities of bread or pies. And, as a bonus, these would be virtually free of the ash inescapable in using a traditional full-sized oven, thanks to the tight lid.

The Dutch oven was also, unlike the hearth oven, portable.[11] For individuals or families on the move, it offered a way to prepare food that did not necessarily involve frying or boiling or roasting on a stick over a flame.

◊ ◊ ◊

The first vessels to be known as Dutch ovens were made of cast iron and, even today, there are many who assume that any true Dutch oven should be made of the same black metal. Tradition is a powerful force, but so is gravity. Over the decades and the centuries, the words "iron" and Dutch oven have seemed to naturally run together—a sort of culinary magnetism dooming the cooks who love them to aches, pains, and muscle strains. Of course, the larger the oven, the greater the pain.

Dutch ovens generally range in width or diameter from 8 to 14 inches—or, in some cases, 16 inches, depth varying from 2 to as much as 6 inches. Even in the small sizes, that's a lot of iron. Cast iron is not particularly dense, as metals go, but its heft is not to be underestimated. A shallow 8-inch oven, with its lid, weighs over 7 pounds. A deepish 12-incher, again with lid, weighs just 17. A deep 16-inch example with its lid on weighs 32 pounds, exclusive of contents. Some go even larger: Phyllis Speer, reigning maven of Arkansas Dutch-oven cooking, owns some twenty-six Dutch ovens, the largest one weighing 150 pounds without its lid.[12]

That's a lot of iron.

Happily, the late nineteenth century saw a metallurgical revolution: the advent of the light and rust-resisting metal aluminum (see chapter on the state rock for all you really need to know about this). Charles Dickens had prophesied in the 1850s that the new miracle metal would give copper and brass a run for their money in making pots and pans. When vast quantities of it became available at cost price after 1880, his prophesy was fulfilled. By 1889, aluminum Dutch ovens weighing less than half as much as their iron twins were on the market, and they have been ever since.

> ### To Make Doughnuts
>
> One quart of milk, three eggs, a pound and a quarter of sugar, three-quarters of a pound butter, a little ginger, one tea cup of yeast, flour enough to make a soft dough, let it rise, then fry in hot lard.
>
> Anonymous, *The Cook Not Mad, or Rational Cookery* (Watertown, NY: Knowlton & Rice, 1831), 36.

---

11   Or relatively so. Dutch ovens weighing as much as 150 pounds have been manufactured, straining the usual understanding of the term as well as the muscles of their bearers.

12   Jeannie Stone, "Flavor: The Glory of the Dutch Oven," *Arkansas Gazette*, July 1 2010, http://www.arkansasonline.com/news/2010/jul/01/flavor-glory-dutch-oven-20100701-0-0/ (accessed June 4 2015).

> ### Ash cakes
> [Mix] a pinch of soda, hot water, a pinch of salt and corn meal. The water must be hot. Make the paste just stiff enough to handle. Rake back a clean place on the hearth, then put the cake down and cover it with hot coals and ashes. When it has cooked done enough you can dust it off with a cloth. You can bake ash cakes in the oven and they're just as good. Don't put any grease on them and very, very little soda.
>
> L. M. Rall of Little Rock, describing her mother's ash cakes, from the WPA "America Eats" files, excerpted in Mark Kurlansky, *The Food of A Younger Land* (New York: Riverhead Books, 2009), 116.

How do the respective materials measure up?

For ease of carry and manipulation, aluminum takes the honors. A 12-inch aluminum oven weighs about 7 pounds as opposed to about 20 pounds for a cast-iron oven.

In spite of the claims of devotees of cast iron, aluminum is probably easier to care for. Aluminum does not rust, so it withstands soap and water with no qualms. Cast iron can also be washed, but care should be taken to protect the "seasoning"—that is, the layer of polymerized oil that seals and protects the cooking surface, imparting a limited non-sticking property to the iron pot and inhibiting rust. Conventional iron-users' wisdom holds that soap should never be used to clean a seasoned oven because it will dissolve the formed protective barrier and embed itself into the pores of the metal where it will return to taint the next meal. Grown men clad in buckskins have been known to break down into tears after seeing their prized Dutch ovens—blackened and greasy inside after years of roasting, baking, frying, and braising—made bright by well-meaning friends or spouses employing such proscribed substances as scrubbing pads, scouring powder, and dishwashing liquid. Phyllis Speer, on the other hand, washes her pots with warm, soapy water, drying them promptly to prevent rust and coating her pots with a film of mineral oil before storing.[13]

As for ease of use, each material has its quirks. Aluminum heats more quickly than cast iron and reacts quickly to temperature changes—so it will cool down quickly as well, requiring a watchful eye on the fire. Its quick temperature transmission also means that it may cook unevenly, unless the heat source is carefully distributed under, around, and atop the pot. Cast-iron ovens, on the other hand, heat slowly, distribute heat more evenly than aluminum, and keep heat longer, making them better choices for cooking on windy days.

Enthusiasts of cast iron are fond of reminding those who use aluminum pots that their light and shiny ovens can melt over a hot fire. There is a grain of truth to this: The melting point of aluminum cast alloy is around 1200° F as opposed to cast iron's melting point of over 2000° F. It is possible to reach temperatures of 1200°F if too many coals are used during cooking, the bottom of the Dutch oven is left in direct contact with the coals, or one's fire-pit is such that prevailing winds create a draft, fanning the coals' heat higher. A little care taken with the fire will, however, minimize chances of a campfire alloy meltdown. Aluminum's quick dissipation of heat, combined with the food inside the pot, should help derail all but intentional metal failures.

Today, Dutch ovens come in a wide variety of sizes, materials, finishes, and even configuration. "Camp

---

13   Stone, "The Glory of the Dutch Oven."

Dutch oven" is a term used to indicate the traditional oven with a flat bottom, integral supporting legs, and the tight-fitting lid with a rim for containing coals. Some vessels are styled Dutch ovens by their makers but lack the legs, flat lid, and even the wire bail handle of the "true gen." They are obviously meant for use in a stove oven or on a stove top. Some feature high-domed lids unsuited to supporting charcoal but which cause moisture to drip back onto the cooking food, basting it. Some are even colorfully finished in porcelain enamel inside and out, providing a smooth and rust-free surface, albeit one that might not hold up to rough camp usage. As such, they might more properly be termed "kitchen ovens" or braising pots, since they are admirably suited to the cooking method in which the main ingredients are first browned, then slowly simmered in a small quantity of liquid. Purists sniff at such vessels sharing the appellation of "Dutch oven," but the proof is in the pudding—or, perhaps, in whatever is braised, roasted, fried, or boiled. The precise configuration of a Dutch oven may be less important than the spirit in which it is used. If the pot is heavy enough, has a tight enough lid, and can be used in high heat, it will serve.

One attraction of the Dutch oven is its versatility. One modern Dutch oven cookbook author asserts that it "substitutes for a host of outdoor cooking utensils."[14] Compensating for this simplification of the kitchen vessel roster, however, Dutch oven enthusiasts of today often end up acquiring a host of subsidiary equipment,[15] the better to use this all-rounder cooking pot. Phyllis Speer's list of necessary accoutrements, aside from the ovens themselves, includes the following:

Hog pan (or oil-changing pan) to contain coals

Shortening (solid vegetable oil)

Mineral oil

Vegetable oil spray

Cast-iron trivet (on which to place the oven lid while checking the food)

Chimney-style charcoal starter (perfect coals in 20 minutes)

Welding gloves

Lid lifter

Plastic "toughies" (scrub pads)

Paper towels

Oak charcoal briquettes ("briquettes are easier than campfire coals")[16]

Most modern Dutch oven authorities recommend using charcoal briquettes, for reasons of convenience, consistency, and lessening environmental impacts on camp sites. This may strike some who embrace the Dutch oven as a chance to return to simpler times through simpler cookery as a cheat or shortcut, but in light of the Dutch oven itself representing a traditional shortcut around heating up a hearth, this somehow seems

---

14   Sheila Mills, *The Outdoor Dutch Oven Cookbook* (New York: McGraw-Hill, 2008), 2.

15   Not to mention multiple Dutch ovens; if one is good, then two, or four, offer all sorts of additional ways to get into trouble while fixing a camp supper.

16   Stone, "The Glory of the Dutch Oven."

appropriate. Formulas or recommendations are found in every Dutch oven cookbook, and an online site devoted to "primitive" camping and cooking offers the best oven techniques, including how many briquettes on top and bottom will produce a desired heat level. These recommendations vary among authors, but on one point all seem to agree: the best method for learning the ways of the Dutch oven is to cook in one.

◇ ◇ ◇

In 1997, the Utah legislature approved House Bill 203, designating the Dutch oven as the official state cooking pot. The measure, sponsored by state representative Craig Buttars, offered no grounds for the designation but simply ordered an annotation of the Utah code to include the oven in the list of state symbols. The measure was signed by Governor Michael Leavitt on March 13. The reasons for the designation were not spelled out in the bill's text. Factors probably included the state's conscious cultivation of memories of its settlement heritage and pioneer lifeways and the location of the International Dutch Oven Society's headquarters in the city of Logan, Utah.

In the 2001 regular session of the Eighty-Third General Assembly of the State of Arkansas, Senator Joseph K. Mahony II introduced Senate Bill 402 to designate the Dutch oven as the official state historic cooking vessel. Senator Mahony represented the Second District, in which is located El Dorado, the hometown of John G. Ragsdale Jr.—engineer, longtime Boy Scout leader, and Arkansas's scholar of the history and use of the Dutch oven. The measure was slightly more verbose than the Utah instrument: justifications for the designation included assertions that "Dutch ovens were used in 1803 when Arkansas was a part of the Louisiana Purchase area;...in 1836 when Arkansas became one of the United States of America; and...have served as cooking vessels and bake kettles on hearths and camping sites of settlers in the State of Arkansas..." It became Act 476 of 2001 and was signed by Governor Mike Huckabee on February 28, 2001.

Dutch oven cooking demonstration at Pinnacle Mountain State Park, near Little Rock.

◇ ◇ ◇

Not to be outdone by their eastern neighbors, the solons of Texas moved in 2005 to designate the Dutch oven as the state's official cooking implement. Senate Concurrent Resolution 9 enumerated previous symbolic designations, pointed to the Dutch oven as "ideal for moist-cooking methods, such as stewing or braising," and invoked both Scouting and the Lone Star Dutch Oven Society in justifying the designation. In the same session, they thoughtfully provided the necessary logistical support for this designation by singling out the chuck wagon as the official state vehicle of Texas.

For further reading:

Acts of Arkansas 2001.

Allen, Ann. *The Orphan's Friend and Housekeeper's Assistant, Composed Upon Temperance Principles...With Variety of Useful Information And Receipts Never Before Published.* Boston: James Munroe & Co., 1845.

Carhart, Arthur H. *The Outdoorsman's Cookbook,* revised edition. New York: Macmillan, 1955.

Haws, Susan. *Dutch Oven Cooking.* Utah State University Summit County Extension Service 2010. http://pioneer.utah.gov/research/utah_symbols/documents/DutchOvenCooking.pdf (accessed August 12, 2015).

Hopkins, Lynn. *Dutch Oven Secrets*, 5th edition. Bountiful, UT: Horizon Publishers, 1994.

Kurlansky, Mark. *The Food of a Younger Land.* New York: Riverhead Books, 2009.

Lone Star Dutch Oven Society. http://www.lsdos.com/ (accessed August 12, 2015).

Mills, Sheila. *The Outdoor Dutch Oven Cookbook.* New York: McGraw-Hill, 2008.

Ragsdale, John G. *Dutch Oven Cooking*, 4th edition. Lanham, MD: Taylor Trade Publishing, 2006.

———. *Dutch Ovens Chronicled: Their Use in the United States.* Fayetteville: University of Arkansas Press, 1981.

———. "Official State Cooking Vessel, a.k.a. Dutch Oven." *Encyclopedia of Arkansas History & Culture.* http://www.encyclopediaofarkansas.net/encyclopedia/entry-detail.aspx?search=1&entryID=530 (accessed August 12, 2015).

Rawson, Hugh. *Wicked Words.* New York: Crown Publishers, 1989.

Smith, Merril D. *History of American Cooking.* Santa Barbara, CA: ABC-CLIO, 2013.

Solem, Barbara. *Batsto Village: Jewel of the Pines.* Medford, NJ: Plexus Publishing, 2014.

Stevens, Molly. *All About Braising: The Art of Uncomplicated Cooking.* New York: Norton, 2004.

Stone, Jeannie. "Flavor: The Glory of the Dutch Oven." *Arkansas Gazette,* July 1, 2010. http://www.arkansasonline.com/news/2010/jul/01/flavor-glory-dutch-oven-20100701-0-0/ (accessed August 12, 2015).

CHAPTER 17: STATE BUTTERFLY

Diana Fritillary: Or, A Huntress that Shows the Dice

Some state symbols are particularly portentous, in the sense of implying big meanings, big ambitions. They are the equivalent of a massive, properly aged porterhouse steak laid out for admiration and eventual consumption, generally by someone who can afford it. They are meant to be improving and inspirational but to have no tincture of fun or whimsy about them—after all, state symbols are supposed to be serious business. On the other hand, some symbols seem to be chosen with a certain commercial consideration in mind, or perhaps a spirit of boasting: "Look and see what we've got!" Such designations can be justified on promotional or educational grounds and are the fundamental stuff of presentations in elementary school classrooms.

And then, there are designations that really need no justification, as their merits are self-evident. Someone—perhaps it was Robert Heinlein?—once wrote, "Kittens need no excuse." Some things deserve the status of symbols simply because it is obvious that they ought to be. Any practical significance is secondary to their beauty or charm. Exhibit "A": the Diana fritillary, Arkansas's official state butterfly.

The Diana (technically known as the *Speyeria diana*)[1] was so designated in 2007, by Act 156 of the

---

1   The "Speyeria" in the Diana's species name honors Dr. Adolf Speyer, a leading German entomologist of the nineteenth century.

Arkansas General Assembly. State Representative John Paul Wells of Logan County introduced the measure, as well he might: Logan County is one of the state's butterfly "hot spots." His measure justified the designation on the grounds of the Diana's educational importance and its value in promoting tourism to Arkansas (this, particularly, had a connection to Logan County). But before these, the measure paid tribute to the beauty of the big butterfly, a quality which, for those lepidopterists, renders the other justifications unnecessary.

The Diana fritillary belongs, like all other butterflies and moths, to the insect order *Lepidoptera*. *Lepidoptera* is Latin for "scaly wing"—which in turn derives from the Greek λεπίς (lepis) meaning scale and πτερόν (pteron) meaning wing. The *Lepidoptera* (which are in fact covered, body and wing, with tiny scales) are among the most successful groups of insects, in terms of proliferation: they can be found on all continents except Antarctica and can thrive in biomes ranging from desert to rainforest and coastal flatlands to mountains. They favor climes that feature flowering plants, and they play an important role in the pollination of these flowers. To date, nearly 180,000 species of *Lepidoptera* have been described worldwide, with North America hosting more than 700 species of butterfly and another 11,000 species of moths.[2]

More than 150 species of butterflies can be spotted throughout the year in Arkansas; of these, about 132 are year-round residents. The Diana fritillary is one of the most spectacular. Diana was the Roman goddess of light and life (Artemis in Greek mythology), later known as the goddess of the moon and hunting, and as a protector of women. "Fritillary" derives from the Latin *fritillus*, meaning "dice-box," referring to the spot patterns that distinguish the Diana's wings. The Diana belongs to the family *Nymphalidae*, or "brushfoots"; this refers to the first pair of legs being relatively short and covered in little hairs, used for cleaning off the mouthparts. The butterflies are large (3.5" or larger wingspan, some measuring 4.5") and, to put it mildly, showy. The Diana exhibits readily visible sexual dimorphism. Males are blackish-brown with orange markings, and the larger females are black with iridescent blue markings. The species was first described by Pieter Cramer in 1777 from a male discovered in Jamestown, Virginia. The female was described in 1864 by W. H. Edwards from examples collected along the Kanawha and Elk Rivers of West Virginia.

The larvae of the Diana are purplish-black caterpillars covered with black branching spines, the lower portions of which are reddish-orange. The larvae favor violets as their host plants. Dianas do not lay their eggs directly on the host; instead, in the fall, the females walk along the ground, laying single eggs under twigs or leaves near the base of the violets. Upon hatching, larvae burrow into the ground to overwinter, emerging in spring to feed and mature. One source notes that the larvae are "elusive," preferring to feed at night.

Adults emerge in late spring, beginning most years in May. Males are the first to fly, emerging a week or more before the females, and are observed to wander widely, looking for females. After mating, males are seldom seen and presumably expire, their reproductive duty done. At the height of summer, the Diana may go into diapause or estivation, a sort of semi-hibernation, awaiting more temperate and moist conditions. The adult Dianas may estivate through August. It is mostly females that emerge to fly in the early fall, looking for places to lay their eggs. These females ward off predators by mimicking the pipevine swallowtail butterfly,

---

2   This figure, supplied by the Lepidopterists' Society, may be too conservative, but the society itself predicts that ultimately, the number of identified *Lepidoptera* species may reach more than 250,000. Lori Spencer, in *Arkansas Butterflies and Moths* (2014), asserts that there are about 265,000 species of butterflies and moths on earth. Of these, some 20,000 are butterflies, the rest moths.

Speyeria diana *male.*

which they loosely resemble; the latter species takes its name from its preferred host plant, from which it feeds. The plant is toxic to most species, thus the butterfly is as well—and the Diana females survive in part by being mistaken for the killer butterflies.

While they are on the wing, Dianas require a high-quality nectar diet. Choice sources include the butterfly milkweed, ironweed, bee balm, red clover, and coreopsis.[3] Their preferred habitat is not well-defined, but Dianas have been reported favoring edges and openings in moist, rich forests and openings in deciduous and pine woodlands near streams. Additionally, Dianas seem to thrive in burned-over forest zones, as this sort of clearing-and-fertilization process tends to encourage flowering plants—including violets, the Diana's exclusive larval host.

Interest in the Diana fritillary increased in the mid-1990s when entomologists began searching for them throughout their historic range and discovered that their natural habitat was diminishing due to such factors as logging, fire suppression, and urban sprawl. They were placed on the federal species-of-concern list and the North Carolina Animal Watch List. The Diana was also identified as a "species of special concern" by the Arkansas Natural Heritage Commission because, while the Diana fritillary is widespread, its populations are scattered and fluctuate greatly between years. It appears most secure in the southern Appalachians and in Arkansas and Missouri, but "secure" is a relative term; threats to the survival of this species are everywhere.

In particular, the Diana is known to be sensitive to habitat change in the form of land clearance either for logging or brush reduction preceding farming or construction. In some parts of the Appalachians, strip mining also threatens the Diana's habitat.[4] Such activity in the nineteenth and early twentieth centuries reduced the overall range and virtually eradicated the Diana fritillary from the Ohio Valley, eastern Virginia, and eastern North Carolina. Today, the Diana is not considered an imperiled species as such, but it remains one "of concern," largely because much about it remains imperfectly understood.

Diana fritillaries seem to do well in moist, mountainous habitats. It is considered rare across its distribution, but is a relatively long-lived butterfly, with adults living four to five months, increasing canny butterfly-chasers' chances of viewing them. The Diana fritillary has been recorded in twenty-seven counties in

---

3   Females tend to be choosy about floral sources; males, on the other hand, are known to take their nutrients by "bellying up" to animal dung.
4   One additional threat to the Diana comes from an unanticipated quarter: white-tailed deer appear to enjoy browsing on the violets that are the Diana's host plants.

Arkansas and is occasionally observed in the mountains of Oklahoma and Missouri.

Much is made of the Diana, particularly at the Mount Magazine Butterfly Festival, held in late June at Mount Magazine State Park, located in the Ouachita mountains more than 2,700 feet above sea level in Logan County. The location is particularly butterfly-friendly—91 of the state's resident butterfly species have been observed on the site—and the Diana fritillary consistently reproduces on the mountain, drawing amateur and professional lepidopterists from across Arkansas and around the continent to what has become both a great celebration of nature and survival, as well as a significant economic boost to the Logan County economy. Another Arkansas event focusing on butterflies is the annual Butterfly Count, held at Queen Wilhelmina State Park in Polk County in mid-July, an intensive one-day census of butterfly populations, including the Diana fritillary, on the flanks of 2,681-foot Rich Mountain.

For further reading:

"Butterflies and Moths of North America." http://www.butterfliesandmoths.org/species/Speyeria-diana (accessed June 28, 2015).

"Fritillaries: Diana Fritillary (*Speyeria diana*)." Xerxes Society for Invertebrate Conservation. http://www.xerces.org/diana-fritillary/ (accessed June 28, 2015).

The Lepidopterists' Society. http://www.lepsoc.org/index.php (accessed June 28, 2015).

Moran, M. D., and C. D. Baldridge. "Distribution of the Diana Fritillary, Speyeria diana, (Nymphalidae) in Arkansas, with Notes on Nectar Plant and Habitat Preference." *Journal of the Lepidopterists' Society* 56 (Autumn 2002): 162–65.

Spencer, Lori A. *Arkansas Butterflies and Moths*, 2nd edition. Little Rock: Ozark Society Foundation, 2014.

———. "Butterflies and Moths." *Encyclopedia of Arkansas History & Culture*. http://www.encyclopediaofarkansas.net/encyclopedia/entry-detail.aspx?search=1&entryID=4754 (accessed June 28, 2015).

———. "Official State Butterfly, a.k.a. Diana fritillary [Butterfly]." *Encyclopedia of Arkansas History & Culture*. http://www.encyclopediaofarkansas.net/encyclopedia/entry-detail.aspx?search=1&entryID=5236 (accessed June 28, 2015).

CHAPTER 18:
STATE BEVERAGE, NUT, AND GRAPE
Drinks and Drupes

Let us now praise (or at least contemplate) the great diversity of foods or consumables that have been chosen as state symbols. Such symbols forge a direct connection to one of the basic concerns of migration, settlement, and development: the challenge of feeding one's self and family. A symbol that is food or drink seldom needs explicit explanation or justification; if it is palatable and of the country, then it will attract its admirers both local and from outside. If it is a workaday food or beverage, it may win friends for its homeliness; if it is distinctive either by flavor or features of culture, preparation, or circumstances of consumption, its followers will revere it as an eccentric and special rarity.

Some thirty-five states have designated or honored something which may fall under the category of "state food." These do not generally include crops (although many are state-grown, all or in part) but are instead mostly prepared items either identified with the culture of a particular state or local items with a regional or national audience. States do not simply designate these as "official food," generally. Instead, many are put in categories including state dessert, state pie, official prepared food (Georgia, for grits...cheese, plain, or otherwise fancified), state snack food (Illinois likes popcorn), state doughnut, state jelly, state meat pie (!), state cuisine (Louisiana, for gumbo—a multi-course meal in every pannikin), state treat, official muffin, official state bean, official dessert emblem (Massachusetts honors the eponymous Boston Cream Pie), official cookie, official appetizer (Rhode Island votes for calamari), state picnic cuisine (South Carolina embraces barbecue…barbecue? South Carolina?), official state bread, and official state pastry.[1]

One of Arkansas's neighbors reaches for success through excess: Oklahoma has designated an entire state meal, a repast worthy of a nineteenth-century holiday blowout. It starts with fried okra, then proceeds to squash, barbecued pork, biscuits and sausage gravy, grits, corn, strawberries, chicken-fried steak, black-eyed peas, and pecan pie. Using calorie figures for given serving sizes from a popular dieter's guide, this light repast rewards the eater with 3,404 calories.[2] Arkansas can offer nothing to equal this, except perhaps a gift card to Franke's Cafeteria in Little Rock.

Arkansas's designated official symbols include several edibles. Other chapters in this volume address the state fruit and vegetable (the South Arkansas Vine Ripe Pink Tomato), the state grain (rice, inevitably paired with its natural home, the Stuttgart soil series), the state floral emblem (the apple blossom, a harbinger of, well, apples), the state mammal (white-tailed deer, foundation of many a happy sport hunter's family dinner), and the official historic cooking vessel (the Dutch oven, suitable for preparing any of these foods—just don't leave the acidic tomatoes in the pot for long if you want to preserve the seasoned surface). The state insect, the honeybee, contributes another edible in the form of its natural sweetener while pollinating both flowers and fruit plants; to this pile of comestibles both in the comb and the field one may add the sheaf of wheat and the beehive depicted on the state seal, the former connected to the farmer's plow also visible on the design. All in all, it can be said that representations of the edible bounty of the state flow through the list of designated state symbols.

But wait, there's more.

Arkansas has not—to date—designated a prepared food or confection as an official state symbol; the fried pie may yet have its day in the legislature. It has, however, singled out three additional agricultural products as state symbols, honoring their producers and acknowledging both their nutritional and economic significance.

State Beverage: Milk

In 1985, the Arkansas General Assembly designated milk the state's official beverage. Act 998 was introduced by State Representative Bobby Glover of the Seventy-Second District (covering Prairie County and part of Lonoke County). It met no opposition, was duly signed by Governor Bill Clinton, and became effective on June 28 of that year. Reasons offered for the designation included milk's healthfulness, the desirability of encouraging milk consumption, and the importance of the dairy sector in Arkansas. The legislation did not specify a type or grade of milk, leaving it up to Arkansans to consume the variety of their choice, from full-fat to "blue."

---

1   Information collated from Netstate (http://www.netstate.com), StateSymbolsUSA (http://www.statesymbolsusa.org), eReferenceDesk (http://www.ereferencedesk.com/resources/state-symbols/), all accessed August 16, 2015, cross-referenced with information provided by various state government websites.

2   Calorie total based on portion-based calorie guide at www.Fatsecret.com, cross-referenced with other diet management and weight-loss online guides, depression from the consultation of which prevents the author from further disclosures.

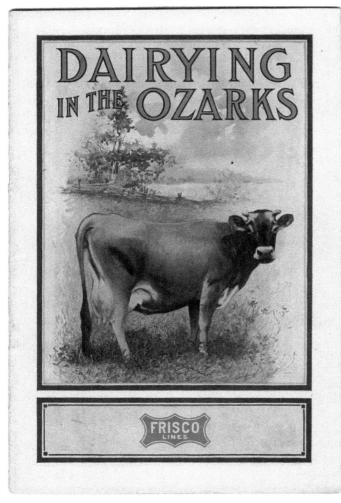

Inducements for dairy farmers, courtesy of the St. Louis & San Francisco Railroad, ca. 1910.

Arkansas was the fourteenth state to choose an official beverage and, of that number, the eleventh to choose milk. (As of 2015, twenty-eight states have made the former move and, of these, twenty have embraced milk; Rhode Island in 1993 designated "coffee milk," a local favorite made with Rhode Island–produced coffee syrup.[3])

Dairy farming has a long history in the Natural State. From colonial through early statehood times, a family's milk generally came from its own dairy cows or through trading with milk-rich neighbors. In 1862, however, the Evergreen Dairy, owned by Eleithet Coleman, began home milk deliveries in Little Rock, the first such in the state. Glass milk bottles would not appear in Arkansas until 1915; Coleman ladled milk from his wagon cans into customers' jars or cans at curbside. As more Arkansans began living in towns and cities, hence isolated from farms, other dairies opened, and it became a usual thing to buy milk, instead of relying on one's family cow.[4]

As demand for commercial products grew, so did the extent of Arkansas's herds. Dairies large and small maintained their own herds, but most dairy cattle remained dispersed in rural districts, one or two per farm; their owners would sell surplus to neighbors or to the nearest town dairy. The 1920 U.S. Census reported that the state had 415,507 dairy cows, 355,200 of them on farms reporting milk production. In the preceding year, the census revealed, Arkansas cows had yielded 87,623,651 gallons of milk, about 190 gallons (or 1,634 pounds) per cow.[5]

The second decade of the twentieth century

3   "Rhode Island Symbols." https://www.ri.gov/facts/factsfigures.php (accessed August 16, 2015).

4   Ginger Penn, "Coleman Dairy," *Encyclopedia of Arkansas History & Culture.* http://www.encyclopediaofarkansas.net/encyclopedia/entry-detail. aspx?entryID=4425 (accessed August 16, 2015); Jodie A. Pennington, "Dairy Industry," *Encyclopedia of Arkansas History & Culture.* http://www. encyclopediaofarkansas.net/encyclopedia/entry-detail.aspx?entryID=4337 (accessed August 16, 2015).

5   United States Bureau of the Census, *Census of Agriculture, 1920* (Washington: Government Printing Office, 1923, 24, Chapter 10, 657–70). http://www. agcensus.usda.gov/Publications/Historical_Publications/1920/Livestock_Products.pdf (accessed August 16, 2015). Milk production per cow for Arkansas can be contrasted with the national average for 1919: 366 gallons, or 3,147 pounds.

saw a beginning of a new trend in Arkansas dairy: a reduction in the size of the herd. Bottled milk, while not yet pasteurized, could nevertheless be shipped and sold farther from its point of production than ever before, lessening the need for herds to be distributed around the state. For a few years, the number of cows declined slightly, but encouragement of milk production by extension agents, combined with ever improving transportation, ensured that the herds would regain their numbers. Dairy herds swelled in size: the high point for Arkansas dairy cows on farms reached 482,000 in 1943. In that year, milk production per cow hit 2,880 pounds (334.8 gallons), a new record for Arkansas.

As dairy farming expanded, the business of processing and marketing milk and other dairy products evolved. In 1939, Little Rock's Coleman Dairy installed pasteurizing equipment and sold its first "Coleman's Pure Milk." This signaled a new direction for Arkansas dairies as customers, especially in towns, came to appreciate the longer life and safety of pasteurized milk. Within a few years, Coleman and other Arkansas dairy processors would sell off their company-owned herds in favor of buying raw milk from producers, allowing the dairies to expand or contract their output to meet market demands.[6] In years to come, milk production per cow would rise while the size of Arkansas's dairy herds would fall, along with the amount of milk used (that is, consumed, sold privately, or made into butter or cheese) on farms where it was produced.[7]

◇ ◇ ◇

Figures from the 1987 Census of Agriculture, roughly contemporary with milk's elevation to the status of state beverage, showed a continuation of trends from mid-century. In 1987, Arkansas's dairy herds numbered about 71,000 head, a far cry from the 1943 peak numbers. The census counted 957 dairy farms, including forty-three in Lonoke and Prairie Counties combined. The market value of Arkansas dairy products sold that year (milk, cheese, butter, whey) was nearly $91 million.[8] More recent figures supplied by the Midwest Dairy Council, a producers' consortium, indicate that, in 2014, Arkansas had about 75 licensed dairy herds, with an average daily production per cow of a cool 3.7 gallons, or 31.8 pounds, which added up to over 96 million pounds of milk, generating some $22 million in milk sales. The trend

Union Creamery, Watson and Aven Creamery, Carlisle (Lonoke County), 1909.

6   Penn, "Coleman Dairy."

7   Donald Blayney, "The Changing Face of U.S. Milk Production," *U.S. Department of Agriculture Economic Research Service Statistical Bulletin* 978 (June 2002). http://www.ers.usda.gov/publications/sb-statistical-bulletin/sb978.aspx (accessed August 16, 2015); U.S. Department of Commerce, U.S. Census Bureau, *United States Census of Agriculture: 1954: Vol. 2, Counties and State Economic Areas,* "Livestock and Livestock Products: Censuses of 1920 to 1954." http:// usda.mannlib.cornell.edu/usda/AgCensusImages/1954/01/34/979/Table-13.pdf (accessed August 16, 2015).

8   U.S. Department of Commerce, Bureau of the Census, *1987 Census of Agriculture* (AC87-A-4) Volume 1: GEOGRAPHIC AREA SERIES, Part 4 : Arkansas State and County Data, http://usda.mannlib.cornell.edu/usda/AgCensusImages/1987/01/04/1987-01-04-intro.pdf (accessed August 16, 2015); David Ware, "Official State Beverage, a.k.a. Milk," *Encyclopedia of Arkansas History & Culture.* http://www.encyclopediaofarkansas.net/encyclopedia/entry-detail. aspx?entryID=3146 (accessed August 16, 2015).

in processing has been toward fewer but larger dairy plants that buy raw milk from producers and turn it into good things. Arkansas has three plants, which each process and produce one or more dairy products.[9]

Not all milk connoisseurs, though, look to the large commercial dairies for their state beverage. There exists in Arkansas a small and wide-flung network of suppliers of raw milk (that is, neither homogenized nor pasteurized, and usually kept free of antibiotics and pharmaceutical helpers such as bovine growth hormones). Why raw milk? Its devotees claim that it strengthens the human immune system and is particularly good for the developing brains and nervous systems of infants and children. They assert that even for children who do not begin life drinking raw milk, later consumption of it may improve or ameliorate autism, behavior problems, frequent infections, deafness, asthma, allergies, and other serious health conditions. But not all agree. With the advent of dairies, dairy producers' cooperatives, and strengthened state health regulations, laws either prohibiting or strictly limiting raw-milk sales were enacted in most states, including Arkansas; the result was the development of stratagems for non-purchase acquisition of raw milk, including consumers' part-ownership of milk cows or goats, which entitled them to a share of milk produced.[10]

Until 2013, sale of raw cow's milk in Arkansas was illegal, although a loophole in state health laws permitted goat farmers to sell up to 100 gallons of goat's milk per month directly to consumers. On April 12, 2013, however, Governor Mike Beebe signed into law HB 1536, a bill allowing the "incidental sale" of raw milk. Under the new law, producers were allowed to sell—at the original production farm—an "average monthly number" of up to 500 gallons of raw goat's milk, cow's milk, or a combination of the two not exceeding that figure. The law set out standards for the raw milk, including that it be "practically colostrum free," and stipulated that the producer/marketer must post a sign at the point of sale containing the name and address of the farm along with a modest disclaimer:

> This product, sold for personal use and not for resale, is fresh whole milk that has NOT been pasteurized. Neither this farm nor the milk sold by this farm has been inspected by the State of Arkansas. The consumer assumes all liability for health issues that may result from the consumption of this product.

You have been warned.

State Nut: Pecan

In 2009, the Eighty-Seventh General Assembly designated the pecan (*Carya illinoinensis*) as the official nut of Arkansas.[11] Act 638, introduced as HB 1906 by Representative Larry Cowling (District 2, Little River County), had twenty-two co-sponsors and was approved on March 27, 2009. The act specifically noted, however, that it did not grant protected status to the pecan, thus ensuring that the nut may be both harvested and consumed.

Many of Arkansas's state symbols have direct or close analogues in its sister-states. Few states, however,

---

9   Midwest Dairy Association. http://www.midwestdairy.com/ot253p205/dairy-in-the-midwest/ (accessed August 16, 2015).

10   Campaign for Real Milk. http://www.realmilk.com/real-milk-finder/arkansas/ (accessed August 16, 2015); see also Kristen Gibson, Kristin Higgins, Harrison Pittman, and Rusty Lumley, "The Promise and Risk of Raw Milk in Arkansas—Analyzing Arkansas' New Raw Milk Law," University of Arkansas Division of Agriculture Public Policy Center, August 2013. http://www.healthy.arkansas.gov/programsServices/environmentalHealth/MilkProgram/Documents/RawMilkArticle.pdf (accessed August 16, 2015).

11   No matter what you're thinking of saying at this point, *don't*. Some jokes are just too easy to make.

have designated official nuts; only four others have taken this step. For what it's worth, however, Arkansas finds itself in the majority in terms of chosen species: Alabama and Texas have similarly honored the pecan. In Texas, in fact, it is both the official state health nut and the official state tree. Oklahoma celebrates it in the form of pecan pie, the hearty sweets course in its official state meal.[12]

The pecan tree is a species of hickory native to much of the South and the Midwest. It has been claimed that George Washington first planted them at his Mount Vernon estate, or that Thomas Jefferson had obtained some examples from the Mississippi River Valley, planted a few, and sent the rest on to Washington. This association of pecans with the Founding Fathers is a curiosity at most, but it provides an excuse to revel in the fact that the pecan is a uniquely American nut.[13]

Pecans first encountered Europeans (or vice versa) in the sixteenth century; Spanish explorers in what is now northern Mexico, Texas, and Louisiana called them *nuez de la arruga*, which roughly translates to "wrinkle nut." Because of their familiarity with the walnut trees of Europe, these early explorers referred to the nuts as *nogales* and *nueces*, the Spanish terms for "walnut trees" and "fruit of the walnut." And what they saw, they tasted, and they decided it was good; Spanish colonizers and missionaries took the pecan back to Europe, then carried them with them ultimately into Asia and Africa.[14] At roughly the same time, English colonizers made contact with the native nations of the eastern coast of North America. There, they found natives who gathered the wild nuts and ate them both as solids and a liquid: ground pecans, mixed with water, formed a nutritious drink, a forerunner of such confections as soy or almond milk.[15]

What to call the nut remained fluid, however, until "pecan" became the most general term, by the early nineteenth century. The name derives from the Algonkian (or Algonquian) word "pakan," meaning something hard enough to require a stone to crack; and so they are, at least the thick-shelled varieties. This name existed cheek by jowl with another: Illinois nuts, so called because examples were early harvested in the Illinois country.[16]

Early attempts to cultivate the pecan met with frustration, since the pecan tree, like the apple, does not

12   Missouri embraces the black walnut and Oregon the hazelnut. New Mexico's state tree, the piñon (or pinyan) pine, produces edible seeds or nuts as well, but so far, that state has not seen fit to make this tree do double duty, unlike Texas's treatment of the pecan.

13   Or fruit; more on this later.

14   National Pecan Shellers' Association. http://www.ilovepecans.org/pecans-101/ (accessed August 16, 2015).

15   William R. Gerard, "Virginia's Indian Contributions to English," *American Anthropologist* 9 (1907): 91. https://books.google.com/books?id=LflDAQ AAMAAJ&pg=PA91&lpg=PA91&dq=powcohicora&source (accessed August 16, 2015). Gerard notes that the pecan or hickory-nut decoction, referred to by Algonkian-speaking natives of Virginia as "powcohickora," added "richness or flavor to their food preparations." The pecan was also employed as a medication; mid-twentieth-century ethnobotanical studies of the Kiowa and Comanche noted that pecans served these Plains nations both as stored food and medication. The Kiowa used a tea of pecan bark to combat tuberculosis, while the Comanche made a poultice of pecan leaves to counter ringworm. Paul A. Vestal and Richard Evans Schultes, *The Economic Botany of the Kiowa Indians* (Cambridge, MA: Botanical Museum of Harvard University), 1939, 20; Gustav G. Carlson and Volney H. Jones. "Some Notes on Uses of Plants by the Comanche Indians," *Papers of the Michigan Academy of Science, Arts and Letters* 25 (1940): 520, cited in "Comanche Ethnobotany," http://www.cfc.umt.edu/cesu/Reports/NPS/UMT/2004/Campbell_Etnobotony%20Report/chaptereight. pdf (accessed August 16, 2015).

16   U.S. Department of Agriculture Germplasm Resources Information Network. http://www.ars-grin.gov/cgi-bin/npgs/html/taxon.pl?9253 (accessed August 26, 2015).

grow "true" to its parent. Pecan trees grown from seed may produce large nuts or small, with thick shells or thin, palatable or sour. Early Spanish colonial arborists experimented with "budding"—grafting individual buds onto rootstock—but ultimately, grafting desirable limbs onto hardy rootstock proved to be the way to wealth. In the 1840s, Louisiana horticulturist A. E. Colomb, working with a slave known only as Antoine, developed a tree bearing only large, thin-shelled nuts. Although the tree itself was destroyed during the Reconstruction period, offshoots survived; these were the founder plants of commercial pecan cultivation.[17]

The pecan is classed as a nut in popular esteem and agricultural production, but *Carya illinoinensis* is botanically considered a drupe—that is, a fruit consisting of a stone or kernel surrounded by something. "Classic" drupes include fleshy fruit with a hard inner layer, such as the peach, plum, nectarine, apricot, cherry, olive, and mango. Botanical opinion includes the fruit of walnuts, pecans, date palms, macadamia nuts, and pistachios as drupes because of their outer, green, fleshy husk and stony, seed-bearing endocarp or inner layer. These latter fruits are also called drupaceous nuts. A "true" nut, on the other hand, is a hard-shelled pod that contains both fruit and seed of the plant, one for which the fruit does not open to release the seed to the world. Chestnuts, hazelnuts, and even acorns are common examples of true nuts. The distinction between drupe and nut, while significant for plant propagation and improvement, is largely lost on those who like them best; pecans easily pass the nut version of the duck test.

The pecan tree is worthy of respect not only for its fruit, but also for its stature, longevity, and, not least, the wood it produces. The pecan may take as long as 200 years to mature; it grows anywhere from 60 to over 120 feet in height. Pecan and its near-twin hickory are among the densest North American hardwoods, and they repay working with hand tools with...more work. Pecan wood bears a reputation of being difficult to machine and to glue; it tends to split, is slow to season, and has a high shrinkage rate. These qualities probably disqualify pecan from being an ideal novice whittler's wood, but its resilience, even grain, and quality of taking finish well lend it to use as a material for tool handles, dowels, wagon-wheel spokes, flooring, furniture, and ladders. Pecan is also prized for its contribution to the preparation of barbecue and other smoked meats; anecdotal evidence collected at cooking competitions suggests that it is esteemed even above hickory by some barbecue champions.

In our neighbor state of Texas, pecans enjoy a dual designation: the tree is designated that state's arboreal emblem, while the nut (or drupe, or fruit—your choice) is honored as the state's official *health* nut. There is method behind this determination: Pecans have a very high concentration of vitamin A, which protects teeth, eyes, and bones. According to the National Pecan Shellers' Association, pecans are high in healthy unsaturated fat, and just a handful a day can lower "bad" cholesterol. They also contain more than 19 vitamins and minerals,

17   Kathleen Purvis, *Pecans* (Chapel Hill: University of North Carolina Press, 2012), 4–5; George R. McEachern, "Propagating Pecans," *Texas Agricultural Extension Service Lawn and Garden Update* (March 2000). http://aggie-horticulture.tamu.edu/newsletters/hortupdate/hortupdate_archives/2000/mar00/h4mar00.html (accessed August 16, 2015).

Pecan Joe's was a small chain of tourist shops offering all manner of pecan products. This location was in Texarkana.

including the aforementioned vitamin A, plus vitamins B and E, folic acid, calcium, magnesium, phosphorus, potassium, and zinc. Just one ounce of pecans, the association claims, provides one-tenth of the daily recommended dosage of fiber. Just imagine what consuming a half pound or so might do! Pecans are also rich in antioxidants, those substances that inhibit harmful oxidation, especially ones used to counteract the deterioration of stored food products.[18] The role and health benefits of such agents remain a subject of debate, but the association, citing USDA studies, asserts that pecans are the most antioxidant-rich tree nut and rank among the top fifteen foods with the highest levels of antioxidants. Thus, those who seek to counteract internal rust, spoilage, or deterioration need look no further than our state nut.[19]

Thanks to the wide range of hardiness in pecan stock, one may find pecan trees and their fruit in virtually any corner of the state. Look for them, one pecan lover suggests, where landowners have cleared other trees, leaving forage for cattle and...pecans, for the cattle's owners. Commercial pecan production in Arkansas is primarily located on alluvial soils near rivers in central, eastern, and southern Arkansas, with another concentration in the southwestern corner. Significant production areas are found along the Arkansas, Mississippi, Red, and St. Francis Rivers. Arkansas's pecans are produced both from native (seedling) trees and from orchards of improved (propagated by budding and grafting) varieties. Most pecans produced in Arkansas come from native groves. Production is encouraged by removal of competing trees and shrubs and thinning to retain trees with highest production, best nut quality, and highest disease resistance. Ground cover under trees (cool-season grasses and legumes) helps with fertilization. Most native pecans are harvested mechanically (the first step consists of literally shaking the trees), although significant amounts are hand harvested by small growers. Farmers manage their pecan orchards to control diseases, insect pests, and weeds. With the improved varieties, yield of marketable nuts is higher and their quality is more consistent but at a price, as "production

18   "Antioxidant," Google online dictionary. https://www.google.com/?gws_rd=ssl#q=antioxidants+definition (accessed August 16, 2015); this seems a rather cold way to refer to the human body, but there it is, folks.
19   "Nutrition in a Nutshell," National Pecan Shellers' Association. http://www.ilovepecans.org/nutrition-in-a-nutshell/ (accessed August 17, 2015). Among the other claims made for the pecan by the association are that pecans help lower cholesterol, may delay age-related motor neuron degeneration, and are suitable for a weight-control diet (oh, that fiber).

Nouveau Powcohickora, a.k.a. blender nut milk

1 cup pecan halves
2 tablespoons of honey
Pinch of salt

Place the pecans in a bowl and cover with at least two inches of water. Let them soak for 12 hours (the longer the pecans soak, the creamier and smoother the milk will be).

Drain the pecans and discard the water. Place nuts, honey and salt in a blender. Add 4 cups of very hot water to the blender and blend on low speed, increasing to high for at least 2 minutes once the crunching sound diminishes.

Strain the pecan "milk" through a tea towel or a fine-mesh sieve into a bowl, pressing down on the solids. Toss or reuse the pecan meal (it makes a good addition to cookies, pancakes, or any batter bread). Before it cools too much, taste the milk; if it needs a little additional sweetness, add a little more honey. Pour into a sterilized sealable jar; kept cold, it should stay good for two or three days at least...but it will disappear long before this.

inputs and management intensity are also higher for improved varieties as compared to native varieties."[20]

What Arkansas pecan growers have wrought is significant: As of 2013, Arkansas had nearly 6,500 acres planted in pecans. Little River and Miller counties were first and second, respectively, in the number of pecan-planted acres, followed by Lonoke, Jefferson, and Phillips Counties; these five accounted for 5,268 of those acres.[21] In that same year, pecan-utilized production[22] from Arkansas was 2.7 million pounds, up from the 2012 production of 2.2 million pounds. The average price per pound was $1.40, a $0.05 decrease from 2012. The total value of the crop was $3.78 million, up from 2012's $2.97 million. Even better news was in store for Arkansas's pecan farmers in 2014, when utilized production rose to 3.5 million pounds, with a market value (in spite of a decline in prices) of $4.6 million.[23]

State Grape: Cynthiana (*Vitis aestivalis*)

Although states have designated various fruits as state symbols, only three have extended this recognition to grapes. In 2001, North Carolina singled out the scuppernong, a native grape that was the first to be cultivated in that onetime English colony. In 2003, Missouri thus honored the Norton, an early American hybrid which became a foundation of German winemaking in that state in the mid-nineteenth century. In 2009, the Arkansas General Assembly followed suit when it designated the Cynthiana, a native grape genetically similar to the

---

20   "Crop Profile for Pecans in Arkansas (2003)." http://www.ipmcenters.org/cropprofiles/docs/ARpecans.pdf (accessed August 17, 2015); in other words, the improved pecans take more work.

21   Carter Dunn and Archie Flanders, "2013 Geographic Distribution of Arkansas Other Crop Acreage" (Fayetteville: University of Arkansas Division of Agriculture Research and Extension, July 2014). http://www.uaex.edu/farm-ranch/economics-marketing/farm-planning/Other%20Crop%20 Distribution_2013.pdf (accessed August 17, 2015).

22   That is, the portion of produced crops that were marketed, and either domestically consumed or exported.

23   U.S. Department of Agriculture, National Agricultural Statistics Service, "Noncitrus Fruits and Nuts 2014 Preliminary Survey" (January 2015). http:// www.nass.usda.gov/Publications/Todays_Reports/reports/ncit0115.pdf (accessed August 17, 2015).

Norton,[24] as Arkansas's official state grape. This action singled out for recognition a presumed native Arkansawyer with a mysterious past, debated parentage, and, very probably, multiple names and even personalities. In other words, something superficially simple instead opened up a wealth of complexities beginning with its very name; in short, it is a symbol worthy of its state.

◊ ◊ ◊

The history of the Cynthiana grape is clouded with competing claims, but most authorities acknowledge its close relationship with the Norton, a hybrid grape developed about 1820 by Virginia physician Daniel Norton, an enthusiastic amateur horticulturist. Norton's own notes indicated that the grape that would bear his name resulted as a hybrid between the "Bland" grape (a native grape of the *Vitis labrusca* type) and "Miller's Burgundy," assumed to be a locally-grown-from-French-stock Pinot Meunier. Recent genetic analysis suggests, however, that Norton may have been mistaken in identifying the "parents" of his hybrid, as genetic markers in modern Norton grapes suggest that the grapes from which the good doctor painstakingly transferred pollen were either Enfariné Noir or Milgrainet varieties, which he also cultivated.[25]

Norton energetically promoted his grape, going so far as to send cuttings to Thomas Jefferson Randolph, nephew of the third president and manager of the Monticello estate. He also sent samples to William Prince Jr., a Long Island nurseryman with a wide reputation. Prince saw potential in Norton's hybrid and propagated it; in 1822, it appeared as "Norton's Seedlings" in Prince's nursery catalog. In 1830, Prince published *A Treatise on the Vine*, in which he referred to what he styled *Vitis nortoni* in glowing

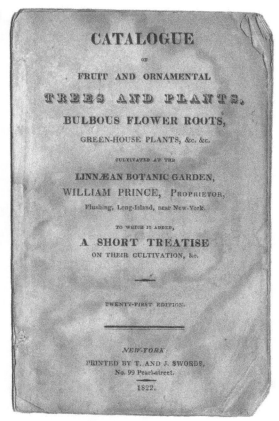

William Prince's nursery catalog of 1822, which offered Norton grape seedlings for sale.

---

24   "Genetically similar" may be considered a cautious understatement; a 1993 study concluded that today's Norton grapes and Cynthianas "may be cultivars derived from the same clonal source." Bruce I. Reisch, Robert N. Goodman, Mary-Howell Martens, and Norman F. Weeden, "The Relationship Between Norton and Cynthiana, Red Wine Cultivars Derived from *Vitis aestivalis*," *American Journal of Enology and Culture* 44, no. 4 (1993): 444. Much literature on both grapes alludes to the touchy question of whether or not they are in fact the same grape; suffice it to say, it's complicated.

25   Rebecca K. R. Ambers and Clifford P. Ambers, "Dr. Daniel Norborne Norton and the Origin of the Norton Grape," *American Wine Society Journal* 36, no. 3 (Fall 2004): 77–87. This article gives a graceful and detailed analysis of Norton's own account of his hybridizing. See also Ed Stover, Malli Aradhya, Judy Yang, John Bautista, and Gerald S. Dangl, "Investigations into the Origin of 'Norton' Grape using SSR Markers," *Proceedings of the Florida State Horticultural Association* 122 (2009): 19–24. The article indicates that the study could not conclusively identify the Norton's parent grape strains, but it cites earlier genetic analysis showing the Norton and Cynthiana to be identical.

terms: "For the purpose of making wine, this is hardly to be excelled by any foreign variety."[26]

Although the Norton was too harsh to find favor as a table grape, it caught on, particularly with German immigrants who found homes in Missouri in the 1830s and 1840s; unlike most native North American grapes, it would produce a red wine with little or no hint of the musty overtaste known as "foxiness." In short, it produced a strong vintage that would withstand comparison with established European types, particularly the red wines of France's Bordeaux region. Moreover, the Norton was winter hardy and pest resistant, qualities that helped balance out relatively small yields of fruit and juice. This combination of qualities may have made it a good candidate for carrying south into Arkansas. This is one possible explanation for the appearance in Arkansas, in the 1850s, of what was believed to be a native grape that was a virtual twin to the Norton: this Arkansas traveler was known as the Cynthiana.[27]

The wine made from Norton grapes proved popular in the post–Civil War years and even found fans in Europe. In 1873, Norton wine from Missouri won top honors at the Universal Exposition of Vienna; five years

later, a Norton red won the same honor at the Universal Exposition of Paris. In years to come, other Norton reds would win international honors, along with wines made from the Cynthiana. The two grapes were recognized as remarkably similar, even without the aid of modern genetic analysis; how something so closely echoing a Franco-American hybrid grape could have found its way to Arkansas, only to be "discovered" growing wild there, was and must remain the stuff of conjecture, as must the origin of its lovely, mellifluous new name. In any event, both Norton and Cynthiana were well established in Missouri—and Arkansas—vineyards by the waning years of the nineteenth century.

Established, yes—but destined for an unwelcome turn. During the late nineteenth

Vineyard in Batesville (Independence County), ca. 1950.

26   Todd Kliman, *The Wild Vine: A Forgotten Grape and the Untold Story of American Wine* (New York: Clarkson Potter, 2010), 54.

27   Hard information on the circumstances of the first appearance of the Cynthiana is scarce; most sources simply assert that the Cynthiana "originated" in Arkansas sometime in the 1850s; it may have been a mislabeled Norton vine imported from Missouri, or else a Norton "sport" or local variant, again, grown from Norton vines from Missouri. No source identifies the origin of the name. Lisa Ann Smiley, P. Domoto, G. Nonnecke, and W. W. Miller, "A Review of Cold Climate Cultivars: Cynthiana/Norton." Iowa State University Horticulture, http://viticulture.hort.iastate.edu/cultivars/Cynthiana.pdf (accessed August 17, 2015).

century, local, state, and national temperance groups shifted away from relying on piety and moral suasion and toward the outright elimination of beverage alcohol. State-level prohibition measures built support and precedent for national Prohibition; with its onset, thriving vineyards full of Cynthiana, Norton, and other wine grapes were uprooted, in some cases replanted with sweet table grapes not usually considered for winemaking. During the period of Prohibition, these same table grapes would be turned to wine by the enterprising, the thirsty, and the desperate, but for law-abiding (or cautious) agriculturalists, vast

Grapes, Springdale, Ark.

expanses of wine grapes had no great allure. For Norton and Cynthiana, grown only in the United States, prospects looked grim.[28] When Prohibition finally ended in 1933, the wine that had been drunk in secret during that time all came from other parts of the world—locations that had never used the Norton grape. So when America began to rebuild its wine regions, people looked to the wines they drank during Prohibition as their inspiration, and those did not, at least initially, include Cynthiana and Norton.

But, the grape did not go away altogether. A few vineyards in New York and Missouri still grew the Cynthiana and its twin, the Norton; the extent of its survival in Arkansas cannot, however, be reliably determined. Post-Prohibition, Arkansas wineries reopened, and new ones appeared in the old strongholds of winemaking, centering on Altus in the Arkansas Valley and Tontitown, in the northwest corner of the state. Much of the post-Prohibition Arkansas wine was made from either Concord grapes or the muscadine, both of which tended to produce the "foxy" quality unbeloved by most consumers. This, plus other factors, led to a steady decline in the number of Arkansas wineries until, by the 1990s, only a handful of hardy perennials remained.

One of these was Cowie Wine Cellars, founded by Robert Cowie in 1967 at Paris, not far from Altus. In 1982, Cowie entered its first competition, the International Eastern Wine competition in New York. More than 700 wines were entered; Arkansas Queen, a 1981 Cynthiana from Cowie, took home a silver medal. One critic hailed the Cowie Cynthiana, asserting it to be "the great American wine of an American grape." By 1982, a minor renaissance of interest in the Norton/Cynthiana was already under way in the Missouri wine country, from which the celebrated Nortons of the 1870s had appeared. This would encourage their Arkansas counterparts

28   During the Prohibition era, apparently Cynthiana and Norton grapes survived in some winemaking districts because their high natural sugar production during fermentation (when compared to most other wine grapes) meant that illegal winemakers would not have to add much sugar to the barrels; thus, they would not have to buy large quantities of sugar, which would drew the attention of revenue agents (Kliman, *The Wild Vine*, 163–65).

to follow suit and take another look at the Cynthiana, deemed a native Arkansawyer.

In 1998, a new factor dropped into place which would have profound consequences for the fame of the Cynthiana. Audrey House, an Oklahoma native but former Little Rock resident, bought twenty acres of land near Altus from the Wiederkehr family, operators of Arkansas's oldest winery. At the time, House was finishing a degree in psychology at the University of Oklahoma but wanted to set hardy roots in Arkansas. The land was available, and it included ten acres of neglected Chardonnay vines. House recruited college friends to come out to the acreage, live in tents, erect buildings, and help her return the vineyard to productivity. Two years later, House was able to purchase thirty additional acres and in 2001 opened a new winery, which she dubbed Chateau Aux Arc.[29]

Wiederkehr Wine Cellars, Inc., Altus (Franklin County), ca. 1960.

In addition to the Chardonnay, the Aux Arc vineyards also grow Zinfandel, Cabernet Sauvignon, Pinot Noir, Petit Sirah, and other European grape varieties, but House's championing of the Cynthiana has attracted particular notice. One of her earliest goals was to produce an estate-grown, estate-bottled Arkansas wine from its premier native grape, and she has enthusiastically pursued it. Chateau Aux Arc not only grows the grape for its own pressings and those of neighboring wineries, but it also propagates Cynthiana seedlings, claiming to be the nation's largest producer of these.[30]

House has also established herself as a partisan for the Arkansas winemaking community. One result of her work was the introduction of House Bill 2193 of the 2009 Arkansas legislative session. The measure, sponsored by State Representatives Beverly Pyle of Cedarville in Crawford County and Kathy Webb of Little Rock, was intended to draw attention to the survival and rising reputation of Arkansas's wine-making traditions. Unlike state symbol designations of a century before, the bill's verbiage was terse: no flowery language hailed the Swiss, German, and Italian winemakers of yore or waxed poetic over the excellence of the state's distinctive native grape. Instead, the bill simply designated the Cynthiana, *Vitis aestivalis*, as the official state grape. No state agency would be required to change any publication or make any effort to reflect this addition to the list of state

29   Chateau Aux Arc, http://www.chateauauxarc.com (accessed August 17, 2015); "Interview with Audrey House," http://wine.lovetoknow.com/wiki/Interview_with_Audrey_House_of_Chateau_aux_Arc (accessed August 17, 2015).

30   "Chateau Aux Arc," video documentary presentation, Alejandro Cordoba, 2012, https://vimeo.com/58262768 (accessed August 17, 2015). Cordoba, a journalism student at the University of the Ozarks, interviewed House on location at Chateau Aux Arc; the segment was aired on KUOZ, the university's television feed.

symbols, although no prohibition against doing so was included. It was perhaps a sign of the times that HB 2193, like the measure that in the same year designated the pecan as the state's official nut, conferred no protected status on the Cynthiana. There would thus be no question of whether or not one might harvest it, press it, or consume the result. The measure was approved on March 24, 2009.

The designation of the Cynthiana in 2009 was particularly timely, given that barely two years previously, in April 2007, Chateau Aux Arc (and its neighboring vineyards) endured four nights of freezing temperatures, which damaged many vines, particularly those of the cold-sensitive *vinifera* varieties.[31] The Cynthiana, however, is considered "moderately hardy" by viticulturalists: presumably the native North American element in its genetics contributes to its ability to withstand brief descents to as low as -10° to -15° F.[32]

In 2010, Arkansas Tech University of Russellville commissioned a study of Arkansas's vineyards and wine-making and their economic significance to the state. The final report, delivered in 2012, confirmed what Audrey House and other Arkansas vintners had already asserted: The wine business was both economically significant and growing. Arkansas grape and wine production and marketing had created the equivalent of 1,668 full-time jobs, with approximately $42 million in wages paid out in 2010. Arkansas's forty grape growers and thirteen active wineries produced nearly 122,000 cases of wine, with a retail value of some $20 million. As impressive were the figures for wine-related tourism: In 2010, about 306,000 tourists had stopped at one or more Arkansas vineyards; those tourists, both Arkansans and out-of-staters, had spent approximately $21 million, slightly exceeding the retail value of the state's wine production. The wine industry's total economic impact on the state, the report concluded, was conservatively estimated at $173 million, a product of "an industry that is a unique partnership of nature, entrepreneurship, artistry and technology."[33]

Of the thousands of gallons of Arkansas wine offered yearly for sale, only a small fraction are made of the Cynthiana. As of this writing, only three vineyards list Cynthiana reds for sale, although investigation in Little Rock package stores uncovered evidence of one more.[34] Thus, it remains, like the Arkansas Black apple, a minority taste, a little overlooked and thus in some sense protected. For now, it is safe in its dual identities. When north of the border or in the vineyards of Virginia, it is Norton, the basis of serious red wines, the sort that should be bought and laid down for some years, in anticipation of their emerging complexity. Once across the line into Arkansas, however, we find Cynthiana, Norton's seemingly identical twin but very much a grape of its own, producing wines of a lighter character, ones suited equally for aging or for drinking young. The Appellation America website offers a wry characterization of these twins: a color sketch of face that is half young man, half

31   Robert G. Cowie, "Chateau Aux Arc Vineyards and Winery," *Encyclopedia of Arkansas History & Culture.* http://encyclopediaofarkansas.net/encyclopedia/entry-detail.aspx?entryID=2566 (accessed August 17, 2015).

32   Take that, Cabernet!

33   "The Economic Impact of Arkansas Grapes and Wine—2010," Frank Rimerman & Co. for Arkansas Tech University, 2012. The Rimerman report also pointed to the potential for expanding vine plantings, lessening Arkansas vintners' reliance on buying grapes from outstate producers. The report did not mention grape varieties by name but alluded to climatic challenges which would, presumably, increase the attractiveness of a hardy, disease-resistant wine grape, suited to local soils and weather conditions.

34   For research purposes, examples of Cynthiana vintages from Chateau Aux Arc, Mount Bethel Winery, Cowie Wine Cellars, and Post Familie Vineyards were located. Further this deponent sayeth not.

woman. The accompanying text is a good-natured résumé of the Cynthiana/Norton relationship:

> You first surfaced in the state of Virginia as Mr. Norton, a man with regal character....Then we met you in Missouri, posing as a demure and elegant lady, impressing with subtle charm. The locals knew you as Miss Cynthiana, their "Cabernet of the Ozarks." As it turns out, you were a little mad, for Mr. Norton and Miss Cynthiana, you are one and the same![35]

For those who know about it, thanks to a chance encounter with a bottle or advice from a friend, Arkansas's state grape, and what is made from it, can remain a secret worth sharing, but not too widely, not too quickly. Too much good fortune, after all, can overwhelm even the most deserving underdog, just as too much prosperity can change people or places almost beyond recognition. It may be enough to acknowledge that a native grape, its parentage unknown—thus a foundling nurtured in the Arkansas wine country—can yield a wine that compares favorably with any red in the land. Like its home state, it is less well known than it might be, is often underrated by those with no first-hand experience of it, and can be a little unpredictable to work with—but it generously rewards those who spend some time with it.

For further reading:

Ambers, Rebecca K. R., and Clifford P. Ambers. "Dr. Daniel Norborne Norton and the Origin of the Norton Grape." *American Wine Society Journal* 36, no. 3 (Fall 2004): 77–87.

Blayney, Don P. "The Changing Landscape of U.S. Milk Production." Washington DC: U.S. Department of Education, 2002. http://www.ers.usda.gov/publications/sb978/sb978.pdf (accessed August 18, 2015).

Chateau Aux Arc. http://www.chateauauxarc.com (accessed August 18, 2015).

Cowie, Robert G. "Chateau Aux Arc Vineyards and Winery." *Encyclopedia of Arkansas History & Culture.* http://encyclopediaofarkansas.net/encyclopedia/entry-detail.aspx?entryID=2566 (accessed August 18, 2015).

———. "Arkansas Historic Wine Museum." *Encyclopedia of Arkansas History & Culture.* http://www.encyclopediaofarkansas.net/encyclopedia/entry-detail.aspx?entryID=2568 (accessed August 18, 2015).

"Interview with Audrey House of Chateau Aux Arc." LoveToKnow. http://wine.lovetoknow.com/wiki/Interview_with_Audrey_House_of_Chateau_aux_Arc (accessed August 18, 2015).

Kliman, Todd. *The Wild Vine: A Forgotten Grape and the Untold Story of American Wine.* New York: Clarkson Potter, 2010.

Lancaster, Guy. "Wineries in Arkansas." *Encyclopedia of Arkansas History & Culture.* http://www.encyclopediaofarkansas.net/encyclopedia/entry-detail.aspx?search=1&entryID=1171 (accessed August 18, 2015).

---

35   Appellation America, http://wine.appellationamerica.com/varietal-index.aspx (accessed August 18, 2015).

Main, Gary. "Growing and Vinting Cynthiana Norton Grapes." *Proceedings of the 24th Annual Horticulture Industries Show*, Fort Smith, Arkansas, January 14–15, 2005. http://www.uark.edu/depts/ifse/grapeprog/articles/ahis05wg.pdf (accessed August 18, 2015).

National Pecan Shellers' Association. http://www.ilovepecans.org/nutrition-in-a-nutshell (accessed August 18, 2015)

Penn, Ginger. "Coleman Dairy." *Encyclopedia of Arkansas History & Culture*. http://www.encyclopediaofarkansas.net/encyclopedia/entry-detail.aspx?entryID=4425 (accessed August 18, 2015).

Pennington, Jodie. "Dairy Industry." *Encyclopedia of Arkansas History & Culture*. http://www.encyclopediaofarkansas.net/encyclopedia/entry-detail.aspx?search=1&entryID=4337 (accessed August 18, 2015).

Pinney, Thomas. *A History of Wine in America from the Beginnings to Prohibition*. Berkeley: University of California Press, 1989.

Purvis, Kathleen. *Pecans*. Chapel Hill: University of North Carolina Press, 2012.

Smiley, Lisa Ann, P. Domoto, G. Nonnecke, and W. W. Miller. "A Review of Cold Climate Cultivars: Cynthiana/Norton." *Iowa State University Horticulture*. http://viticulture.hort.iastate.edu/cultivars/Cynthiana.pdf (accessed August 18, 2015).

University of Arkansas Division of Agriculture, Viticulture and Enology Research Program. "American Viticultural Areas in Arkansas: Uncorking Arkansas's Wine Country." http://www.uark.edu/depts/ifse/grapeprog/winetrail/viticultural%20areas.htm (accessed August 18, 2015).

Ware, David. "Official State Beverage, a.k.a. Milk." *Encyclopedia of Arkansas History & Culture*. http://www.encyclopediaofarkansas.net/encyclopedia/entry-detail.aspx?search=1&entryID=3146 (accessed August 18, 2015).

———. "Official State Grape, a.k.a Cynthiana Grape." *Encyclopedia of Arkansas History & Culture*. http://www.encyclopediaofarkansas.net/encyclopedia/entry-detail.aspx?search=1&entryID=3118 (accessed August 18, 2015).

———. "Official State Nut, a.k.a. Pecan." *Encyclopedia of Arkansas History & Culture*. http://www.encyclopediaofarkansas.net/encyclopedia/entry-detail.aspx?search=1&entryID=5923 (accessed August 18, 2015).

CHAPTER 19: STATE DINOSAUR

Solo 'Saur: *Arkansaurus fridayi*, the State's Only Dino

To begin with, let us imagine a particular place not as it is—a quiet, landlocked farm district—but as it was: a vast expanse of prime seafront property. The coast stretches along a southwest-northeasterly line, in some places meeting the sea as bluffs, in others becoming a gentle, sloping coastal plain. The fertile ground is covered with ferns, brush, and flowering plants; above them rise clumps and groves of conifers and cycads (seed-bearing plants with stout trunks and leaf-heads resembling palm trees). This is a warm clime and moist, with plenty of carbon dioxide in the air. The vegetation is lush, a riot of green life.

This abundance is not confined to green things. Everywhere there is animation, interaction, subsistence, and predation: this place is alive. Above the foliage, pterosaurs glide through the air, searching for insects and other small prey on the ground. In the warm, shallow sea, scores of ammonites, belemnites, other mollusks, and fish are hunted by mosasaurs, great marine reptiles which must compete and contend with sharks, which are fellow scavengers/predators. Underfoot, the ancestors of ants and other insects scurry and burrow; above the ground, protobutterflies and bees carry on the work of pollenating flowering plants. And, moving across the land, are larger creatures, too: some quadrupedal, some bipedal. Some are vegetarian, others omnivorous flesh-eaters. The bipedal flesh-eaters are distinctly predatory or, at least, opportunistic.

Now, visualize a corner of this scene: over there, behind a clump of short trees—early magnolias, possibly—lurks a theropod, a "bird footed" bipedal dinosaur, with short, muscular forearms instead of wings. It's hard to tell its height—it is keeping its head down as a herd of sauropods lumbers past—but it looks about ten feet long, perhaps longer. It is covered in short feathers, with a more prominent dorsal crest. It is an omnivorous predator but not the biggest one on the block, so it is cautious, waiting for the right moment to go foraging.

It's lunch time in the early Cretaceous, and you're in Lockesburg, Arkansas.

◇ ◇ ◇

The town of Lockesburg is located near the center of Sevier County in southwestern Arkansas, at the juncture of State Highways 24 and 71. The first incorporated town in Sevier County, it was once the county seat but was bypassed by the Kansas City, Pittsburg and Gulf railroad in 1897; county government moved to DeQueen a few years later. Lockesburg survived, however, and its few dozen businesses were supported by farming and sawmill jobs. Its population has slowly increased since 1960: in 2000, Lockesburg topped 700 inhabitants for the first time since 1910.

Arkansas Highway 24 extends about nineteen miles from Lockesburg, west to the Oklahoma state line. Farms and homes line the road; fields extend past the trees and bushes lining the borrow ditches. A half mile or so west of town, a sand and gravel operation looms on the south side of the highway. Highway 24 traverses first the lower-Cretaceous Trinity zone (with a stratigraphic range covering the late Aptian and early Albian ages, approximately 115 to 106 million years ago), then goes through Quaternary (no more than two million years old, give or take an epoch) terrace and alluvium zones before crossing the Little Cossatot River, then heads back into the Trinity on the river's west side. The Trinity zone consists of gravel, sand, clay, gypsum, celestine, and barite. These sediments originated to the north, in the Ouachita Mountains, and were deposited following a "major unconformity"[1] on an upturned and eroded Paleozoic surface in a shallow, coastal marine environment.

Lockesburg's water tower bears the name of its schools' sports mascot, a small woodland hawk dubbed "blue darter" because of its slate-blue back and its quick movements when swooping or tracking prey through brush.

On an August day in 1972, Lockesburg gas station owner Joe B. Friday noticed buzzards flying above a disused gravel pit located on his property along Arkansas Highway 24. In addition to his business, Friday ran cattle, and he thought that one of his animals might have died or fallen into difficulties.

---

1   An unconformity is a gap in the geologic record that indicates an episode or episodes of crustal deformation, erosion, and sea-level variations. Unconformities manifest themselves in surfaces between two rock bodies that constitute a substantial break (hiatus) in the geologic record (sometimes people say, inaccurately but understandably, that "time" is missing; it's not missing, but it HAS been messed with). Adapted from: http://www.indiana.edu/~geol105b/images/gaia_chapter_6/unconformities.htm (accessed August 17, 2017).

He found instead, sticking out of a clay bank flecked with color, what appeared to be bones, (literally) as hard as rocks. According to a 2014 *Arkansas Life* article, Friday dug out the fossils, then displayed them for some months in his service station. Thus began the modern story that culminated with, in 2017, the designation of the state's official dinosaur, *Arkansaurus fridayi*.

◇ ◇ ◇

What we know as Arkansas and the modern practice of research into and interpretation of fossil remains are roughly contemporary with each other. When Arkansas organized, first as a territory and then as a state, there were no dinosaurs as such; the term had not yet been invented. "Scientists," too, were new on the block: the term was coined in 1834. Scientists were preceded, however, by individuals who were variously dubbed natural philosophers, curators of nature, nature-peepers, and other sobriquets. Some of the most ingenious of these studied petrified skeletal remains and sought to understand the creatures they had been. These were the first of what have been called, since the term was coined in 1822, paleontologists.[2] Twenty years later, English zoologist and paleontologist Richard Owen suggested a general name for the remains of creatures that seemed to be related to modern lizards: Owen called them dinosaurs.

Paleontology studies the history of life on Earth by the discovery, study, and analysis of information from fossils. Fossils are the durable remains of plants, animals, fungi, bacteria, and single-celled living things; their organic materials and pores are replaced and filled by minerals, creating archival copies of life long gone. Paleontologists use these fossil remains to understand different aspects of extinct and living organisms. Individual fossils may contain information about an organism's life and environment; the behavior of organisms also can be deduced from fossil evidence, as well as their evolutionary history. Paleontologists infer, for instance, that whales evolved from land-dwelling animals: fossils of extinct animals closely related to whales exhibit front limbs like paddles, as well as tiny rear limbs instead of the boneless flukes of modern cetaceans.[3]

Fossils were studied by Greek and Roman philosophers in the Classical period; they were recognized as the remains of living things, but their nature remained conjectural. Some speculated that they were the remains of mythical beasts such as dragons or griffins, while Christian-era philosophers would suggest that fossils were the leftovers of creatures destroyed in the biblical great flood.[4]

By the late seventeenth century, natural philosophy had advanced sufficiently so that inquirers, while still wrestling with the question of just how to reconcile tangible evidence with the biblical accounts of the world's inception, could nevertheless examine fossil remains with an exacting curiosity. Nicolaus Steno, a Danish physician, natural philosopher, and cleric, proposed a process which explained how solid organic objects could

---

2   In 1822, Henri Marie Ducrotay de Blainville, editor of *Journal de Physique*, coined the word "palaeontologie" to refer to the study of ancient living organisms through fossils.

3   Flukes contain no bones; instead, they are made of dense tissue surrounded by a network of arteries and veins. The development of flukes replacing the tiny vestigial legs, perhaps as recently as 38 million years ago, marked the last step in the whale's evolution from land animal to water animal.

4   For extended discussion of the classical approach to making sense of fossils, see Adrienne Mayor, *The First Fossil Hunters: Paleontology in Greek and Roman Times* (Princeton, NJ: Princeton University Press, 2000). The term "fossil" derives from the Latin *fossilis*, meaning "dug up," which in its turn derives from *fossus*, the past participle of the verb *fodere*, "to dig." It survives in English in the form of "fosse," a moat or ditch dig around a castle, and in the verb "fossick," meaning to rummage around or dig through something, such as abandoned gold workings, gravel pits, or archival collections.

be preserved, in a petrified state, in layered deposits; in a treatise published in 1669, he laid out basic principles of the modern disciplines of geology and stratigraphy, as well as paleontology.[5]

The type of fossils found in any particular place depends upon the terrain that existed when the matter that became petrified was first deposited. In the case of Arkansas, an operative description of its early profile might be "seaside views, with predators."

Representative examples of all the major fossil groups have been found in Arkansas. The state's most commonly reported fossils are from echinoderms, mollusks, brachiopods, bryozoans, and cnidarians (corals and jellyfish). Chordate fossils (bones) are less frequently found, and almost all of these (so far, at least) have been from fish, small marine reptiles, and mammals.

Different types of fossils are present in each of the physiographic areas or "provinces" of Arkansas. The majority of Arkansas fossils are found in sedimentary rock—limestone and shale—from the Ozark Plateau. Most of the rocks in this region formed in shallow seas where marine invertebrates thrived. The Arkansas River Valley does not contain the variety of marine fossils present in the Ozarks, but trace fossils (fossils consisting of imprints or marks left by an organism, as opposed to physical remains) and plant or tree fossils do occur.

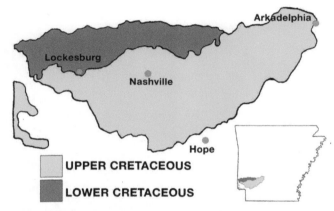

*Location of Cretaceous formations in the state in relation to the community of Lockesburg, where **Arkansaurus's foot bones were** found.*

Fossils are rarest in the Ouachita Mountains, principally because the environment in which the rocks formed was not a setting where most marine animals could live. Graptolites (marine creatures which formed net-like colonies and became extinct over 300 million years ago) and some trace fossils make up most of the macro fossils found in the area.

The Mississippi River Alluvial Plain consists mostly of recent unconsolidated sediments, so the likelihood of finding fossils in this region is very slight. However, remains from large mammals such as mammoths, mastodons, dire wolves, and saber-toothed cats have been found here. The West Gulf Coastal Plain is mostly fossil-free except for its western portion: here, Cretaceous-age rocks outcrop at the surface. Fossils from this region include invertebrate remains such as oyster shells, clams, and snails, and such vertebrates as sharks and marine reptiles and one (to date) lonely dinosaur.[6]

---

5   Hans Kermit, *Niels Stensen, 1638–1686: The Scientist Who Was Beatified* (Leominster, UK: Gracewing, 2003), 108 – 129. See also footnote (2). Early stratigraphers such as Steno firmly established the general principle that in geology, as in piles of papers on scholars' desks, the oldest stuff is, absent any catastrophic unconformity, on the bottom.

6   See Thomas Freeman, *Fossils of Arkansas: An Introduction to Paleontology Illustrated with Common Fossils of Arkansas* (Little Rock: Arkansas Geological Commission, ca. 1966) for general information.

Lunchtime in Lockesburg: Artist Brian Engh's conjectural representation of Arkansaurus fridayi in its lush Cretaceous context. Engh notes that the "animal is reconstructed based on related species that we have more complete skeletons of, but we really don't know exactly what its head would

The Cretaceous is defined as the period between 145.5 and 65.5 million years ago. It was the last period of the Mesozoic Era, which followed the Jurassic and ended with the extinction of the dinosaurs (except birds). Its name derives from the period's association with large chalk beds in north-central France studied in the 1820s by Belgian geologist Jean-Baptiste-Julien d' Omalius d'Halloy. These beds were created by the deposited shells of prehistoric marine invertebrates; the term **Cretaceous** issues from the Greek word *creta*, or "chalk."

By the beginning of the Cretaceous, the supercontinent dubbed Pangea[7] was already rifting apart.[8] By the mid-Cretaceous, it had split into two great masses which in turn became several smaller continents: Euramerica, which over time resolved itself into Europe, the Atlantic islands, and North America; and Gondwana, from which issued today's Africa, South America, Australia, and Antarctica. This created large-scale geographic isolation, causing a divergence in evolution of life forms on the respective land masses. The rifting also generated extensive new coastlines and a corresponding increase in the available expanses of near-shore habitat. Additionally, seasons began to grow more pronounced as the global climate became cooler. Forests evolved to look similar to present-day forests, with oaks, hickories, and magnolias becoming common in North America by the end of the Cretaceous. Although the era was cooler than what had preceded it, it was still warm: polar ice caps were practically nonexistent and, in fact, forests grew on the continent of Antarctica.[9]

Cretaceous Arkansas encompassed both the high plateau known today as the Ozarks and the inland body known variously as the Western Interior Seaway, the Cretaceous Sea, or the Niobraran Sea. Arkansas's prime seashore property zone ran southwest-northeast on a gentle curve, from Mena to near Pocahontas. The seas that covered nearly half of today's state were shallow, warm, and full of life, including predatory marine reptiles such as plesiosaurs and mosasaurs. Other marine life included sharks and advanced bony fish including *Pachyrhizodus*, *Enchodus*, and also the sixteen-foot-long *Xiphactinus*—a fish larger than any modern bony fish. Other sea life included invertebrates such as mollusks, squid-like belemnites, and plankton.

The Western Interior Seaway was also home to early birds, including the flightless *Hesperornis*, which had stout legs for swimming through water, as well as the tern-like *Ichthyornis*, an early avian with a toothy beak. *Ichthyornis* shared the sky with large pterosaurs such as *Nyctosaurus* and *Pteranodon*.

But what of the creatures of the land? During the 1980s, the fossilized tracks of dinosaur herds were discovered in southwestern Arkansas. The Nashville Sauropod Trackway, in a gypsum mine near Nashville,

7   A coinage by geotheoretician Alfred Wegener, who first used this Greek-derived term about 1920, having deduced the existence of this supercontinent some years earlier.
8   "Rifting" = "drifting," or close enough. Continental rift is the process of deformation of lithospheric plates due to lateral stress; as a result, a gap is formed at the deformed region. Slowly this widens to become a sea or even an ocean basin. A good example of this is the Red Sea: it formed as a result of rift between Arabian and African plates of the supercontinent known as Gondwana. Continental **drift** (championed by Alfred Wegener) is the movement of...well, continents. Plate tectonic theory, which came into favor in the 1960s, effectively incorporated both, positing that the earth's surface is made up of plates about fifty miles thick, which include both continents and ocean regions. Scientific opinion drifts much more quickly than the continents or geologic plates, causing rifts between scholars. And so it goes.
9   The first to discover this was polar explorer and adventurer Robert Falcon Scott, who found fossil plants on his successful but ultimately fatal 1912 expedition to the South Pole. He diligently collected some thirty-five pounds of specimens, which he hauled along with him to his death. When his body was found, next to it was a fossil of the *Glossopteris indica*, an extinct beech-like tree from 250 million years ago.

Arkansas, yielded literally thousands of dinosaur footprints, most of them belonging to sauropods (the huge, four-footed plant eaters of the late Jurassic period, typified by *Diplodocus* and *Apatosaurus*). Clearly, herds of sauropods traversed this region of Arkansas during their periodic migrations, leaving footprints (possibly separated by millions of years) up to two feet in diameter.[10] Other than these tracks, dinosaurs did not leave much trace of their passage through Arkansas.

Except for one.[11]

After Joe Friday found the mysterious fossilized bones, he displayed them in his shop, attracting local interest. Apparently, the idea that these were dinosaur remains was not raised, perhaps because no dinosaur remains had ever been found in Arkansas.[12]

Eventually, a local named Doy Zachry, home from his studies at the University of Arkansas (UA) at Fayetteville, took the fossils to show to one of his instructors, geology professor James H. Quinn. Quinn identified the fossils as the foot bones of a dinosaur of undetermined type and subsequently visited Lockesburg, looking for what else might have survived in the gravel pit. Quinn and members of his team found additional pieces of fossil bone, apparently belonging to the same skeleton; he assembled the fossils into a conjectural reconstruction of the foot, using clay to fill in gaps. Quinn could not match the bones to any other known species of dinosaur, but he deduced that it had been

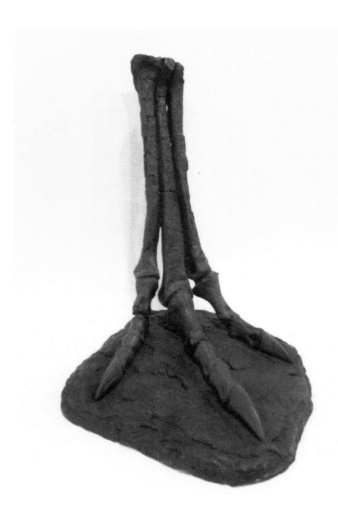

Reconstruction of Arkansaurus fridayi foot, incorporating casts of the surviving bones and elements deriving from more complete theropod skeletons.

---

10   Anastasia Teske, "Nashville Sauropod Trackway," *Encyclopedia of Arkansas History & Culture.* http://www.encyclopediaofarkansas.net/encyclopedia/entry-detail.aspx?entryID=3815 (accessed August 17, 2017).

11   Lack of evidence did not, however, dissuade Mr. Ken Childs of Beaver (Carroll County) from creating a prehistoric theme park, John Agar's Land of Kong, later renamed Dinosaur World, which featured more than 100 figures of dinosaurs, cavemen, and (yes) King Kong, spread across some sixty-five acres, which probably were above water level during the Cretaceous. The park closed in 2005. http://www.roadsideamerica.com/story/8415 (accessed August 17, 2017).

12   Paul McDonnold, "Them Dry Bones," *Arkansas Life* (September 2014). http://arkansaslife.com/them-dry-bones/# (accessed August 17, 2017).

bipedal, bird-like, and carnivorous, possibly related to *Ornithomimus*, an ostrich-like dinosaur named in 1890 by O. C. Marsh. Quinn also gave the mysterious saurian a *nomen nudem* (literally, "naked name," meaning a working or unofficial moniker): he dubbed it "Arkansaurus fridayi," honoring its discoverer. Friday, for his part, donated the bones to UA and in return received a full-size cast replica of them.[13]

Quinn intended further study of the Lockesburg find, but he died in 1977. Subsequent explorations of the gravel pit by teams from UA, Texas Tech University, and, finally, Joe Friday himself yielded no additional petrified remains.

In 1995, Dr. James Kirkland, paleontologist for the Dinamation International Society,[14] examined the bones at Fayetteville. Kirkland noted *Arkansaurus*'s similarity to remains of a dinosaur he had recently recovered from a Cretaceous-era formation in Utah; that creature's ankle structure virtually duplicated that of *Ornitholestes* ("bird robber"), a small, predatory carnivore discovered in a Wyoming excavation in 1900. Kirkland concluded that *Arkansaurus* was similar to his newly discovered big lizard, but it was earlier and larger. In the late 1990s, the fossils were lent to Dr. Dan Chure, a paleontologist at Dinosaur National Monument in Utah. Chure concluded that Quinn had been right: *Arkansaurus fridayi* was likely related to *Ornithomimus*. Chure suggested that it represented a primitive example, the earliest known instance of this species.

Most recently, *Arkansaurus* has been analyzed by ReBecca Hunt-Foster, a paleontologist with the Bureau of Land Management in Utah. In 2002, as an undergraduate student in geosciences at UA in Fayetteville, she examined *Arkansaurus*'s remains, prompted by a conversation with James Kirkland and by the encouragement of UA geologist Dr. Doy Zachry; Zachry was the undergraduate student had first brought the bones to the attention of James Quinn. Hunt-Foster wrote a research publication for the 2003 Arkansas Undergraduate Research Conference, determining that the remains of *Arkansaurus* were of uncertain affinity but were likely from a relative of *Ornithomimus*, agreeing with Quinn's and Chure's earlier evaluations.[15]

Undergraduate paleontologist ReBecca Hunt examining* Arkansaurus fridayi *remains, 2002.

In 2016, Hunt-Foster revisited the topic. In the intervening years, more research on ornithomimid dinosaurs had been done, so she was better able to compare the remains of *Arkansaurus* to those of other known ornithomimids, especially remains found elsewhere in North America. Her judgment was

---

13   McDonnold, "Them Dry Bones."

14   Dr. Kirkland currently serves as State Paleontologist for Utah. The Dinamation International Society was a Fruita, Colorado–based nonprofit corporation specializing in "participant-funded dinosaur excavations." See William Panczner, *A Traveler's Guide to Tracking Dinosaurs in the Western United States* (Frederick, CO: Renaissance House, 1995), 48.

15   ReBecca Hunt, "An Early Cretaceous Theropod Foot from Southwestern Arkansas," *Proceedings Journal of the 2003 Arkansas Undergraduate Research Conference* (2003): 87–103.

that the fossils from Arkansas represent a unique taxon that would have lived in the Early Cretaceous and likely roamed the southern portion of the United States and, possibly, Mexico. It represents one of the oldest known North American ornithomimids, which lived in an age in which most other studied, comparable examples have been found in Asia and Europe; it would have been a kind of "great-grandfather/grandmother-dinosaur" of Marsh's *Ornithomimus*.[16]

ARKANSAURUS FRIDAYI

1m

Illustration by Brian Engh
DONTMESSWITHDINOSAURS.COM

Predator and (anachronistic) prey: Arkansaurus fridayi with motivated human, for scale. Arkansaurus would probably have targeted small lizards, avians, or mammals (a.k.a. "snack food of the Cretaceous").

Reconstructing the appearance and characteristics of *Arkansaurus fridayi* requires generalizing from what is known about its contemporaries and probable "kin." An Arkansas Geological Survey publication from 1998 suggests that *Arkansaurus fridayi* was a bipedal, swift-moving hunter, primarily carnivorous but possibly supplementing its diet with fruits and plant leaves; it stood between six and fifteen feet tall, with a slender neck and tail, a small head, and relatively long forearms featuring opposable digits.[17] Subsequent reconstructions have modified *Arkansaurus*'s presumed appearance somewhat, giving it a shorter, thicker neck and tail, as well as short feathers. Ultimately, though, such reconstructions are at the mercy of how much—or how little—can be found of the original creature...and in the case of Arkansas's state dinosaur, not much remains. Paleontologist Hunt-Foster summed up the problem for *Arkansas Life* in 2014:

> "We can kind of tell what family it belongs to," [Hunt-Foster] says, "but not any resolution beyond that." Drawing an analogy, she explains that there are many kinds of dogs, from Chihuahuas to Great Danes. All are dogs. Likewise, the *Arkansaurus* is a dinosaur. We just don't know what kind. Possibly, we never will.[18]

Most states (though not Arkansas) have designated official state fossils. In addition, ten—actually, nine, plus the District of Columbia—have, to date, designated official state dinosaurs. Arkansas is the most recent to do so. In January 2017, State Representative Greg Leding of Fayetteville introduced a resolution in the state House of Representatives recognizing *Arkansaurus fridayi* as the state's official dinosaur.

The germ of the measure did not originate with Leding, however, but rather with a young constituent:

16   ReBecca Hunt-Foster, communication with the author, June 26, 2017.
17   Angela K. Braden, *The Arkansas Dinosaur, "Arkansaurus fridayi"* (Little Rock: Arkansas Geological Survey, 2007 [revision of 1998 edition]), 4–5.
18   McDonnold, "Them Dry Bones."

Fayetteville High School student and paleontology enthusiast Mason Cypress Oury. In 2013, while gathering information on colleges with paleontology programs, Oury found a list of states with officially designated dinosaurs or fossils: he noticed that Arkansas was not one of them, and an idea was born: to confer official honors upon what Oury called "the only dinosaur that bleeds Razorback Red."[19] In March of that year, Oury started an online petition drive, seeking signatures enough to persuade the Arkansas Assembly to designate *Arkansaurus fridayi* the state's official dinosaur. Although the campaign stalled in 2013 and 2014, Oury persisted; in 2015 and 2016, he attracted press coverage and was able to persuade State Representatives Greg Leding and David Whittaker to champion his proposal. According to Oury, the "sell" was not difficult: "All of the representatives I've emailed, they're like 'Yeah, this would be fun, let's do that, woo!...In a way, I've awakened the inner child in everyone."[20]

On January 10, 2017, Leding introduced House Concurrent Resolution 1003, conferring official designation on *Arkansaurus*. It proclaimed:

> The Ninety-First General 17 Assembly of the State of Arkansas will select an official state dinosaur from the known population of dinosaurs represented in Arkansas's fossil record: *Arkansaurus, Paluxysaurus,* and *Acrocanthosaurus*; and...*Arkansaurus fridayi* shall be selected, since it is unique to the State of Arkansas, brings recognition to the State of Arkansas, and promotes an interest in paleontology in Arkansas."[21]

The resolution attracted favorable press attention and several willing co-sponsors. It was slightly amended to more clearly reflect the known fossil record of dinosaurs in Arkansas: "the known population of dinosaurs represented in Arkansas's fossil record: *Arkansaurus*, sauropod dinosaur, and theropod dinosaur tracks of currently uncertain taxonomic affiliation."[22] The Arkansas House unanimously approved HCR 1003 on January 23, 2017, and the Senate followed suit on February 16, with Oury observing the vote. The next day, Governor Asa Hutchinson signed the measure into law.

ReBecca Hunt-Foster serves (as of 2017) as the Bureau of Land Management's sole district paleontologist, based at the BLM Canyon Country District in Moab, Utah. The cast of the reconstructed *Arkansaurus* foot prepared by the late Dr. James H. Quinn is still in the Friday home in Lockesburg. The petrified remains of *Arkansaurus fridayi* are at the Fayetteville headquarters of the Arkansas Archaeological Survey, where the collections of the former University of Arkansas Museum (of which they are a part) are held. Cypress Oury, whose interest led to the dinosaur's designation, is as of 2017 a student at the University of Arkansas at Fayetteville, considering both archeology and paleontology as paths of study.

---

19   Jacqueline Ronson, "Teen Pushes for the 'Arkansaurus' to Be Named State Dinosaur of Arkansas," *Inverse*, March 10, 2016. https://www.inverse.com/article/12685-teen-pushes-for-the-arkansaurus-to-be-named-state-dinosaur-of-arkansas (accessed August 17, 2017).

20   Ibid.

21   Arkansas House of Representatives, Concurrent Resolution 1003, filed January 10, 2017.

22   House Concurrent Resolution 1003 (as amended) http://www.arkleg.state.ar.us/assembly/2017/2017R/Bills/HCR1003.pdf (accessed August 17, 2017).

For further reading:

Braden, Angela K. *The Arkansas Dinosaur, "Arkansaurus fridayi."* Little Rock: Arkansas Geological Survey, 2007.

Chandler, Angela. "Official State Dinosaur." *Encyclopedia of Arkansas History & Culture.* http://www.encyclopediaofarkansas.net/encyclopedia/entry-detail.aspx?entryID=3438 (accessed August 24, 2017).

Freeman, Thomas. *Fossils of Arkansas: An Introduction to Paleontology Illustrated with Common Fossils of Arkansas.* Little Rock: Arkansas Geological Commission, ca. 1966.

Glut, Donald F. *Dinosaurs: The Encyclopedia.* Jefferson, NC: McFarland & Co., 1997.

McDonnold, Paul. "Them Dry Bones." *Arkansas Life* (September 2014). http://arkansaslife.com/them-dry-bones/# (accessed August 24, 2017).

Unklesbay, A. G. *The Common Fossils of Missouri.* Columbia: University of Missouri Press, 1955.

Conclusion

Room for Some More?

At some point, it may be possible that a state will arrive at a sufficiency, even a surfeit, of symbols. Where is that line? Iowa has a total of eight official symbols, while Massachusetts has forty-four. In Missouri in 2015, that level of sufficiency was apparently reached, at least in the estimation of Representative Tom Flanigan of Carthage, who introduced HB 1350, a measure that would cap state symbols at the then-current twenty-eight. The legislation targeted pending bills such as the one to anoint "Jim the Wonder Dog" as the state Wonder Dog and "Old Drum" the state historical dog, along with one to name the white-tailed deer as the state game animal.

Flanigan suggested that the legislature could probably come up with many more, but "you diminish the ones you've already decided are state symbols."

Ultimately, the Missouri legislature dodged designations and limitation alike. "Jim the Wonder Dog"—a Llewellyn setter famed in the 1930s for his alleged ability to answer questions, predict the sex of unborn babies, and pick Kentucky Derby winners—remained undesignated. So did both the white-tailed deer and the proposed historical dog "Old Drum," whose death was the subject of an 1870 Missouri Supreme Court case. However, HB1350 also failed to win approval, leaving the door open for these, and perhaps other, proposed designations to see the light of day in times to come.

In Arkansas, no such artificial cap has been imposed. Thus, the way lies open for future advocates and enthusiasts of state curiosa, products, and the like to make the case for their darlings' designation. Perhaps in editions to come, chapters will be reserved for the state game fish (brown trout, anyone?), state snack food (I nominate the fried pickle, pride of Atkins), state dessert (fried pie, pecan pie, or any pie from DeValls Bluff), state game bird (make mine mallard) or state historical boat (a well-used 1968 Ranger, maybe?). Suggestions have been made for a state firearm (I would opt for a well-worn field-grade Winchester Model 12, or, if money is no object, an HE grade Super Fox 12-gauge double with 32-inch barrels) and a state historical knife (the bowie knife, naturally); surely, there are other official talismans in prospect.

Whatever the choices may be, chances are that they too will be signposts for those who seek them: threads of Arkansas's settlement and development and even Arkansans' pride will run through each story. They will speak volumes to any who will listen. Stories will abound of past aspirations; of large ventures, discoveries, and recoveries; and of politicians and private citizens recognizing things that make up the essence of the state of Arkansas.

Image Credits

7: (Top to bottom) *Apple Blossom Time*, postcard, PHO 19-213, courtesy of the Butler Center for Arkansas Studies (hereafter the Butler Center); *Group holding Arkansas state flag*, 1955. Harris & Ewing Collection, Library of Congress; *Mockingbird decal*, collection of Jen Hughes; *Ozark farm scenes*, unidentified location, Ark. ca. 1930, postcard, PHO 14-114, courtesy of the Butler Center. **12:** Illustration from *Arkansas in 1892–93 for the World's Columbian Exposition*, Arkansas World's Fair Directory. Little Rock: Arkansas Democrat Company, 1893. **13:** *Samuel Calhoun Roane*, courtesy of the Arkansas History Commission (hereafter AHC). **14:** *Territorial seals*, courtesy of AHC. **15, 16:** Office of the Secretary of State. **18:** *Arkansas State girl, seal and flower (Apple Blossom)*, undated, postcard, PHO 19-168, courtesy of the Butler Center. **20:** *John Chapman*, illustration from *H. S. Knapp—A History of the Pioneer and Modern Times of Ashland County*. Philadelphia: J. B. Lippincott & Co., 1862. **21:** *Packing scene at "Appledale" H. W. Gripple's Famous Apple Orchard*, unidentified location, Benton County, Ark., ca. 1915, postcard, PHO 14-124, courtesy of the Butler Center. **22:** *Map of the Arkansas Land Grant of the St. Louis, Iron Mountain and Southern Railway, Little Rock to Texarkana [and] Little Rock to Missouri Line*. St. Louis: Woodward & Tiernan Printing Company, 1878. **23:** *Apple orchard in bloom, Springdale, Washington County, Ark.*, ca. 1926, postcard, PHO 14-56, courtesy of the Butler Center. **25:** (Top, left to right) *Malus domestica: Rutherford*, Bertha Heiges, 1896; *Malus domestica: Arkansas*, Amanda Almira Newton, 1906; *Malus domestica: Arkansas Sweet*, Deborah Griscom Passmore, 1906. (Bottom, left to right) *Malus domestica: Arkansas Red*, Deborah Griscom Passmore, 1899; *Malus domestica: Arkansas Beauty*, Royal Charles Steadman, 1916; *Malus domestica, Arkansas Black*, Deborah Griscom Passmore, 1895. U.S. Department of Agriculture Pomological Watercolor Collection. Rare and Special Collections, National Agricultural Library, Beltsville, Md. **28:** *Arkansas, the World's Orchard*, courtesy of AHC **30:** Office of the Secretary of State. **31:** *James Miller*, illustration from Fay Hempstead, *Historical Review of Arkansas; Its Commerce, Industry and Modern Affairs*, Vol. 1. Chicago: Lewis Publishing Company, 1911, p. 85. **32:** Illustration by Jen Hughes. **33:** Illustration from *Glimpses of the World's Fair: A selection of gems of the White City seen through a camera*. Chicago: Laird & Lee, 1893. **35:** USS *Arkansas*, National Archives & Records Administration. **36-37:** Courtesy of AHC. **38:** Courtesy of AHC. **39:** Jefferson Co. Historical Society. **41:** https://arkansasflagwabbasekamemorial.wordpress.com/ **42:** Courtesy of *The Pine Bluff Commercial*, http://www.pinebluff.com. **44:** *Plate 12 Mockingbird* by Louis Agassiz Fuertes, from *Birdcraft: A field book of two hundred song, game and water birds*, Mabel Osgood Wright with eighty full-page plates by Louis Agassiz Fuertes. New York: Macmillan, 1897. **45:** *Mockingbird*, from the *Birds of America Series (N4)* for Allen & Ginter Cigarette Brands, lithograph card, 1888. www.metmuseum.org. **46:** *Mockingbird* lithograph by John James Audubon. *Birds of America*, 1840 (octavo edition). **47:** *Arkansas state bird* postcard, signed by artist Ken Haag, 1968. Collection of Jen Hughes. **48:** *Mockingbird and Apple Blossom* 20-cent stamp, 1982. Collection of Jen Hughes. **50:** Illustration from "Report upon the forestry investigations of the U.S. Department of Agriculture 1877–1989," Bernhard Eduard Fernow, United States Department of Agriculture, Washington, Govt. printing office, 1899. **51:** Courtesy of AHC. **55:** *Log train for G. F. Bethel Saw Mill; Mansfield, Ark.*, 1903, courtesy of AHC. **56:** *Arkansas Lumber Company*, courtesy of AHC. **58:** *In the timber region, Arkansas*, Wittenberg & Sorber, St. L. engraving, ca. 1896. Illustration from: *Arkansas. Statistics and information showing the agricultural and mineral resources*, Missouri Pacific railway company, 17th ed., ca. 1896, p. 43. **61:** *Map of the Arkansas Land Grant of the St. Louis, Iron Mountain and Southern Railway, Little Rock to Texarkana [and] Little Rock to Missouri Line*. St. Louis: Woodward & Tiernan Printing Company, 1878. **64:** *Diamond Age*, photo by Steve Jurvetson. **68:** *Spot where first diamond was found in Arkansas, Murfreesboro, Pike County, Ark.*, ca. 1920, PHO 10-193, courtesy of the Butler Center. **69:** *John Huddleston and Samuel Reyburn*, 1906. Arkansas diamond mining research collection. BC.MSS.08.15, courtesy of the Butler Center. **70:** *Prospecting for diamonds, Arkansas*, Bain News Service, George Grantham Bain Collection, Library of Congress, n.d. **71:** *Group of diamond miners, Murfreesboro, Pike County, Ark.*, ca. 1920, PHO 10-295, courtesy of the Butler Center. **72:** *Nashville News*, newspaper supplement, ca. 1911, Arkansas diamond mining research collection, BC.MSS.08.15, courtesy of the Butler Center **74:** *Pisolitic bauxite 3*, photo by James St. John. **77:** (Top to bottom) *General office of the Aluminum Company of America, Bauxite, Saline County, Ark.*, ca. 1910 postcard, PHO 10-59; *South view of mill, Bauxite Company, Bauxite, Saline County, Ark.*, ca. 1911 postcard, PHO 10-57; *Milling Bauxite Plant, American Bauxite Company, Bauxite, Saline County, Ark.*, ca. 1906 postcard, PHO 10-58—all courtesy of the Butler Center. **78-79:** *The Bauxite Mines*, mural by Julius Woeltz for the U.S. Post Office in Benton, Ark., 1942. Photo from the Carol M. Highsmith Archive collection, Library of Congress. **80:** *Loading cars with bauxite, Bauxite, Ark.*, 1912. PHO 10-471, courtesy of the Butler Center. **82:** Office of the Secretary of State. **84:** Courtesy of Mount Ida Chamber of Commerce. **85:** *American Journal of Science*, 1880, p. 576. New Haven: J. D. & E. S. Dana. **86:** *James A.*

Bauer, 1958. Photo by Ernie Deane, courtesy of AHC. **87:** *Quartz Crystal Cave and Museum, Hot Springs, Ark.* undated, color tint postcard, PHO 17-369, courtesy of the Butler Center. **89:** Henry Schoolcraft, "Annual report of the Board of Regents of the Smithsonian Institution," p. 277. Smithsonian Institution; Board of Regents; United States National Museum. Report of the U.S. National Museum; Smithsonian Institution. Report of the Secretary, 1846. Washington: Smithsonian Institution **90:** *Quartz vein in sandstone (Coleman Quartz Mine) 3.* Photo by James St. John. **91:** Courtesy of Arkansas Department of Parks and Tourism (hereafter ADPT) **92:** *Adult female worker honey bee,* courtesy of CSIRO. **94:** Wikimedia commons. **96:** Unknown, Tetradrachm, about 390–300 B.C., Silver, J. Paul Getty Museum, Villa Collection, Malibu, California, Gift of Lily Tomlin. **99:** Photo by Mary Hightower, courtesy of University of Arkansas System Division of Agriculture. **102:** Illustration from *The Arkansaw bear; a tale of fanciful adventure,* by Albert Bigelow Paine and Frank Ver Beck, 1898. **105:** *Square dancing children,* courtesy of AHC. **106:** *Sandford Faulkner gravestone dedication at Mount Holly Cemetery,* 1955, courtesy of AHC. **106:** Office of the Secretary of State. **108:** *Records of early American dances: as revived by Mr. and Mrs. Henry Ford.* Henry Ford, Benjamin Lovett. Square Dance History Project. **111:** Courtesy of ADPT. **113:** Illustration from *The Arkansaw bear; a tale of fanciful adventure,* by Albert Bigelow Paine and Frank Ver Beck, 1898. **114 :** *Migrant family from Arkansas playing hill-billy songs,* Farm Security Administration emergency migratory camp. Calipatria, California, photo by Dorothea Lange, February 1939. **116:** *Arkansas Traveler/Clementine* picture disc, 1948. Record Guild of America. Collection of Jen Hughes. **117:** *Arkansas: The official state song,* sheet music pamphlet, 1968, courtesy of AHC. **120:** *The Arkansas Traveller* and *The Turn of the Tune,* lithographs by Currier and Ives. Office of the Secretary of State. **122:** *Wayland Holyfield,* courtesy of the artist. **126:** U.S. Department of Agriculture. **129:** Courtesy of AHC. **131:** Collection of Jen Hughes. **132:** *Hog Heaven Produce, Bismarck,* courtesy of ADPT. **133:** Courtesy of ADPT. **136:** U.S. Fish and Wildlife Service. **137:** *Virginia deer.* Image from, Augustus A. Gould, et al., "A System of natural history : containing scientifci [*sic*] and popular descriptions of man, quadrupeds, birds, fishes, reptiles and insects" (1834), p. 343. Boston : Carter, Hendee, & Co. Brattleboro, Vt. Published by Peck & Wood. **138:** Eadweard Muybridge. *Animal locomotion: an electro-photographic investigation of consecutive phases of animal movements.* 1872–1885. Published under the auspices of the University of Pennsylvania. Plates printed by the Photo-Gravure Company. Philadelphia, 1887. **141:** U.S. Fish and Wildlife Service. **144:** Collection of Jen Hughes. **146:** Collection of Jen Hughes. **147:** Jeff. Davis! "As women and children." Philadelphia: For sale 304 Chestnut Street, ca. 1865. Library of Congress Prints and Photographs Division, Washington DC. **149:** Collection of Jen Hughes. **151:** Collection of Jen Hughes. **152:** *Land of Opportunity postcard,* ca. 1950s. **153:** Photo by Jorden Vincent. **156:** U.S. Department of Agriculture. **157:** *Carlisle Rice Mill Company, Carlisle, Lonoke County, Ark.,* ca. 1960, postcard, PHO 14-9, courtesy of the Butler Center. **158-159:** *Train load of rice, Ark.,* 1912, PHO 14-199, courtesy of the Butler Center. **163:** *Pumping station, F. Kiech Rice Farm, Nettleton, Ark.,* undated, postcard, PHO 14-186, courtesy of the Butler Center. **165:** *Plowing rice fields, near Stuttgart, Arkansas County, Ark.,* ca. 1925, PHO 14-67, courtesy of the Butler Center. **168:** *Dutch oven,* stock photo. **171:** *Cook lifting lid full of coals from dutch oven used for baking bread near Marfa, Texas,* photo by Russell Lee, May 1939. Farm Security Administration, Office of War Information Photograph Collection, Library of Congress. **172:** *Making a Buckaroo Breakfast,* Leslie J. Stewart (depicted), photo by Linda Gastanaga, July 1978. Paradise Valley Folklife Project Collection American Folklife Center, Library of Congress. **175:** *Placing Biscuits into a Preheated Dutch Oven,* photo by Suzi Jones, July 1978. Paradise Valley Folklife Project Collection, American Folklife Center, Library of Congress. **176:** Courtesy of ADPT. **178:** U.S. Fish and Wildlife Service. **180:** *Male Diana fritillary,* photo by Megan McCarty. **182:** Humphreys' Dairy bottle cap, collection of Jen Hughes. **184:** Courtesy of AHC. **185:** *Union Creamery, Watson and Aven Creamery, Carlisle, Lonoke County, Ark.,* 1909, postcard, PHO 10-407, courtesy of the Butler Center. **189:** *Pecan Joe's, Texarkana, Ark.,* undated, postcard, PHO 10-441, courtesy of the Butler Center. **191:** William Prince catalog, 1822. Used by permission, Ethel Zoe Bailey Horticultural Catalogue Collection, L. H. Bailey Hortorium, Dept. of Plant Biology, Cornell University (all rights reserved). **192:** *Vineyard of Concord grapes, Batesville, Independence County, Ark.,* ca. 1950, PHO 14-157, courtesy of the Butler Center. **193:** *Vineyard, Springdale, Washington County, Ark.,* ca. 1930, postcard, PHO 14-57, courtesy of the Butler Center. **194:** *Wiederkehr Wine Cellars, Inc., Altus, Franklin County, Ark.,* ca. 1960, postcard, PHO 10-7, courtesy of the Butler Center. **198:** *Arkansaurus fridayi* cast from Arkansas Geological Survey. **199:** *Lockesburg Waterworks,* photo by Valis55, Wikimedia Commons. **201:** Arkansas Geological Survey **202:** Illustration by Brian Engh, www.dontmesswithdinosaurs.com. **204:** *Arkansaurus fridayi* cast, courtesy of University of Arkansas Museum. **205:** Courtesy of ReBecca Hunt-Foster. **206:** Illustration by Brian Engh, www.dontmesswithdinosaurs.com.

Printed in the USA
CPSIA information can be obtained
at www.ICGtesting.com
JSHW041748121123
51672JS00003B/7

9 781935 106845